CONSCIENCE AND ITS CRITICS

Conscience and Its Critics

Protestant Conscience, Enlightenment Reason, and Modern Subjectivity

Edward G. Andrew

UNIVERSITY OF TORONTO PRESS
Toronto Buffalo London

© University of Toronto Press 2012
Toronto Buffalo London
www.utppublishing.com

ISBN 978-0-8020-4859-2 (cloth)
ISBN 978-1-4426-1487-1 (paper)

Canadian Cataloguing in Publication Data

Andrew, Edward, 1941–
Conscience and its critics : Protestant conscience, enlightenment reason, and modern subjectivity

Includes bibliographical references and index.
ISBN 978-0-8020-4859-2 (bound).   ISBN 978-1-4426-1487-1 (pbk.)

1. Conscience – History.   2. Reason – History.   I. Title.

BJ1471.A52 2000   170   C00-931917-4

This book has been published with the help of a grant from the Humanities and Social Sciences Federation of Canada, using funds provided by the Social Sciences and Humanities Research Council of Canada.

University of Toronto Press acknowledges the financial assistance to its publishing program of the Canada Council for the Arts and the Ontario Arts Council.

University of Toronto Press acknowledges the financial support for its publishing activities of the Government of Canada through the Book Publishing Industry Development Program (BPIDP).

To T.

Contents

Acknowledgments   ix

Introduction   3

1 Christian Conscience and the Protestant Reformation   12

2 Conscience Makes Cowards of Us All   34

3 Conscience Makes Heroes of Us All   50

4 Hobbes on Conscience outside and inside the Law   63

5 Enlightened Reason versus Protestant Conscience in John Locke   79

6 Aristocratic Honour, Bourgeois Interest, and Anglican Conscience   99

7 Professors and Nonprofessors of Presbyterian Conscience   114

8 Conscience as Tiger and Lamb   131

9 Individualist Conscience and Nationalist Prejudice   153

Conclusion   177

Notes 191

Bibliography 229

Index 247

Acknowledgments

I am grateful to Judith Baker, Darin Barney, John and Susan Beattie, David Dyzenhaus, André and Brydon Gombay, Ian Hacking, Simon Kow, John and Catherine Lu, Nathan McCune, Alice Ormiston, Tom Pangle, Gordon Schochet, and Tetsuji Yamamoto for interesting conversations on the theme of this book. They will know better than I where I pinched their ideas without citation. I am particularly indebted to Donna Andrew, Ronnie Beiner, and Ed Hundert, who read the manuscript and made valuable suggestions for improvements. Beiner is the kind of colleague that makes university life bearable for those of us who experience an intense threat to liberal education. The stand of conscience exhibited by my recently reinstated colleague at the University of Toronto, Kin-Yip Chun, has challenged the reasons of the comfortably situated and demonstrated that conscience is not a culturally specific product.

The research for this book was made possible by the Social Sciences and Humanities Research Council. I am most grateful that funds were available for such a spectral, cloudy and useless subject as conscience. The publication of this book has been made possible by a grant from the Aid to Scholarly Publications of Canada.

I am grateful to Virgil Duff and Anne Laughlin of the University of Toronto Press, and to Matthew Kudelka, for amending my prose and often improving it, and to Jean Colens, for assisting in proofreading and for compiling the index.

CONSCIENCE AND ITS CRITICS

Introduction

The first article of the Universal Declaration of Human Rights declares: 'All human beings are born free and equal in dignity and rights. They are endowed with reason and conscience and should act towards one another in a spirit of brotherhood.' The Preamble to the Declaration asserts that violations of human rights 'have outraged the conscience of mankind,' and the 18th Article declares the right to freedom of conscience.[1] My aim in this book is to consider the meanings that have been attached to the word 'conscience' and to establish whether we can glean any stable and consistent meaning from the history of its usage. What conceptual relationship does conscience bear to 'reason'? Are reason and conscience identical twins, or are they harmonious sisters, or are they, like Cain and Abel, warring brothers?

Conscience and Its Critics: Protestant Conscience, Enlightenment Reason, and Modern Subjectivity examines the evolution of the meanings of conscience from the sixteenth to the nineteenth centuries. In the past fifteen years, I have written two other books on liberalism and the languages of moral subjectivity. *Shylock's Rights: A Grammar of Lockian Claims* (Toronto, 1988) and *The Genealogy of Values: The Aesthetic Economy of Nietzsche and Proust* (Lantham, 1995) explored rights as the personalization of right and values as the privatization of common goods. Conscience is an integral part of moral subjectivism. Rights function to protect choices; values are what are chosen; conscience sanctifies the choice. The rights of conscience are more than an important human value: they are the basis of human rights. In their opposition to the language of natural rights, Bentham and Burke perceived irrational conscience to be the spurious source of natural rights. That is, if individuals themselves do not judge whether their own rights have been violated or safeguarded – a position that Burke and Bentham considered dangerous nonsense – then all rights are civil rights, the offspring of positive law and the interpretation of civil authorities.

Luther's and Montaigne's conceptions of conscience have often been cited as sources of modern subjectivism, in that they broke with the rationalism of Thomistic natural law. I will examine these claims in the first two chapters of the book, the first dealing with the theology of conscience and the second with Shakespeare's Hamlet. The magnificently conflicted figure of Hamlet, who combined the moral imperatives of Lutheran conscience with the reflective and sceptical consciousness of Montaigne, anticipates the dynamic tensions of modern subjectivism. Having interpreted the multiple meanings of conscience in Shakespeare's *Hamlet*, and their relationship to conceptions of prudence and honour, I will have set the stage for an analysis of the place of conscience in seventeenth- and eighteenth-century thought.

Perhaps the most remarkable development in the meaning of conscience occurred in the first half of the seventeenth century when, as C.S. Lewis observed, '*conscience*, so to speak, passed from the witness-box to the bench and even to the legislator's throne.'[2] This dramatic evolution is reflected in the transition from Hamlet's cowardly conscience (see Chapter 2) to Milton's heroic conscience (see Chapter 3). As Lewis pointed out, this was the era when forensic metaphors for conscience as witness and prosecutor of God's will, and as judge of divine law, gave way to metaphors of autonomy or self-legislation. Witnesses, prosecutors, and judges are backward looking, judging guilt or innocence in relation to existing laws; in this they are distinct from legislators, who deliberate about the future and make new rules to accommodate new situations. Until the mid-seventeenth century, conscience was generally retrospective: it meant individual self-awareness conjoined either to divine law (in the case of Luther) or to custom (in the case of Montaigne); judging oneself in relation to existing norms to ascertain guilt or innocence; and not deliberating about the future and then crafting new rules appropriate to those deliberations. Hamlet's conscience that makes cowards of us all was backward looking or retrospective; in contrast, Milton's conscience was prospective in that it made heroes of common men and women, empowered the saints into battle, and supplanted existing law with the dictates of the inner guide.

Thomas Hobbes feared the revolutionary character of Milton's conscience but he did not retreat to Hamlet's cowardly conscience. Although he was fearful of the antinomian character of Protestant conscience and sceptical of its claims to certainty, Hobbes espoused the egalitarianism of the Levellers and – more surprisingly – supported their position on jurors as judges of law. Chapter 4 discusses the reason/conscience relationship as analogous to the judge/jury relationship in the mid-seventeenth century, and presents Hobbes as the foremost English political philosopher because he found a home for conscience within the law – within the rights of defendants and of jurors – instead of leaving conscience homeless, as did later English political theorists.

Chapter 5 analyses Locke, who was a Hobbesian in his philosophy and a Miltonian in his politics, and thus an inconsistent blend of Enlightenment reason and Protestant conscience. The eighteenth-century Enlightenment embraced Locke's rejection of conscience as an innate practical principle, not his revolutionary politics based on conscience and natural law. Indeed, a major thesis of this book is that Enlightenment thinkers welcomed Locke's substitution of public opinion (social approval or disapproval) for natural law and the rights of conscience. Chapter 6 assesses the opposition between Mandeville and Shaftesbury and discusses how Bishops Berkeley and Butler upheld Anglican conscience against the bourgeois prudence of the former and the aristocratic code of honour of the latter. Chapter 7 explores the Scottish Enlightenment in the context of the politics of the Scottish universities; Hume was not a professor, while Hutcheson and Smith professed enlightened versions of Presbyterian conscience. Smith's theory of conscience as the 'impartial spectator' is presented as the high water mark of naturalistic reconstructions of conscience within the horizons of Enlightenment social psychology. Chapter 8 examines the place of conscience in the radical politics of Paine, Wollstonecraft, Godwin, and Blake. For the radical thinkers, conscience was the voice of dissent from the consensus that the inequalities of commercial societies are inevitable; it was also the voice of certainty – not of enlightened scepticism or indifference – that oppression is wrong. In the clear, powerful voice of Blake, conscience denounced Enlightenment reason as oppressive and conformist. Chapter 9 explores the conflicting sources of John Stuart Mill's doctrine of conscience and its claims to liberty: the Enlightenment educational theory and practice of James Mill, Coleridge's championing of conscience over consciousness (where Mill is introduced to the active self of German idealism), and De Tocqueville's analysis of the tyranny of public opinion. Reacting to the tyranny of public opinion and to the conformism of bourgeois public opinion, Mill affirmed an individualism of conscience; this was not a swing back to seventeenth-century individualism from eighteenth-century sociability, but rather a purportedly post-Protestant conception of conscience. I say post-Protestant to distinguish Mill's liberalism from the secular humanism of Auguste Comte, whose thought, Mill contended, bore the marks of the Catholic heritage that Comte disavowed. Mill's account of conscience was weakened by the Enlightenment prejudices he imbibed from his father. If conscience is ultimately based, as Mill thought, in 'the desire to be at unity with our fellow creatures'[3] (i.e., in Enlightenment sociability), it does not accord with the common usage of conscience as nonconformist, or with Mill's championing of individuality and integrity in the face of public opinion or social censure.

Although the language of conscience appeared cloudy and spectral to the light of reason – a misty and superstitious relic (like the ghost of Hamlet) to be cleared away by the sun of the Enlightenment – liberal democratic notions of liberty, equality, and identity are tied up with popular notions of conscience. The basic liberal right is freedom of conscience, but it is unclear to what extent freedom of conscience is limited to the sphere of belief and thought, and whether it encompasses freedom of association as well as freedom of speech, and whether it extends to conscientious objection and civil disobedience. Our claims to equality are gauged in terms of conscience; we are equal in terms of our moral choices, whereas we may be unequal in terms of our capacity to calculate consequences. (The argument of Hobbes that we are equal in terms of our vulnerability to violent death, and that of Bentham that we are equal in terms of our susceptibility to pain and pleasure, do not seem to have the moral purchase of an equality in terms of what matters most – our moral choices.) Finally, our identity is constituted by our moral (not our consumer or aesthetic) choices – our consciences, not by our consumer habits or tastes. Although post-Lockean philosophy maintained that human identity is self-consciousness located in memory or habit, conscience, as William Blake and Immanuel Kant maintained, is active and forward looking; it is not the backward-looking glance of memory, nor is it the ties of habit. One makes oneself through one's moral choices; in contrast, memory may preserve how one has been made, and habit may passively reproduce one's given identity.

Since we conclude with Mill, we do not assess the ideas of Sigmund Freud, except for his misinterpretation of Hamlet. However, since the Freudian truncation of conscience as superego has become the received wisdom of our time, I should say a few words about Freud's relationship to the history of ideas about conscience. Freud's opposition of the conscious ego (reason) to the unconscious superego (conscience) follows the trajectory of Enlightenment reason at war with irrational conscience. The rejection of conscience as an innate practical principle, and its reformation as the contingent product of one's upbringing and social circumstances, was proclaimed in Locke's *Essay concerning Human Understanding* and restated by the eighteenth-century Enlightenment before being rechristened or dechristened as the Freudian superego. In the post-Lockean Enlightenment, the elevation of consciousness as the basis of personal identity accompanied the rejection of conscience as an innate practical principle; this of course was before Freud identified the self as the conscious ego, distinct from the unconscious superego. The superego, whatever its formation, stands opposed to sensuous desire. These elements of Freudian doctrine are all questionable. Thinkers as diverse as Montaigne and Kierkegaard have thought conscience constitutive of selfhood or personal identity; thinkers as diverse as Shaftesbury and Rousseau have perceived conscience as innate; thinkers as diverse as Blake and Mill have perceived conscience as friendly to desire, not inimical to it. One purpose of this book is to free reflections upon conscience from the blinkers of Freudian doctrine.

This study does not discuss continental thinkers except to provide background or context for British thinkers. Conscience is a difficult enough word to pin down in English; the difficulty would be compounded if we were to add to our considerations the French *conscience*, which combines the English words 'conscience' and 'consciousness' (the latter coined by Ralph Cudworth in *The True Intellectual System of the Universe* in 1678 and popularized in Locke's *Essay concerning Human Understanding*). The German translation of Locke's *Essay* led to the coining of the word *Bewusstsein* (consciousness), the meaning of which had previously been contained in the word *Gewissen* (conscience). Also, by extending our exploration of the evolution of conscience to continental Europe we would be losing the specific relationship I wish to maintain between ideas of conscience and the events and practices of British political history. I conclude my narrative with

John Stuart Mill, for the purpose of highlighting the antagonistic relationship between reason and conscience. Had I concluded with Immanuel Kant, as some writers have done,[4] the message might have been that Protestant conscience and Enlightenment reason are readily harmonized. Kant has been taken to be the exemplar of Enlightenment, but his opposition to empiricism, sensualism, and utilitarianism was not characteristic of Enlightenment thinkers. In addition, I do not think that Kantian autonomy as moral law is the last word on conscience, for two reasons.[5] *First*, from a Nietzschean or post-Enlightenment perspective, the autonomous individual is beyond good and evil, and not yoked, as Protestant conscience is, to Christian standards of good and evil. That is, to the extent that moral autonomy is distinct from Protestant conscience, it approaches Nietzschean immoralism. *Second*, to collapse conscience into the Kantian moral law is to lose what is distinctive about conscience – its antinomian character. Like equity, conscience stands outside – but attached to – systems of law as a standard for their correction in particular cases. Also, conscience prescribes for oneself, not for others; reason, whether utilitarian calculation or Kantian practical reason, prescribes for others as well as oneself. As Gilbert Ryle wrote: 'We limit the verdicts of conscience to judgements about the rightness or wrongness of the acts only of the owner of that conscience. It is absurd to say, "My conscience says that *you* ought to do this or ought not to have done that." Judgements about the morality of other people's behaviour would not be called verdicts of conscience.'[6]

Rational autonomy tends to universalism, conscience to particularism. To the extent that rational autonomy approaches legal formalism or bureaucratic ethics, conscience – always in tension with law – will pull away from it. To restate the relationship in political terms, Kantian autonomy tends toward republican rule of law, conscience toward egalitarian libertarianism or anarchism.

Reason and conscience are protean terms; sometimes they have been identified with each other (by Butler, Kant, and Wollstonecraft, among others) and sometimes differentiated (by Locke, Rousseau, and Blake, among others). To the extent that reason is seen as prudential calculation, reason and conscience diverge. To the extent that reason supplies the moral rule of doing as one would be done by, reason and conscience tend to converge (although the antinomian character of conscience prevents it being collapsed into the Kantian moral law). On the other hand, to the extent that reason becomes equated with public opinion – and it is the position of this book that a major strand of the Enlightenment equates reason not with one's own judgment but with public opinion – then reason and conscience diverge. Conscience emphasizes not that judgment be rational, but that it be one's own. However, the stark opposition of irrational conscience and conscienceless reason is an ideal type, because proponents of the irrationality of conscience did not see themselves as conscienceless, and opponents of Enlightenment reason did not see themselves as irrational.

The hypothesis tested in this book is that modernity is the product of tensions between Protestant conscience and Enlightenment reason, not a harmonious conjunction of the two. Whether these archetypes are useful in interpreting individual thinkers and schools of thought will be a matter of debate. Certainly neither Protestantism nor Enlightenment is unitary or easily defined. Indeed, one of the recurring questions in this book is why, unlike France, Scotland, America, and Germany, England did not develop a group of thinkers who were readily identifiable as part of the Enlightenment. The difficulty of characterizing the Enlightenment is perhaps evident in a recent characterization of the Enlightenment project as 'the effort to limit God's control over earthly life while keeping him essential to morality.'[7] Does this statement mean that the Enlightenment aimed to replace ecclesiastical control of society with individual conscience? Hume, Voltaire, and Diderot favoured an established church to replace ecclesiastical control of society (as opposed to separation of church and state). Also, one might ask what kind of morality it is that relinquishes 'control over earthly life.' Finally, even if one includes Deists among those who think God essential to morality, one would have to exclude Hume, Diderot, Helvétius, D'Holbach, and Bentham from one's model of Enlightenment thought. Perhaps the conclusion to be derived is that one cannot characterize definitively movements such as the Enlightenment.

Nevertheless, I employ ideal types that I hope do not do much violence to the complexity and variety of intellectual history. The typology I use locates equality on the side of conscience and inequality on the side of reason; humans are equal in their moral choices, but unequal in their ability to calculate. Also I put certainty on the side of Protestantism and scepticism on the side of Enlightenment – the zeal and intolerance of Milton, Jurieu, and Locke with the former, and the sceptical tolerance of Hobbes, Hume, Voltaire, and Diderot with the latter. A corollary of this view is that freedom of conscience, which tends toward the separation of church and state, should not be confused with sceptical indifference to religion (fostered, as Hobbes, Hume, Voltaire, and Diderot thought, by the supremacy of the state in matters of religion). Furthermore, I place individuality – each person her own priest – on the pole of Protestantism, while linking sociality to the opposite pole of Enlightenment. David Hume understood solitude to be part of 'the whole train of monkish virtues' and thus useless to oneself and to one's fellows.[8] Denis Diderot broke his friendship with Rousseau when Diderot asserted that 'the virtuous man reveres society; the wicked only avoids it.'[9]

An account of the history of the conflict between reason and conscience (or between rational judgment and one's own judgment) may help clarify contemporary self-understanding. Thoughtful questioning about conscience is essential if we are to revive the liberal tradition and prevent the rights of conscience from descending into a ritualistic incantation. Can we talk of freedom of conscience without having a clear idea of what conscience is? Does freedom of conscience just mean freedom for Protestant religions, or those forms of interior faith without public ceremonies or common rituals? Is it confined to freedom of thought, as distinct from freedom of action (i.e., justifiable actions that we call conscientious objection, dissent, or civil disobedience)? If freedom of conscience includes freedom of speech, does the Kantian and Benthamite licence to speak freely go hand in hand with the duty to obey punctually? Would liberal democrats do better to take the Hobbesian path of institutionalizing conscience within the law (as Hobbes did for defendants and jurors, whereby jurors were to declare the law, and not just establish whether the accused did what he was charged with doing)? Or would they be better off taking the Lockean path, and authorizing a role for conscience outside the law (i.e., in the judgments of individuals when the government has abused its trust)?

As a preliminary step toward addressing these questions, this study sets forth a history of thoughtful attempts in Britain to characterize conscience; these are analyzed in the context of the Protestant Reformation, the English Civil War, the Glorious Revolution, the European and American Enlightenment, and the French Revolution. If the reader thinks that my account of the campaign of Enlightenment reason against Protestant conscience is indecisive, I will not be dismayed. A decisive victory of reason over conscience, or vice versa – of Hume over Milton or of Blake over Locke – would deprive our tradition of a vital tension that has made us what we are. Whether the tension between reason and conscience has resonances for other traditions, which have subscribed to the Universal Declaration of Human Rights, is a matter for those who inhabit these traditions to decide. Autonomous reason prescribes universal rules; conscience does not prescribe for others.

Chapter 1

Christian Conscience and the Protestant Reformation

The Universal Declaration of Human Rights asserts that all human beings are endowed with reason and conscience. A difficulty with this formulation is that the word 'conscience' (or *syneidesis*, or *Gewissen*, or *conscientia* and its derivatives) is a Western and almost exclusively Christian word. Despite Hitler's claim that 'conscience is a Jewish invention. It is a blemish, like circumcision,'[1] the Old Testament equivalent for conscience was *leb* (heart).[2] There are no Sanskrit, Chinese, or Japanese words for conscience, although the Chinese *liang xing* and the Japanese *ryo shin* (both literally mean 'good heart') are used to translate the foreign idea. Could we then say that the relationship of reason to conscience is analogous to the relationship of head to heart?

The heart is internal or hidden; likewise, conscience connotes interiority. The old English *inwit*, which James Joyce attempted to revive in *Ulysses*, brings out this innermost aspect of humanity. The heart may have its reasons, but it does not usually provide them. Reason and speech belong together (*logos* means both reason and speech), whereas conscience is 'dumb'; as Martin Heidegger said, 'Only in keeping silent does the conscience call.'[3] Conscience, unlike reason, does not communicate; if the call of conscience is heard more clearly away from the crowd, it addresses oneself, not others. Its reasons – 'I could not live with myself if I did that,' or 'I should not want to become the kind of person who participates in that' – are not communicable; if stated publicly, they are self-promotion.

Thus conscience, like the heart, is *alogos* (speechless); yet it does not bear the heart's connotation of love, compassion, or benevolence. Jean Calvin wrote: 'He who trusts only his conscience and neglects reputation is cruel.'[4] Two centuries later, enlightened adversaries of conscience echoed Calvin's proposition. Indeed, the thesis of this book is that the inner-directedness of conscience may be in inverse relationship to responsiveness to others. In *Julie or the New Heloise*, Rousseau's St-Preux writes to his beloved Julie after leaving the land of Calvin for the country of *les philosophes*: 'Republican austerity is not good form in this country; here more flexible virtues are required, ones that can more easily bend to the interests of friends and protectors.'[5] The goodheartedness of eighteenth-century moralists constituted a rejection of seventeenth-century individualism, whether Hobbesian egoism or Miltonian conscience. The post-Enlightenment reintroduction of conscience as Victorian duty seemed heartless to sentimentalists both then and now. That is, good-heartedness (Shaftesbury's, Hutcheson's, Hume's, Diderot's and Smith's benevolence) is an enlightened alternative to individual conscience, not an elaboration of it. Conscience is conceptually distinct from both prudential self-love and estimable benevolence; as Bishop Butler indicated, one of the functions of conscience is to adjudicate between prudence and benevolence. Conscience, then, is not a warm heart.

Conscience, as distinct from heart, derived from the New Testament. Saint Paul developed the idea of conscience to distinguish his new faith in Christianity from his old belief in Judaism; he sharply distinguished law from love, and the mere observance of the law, or works, from faith (Galatians 2:16–21; Romans 3:21–31). In Pauline doctrine, conscience replaced ritual observance. For instance, with respect to ceremonial feasts and dietary laws, Saint Paul wrote (Romans 14:14): 'I know, and am persuaded by the Lord Jesus, that *there is* nothing unclean of itself: but to him that esteemeth any thing to be unclean, to him *it is* unclean.' While no food is obligatory or forbidden, it is not an act of love to give offence to others by eating things that others hold deeply to be unclean.

If Saint Paul's view of conscience stands opposed to Judaic Law, it has an ambiguous relationship to secular law. Paul counselled Christians to obey all worldly authorities not only from a prudent fear of the law 'but also for conscience's sake' (Romans 13:5). Pauline doctrine was conservative with respect to conscience and secular authority; yet Milton and Locke, among others, would later use Paul's teachings on conscience as a basis for disobeying worldly authorities. However, it was Saint Paul's teaching on the innateness of conscience that the post-Lockean Enlightenment decisively opposed. Arguing against the position that only those who heard the Law delivered from Mount Sinai are saved, Saint Paul wrote (Romans 2:14–16): 'For when the Gentiles, which have not the law, do by nature the things contained in the law, these, not having the law, are a law unto themselves: Which shew the work of the law written in their hearts, their conscience also bearing witness, and their thoughts in the mean while accusing or else excusing one another; In the day when God shall judge the secrets of men by Jesus Christ according to my gospel.'

For Saint Paul, conscience was not identical with the natural law engraven in the hearts of all mankind; rather, he saw conscience, along with the conflicting thoughts we have with respect to whether our actions are justified or reprehensible, as associated with the innate sense of right and wrong. For later Christians, conscience came to mean the God-given sense of right and wrong, coupled to self-awareness in the shadow of God's impending judgment upon us all. Conscience was the God-given mirror by which Christians were able to view their innermost selves and by means of which they could remove unsightly blemishes from their souls before going on to the great party in the sky.

Yet the term *conscience* as it was used in the Bible did not convey the sense of individual subjective certainty that it came to have after the Protestant Reformation. In his thoughtful study *Conscience in the New Testament*, C.A. Pierce pointed out that individuality is not a significant element in Biblical accounts of conscience; he then drew our attention to the *con* in *conscientia* (the *syn* in *syneidesis*): 'It is as members of the Church and not primarily individuals that they have sure knowledge of God. This *knowledge* could not have so sufficient a reality as to uphold a man in face of unjust suffering, were it not fundamentally a *shared knowledge*.'[6] Pierce thought that conscience has become such a vague and amorphous term that it has clouded all ethical discussion; and that when churches abandon individuals to their consciences, they are depriving them of the assistance and light they are entitled to expect from their communion.[7] With respect to the New Testament, Pierce wrote: 'It may with some plausibility be advanced that the most comprehensive single rendering of conscientia in English would be *common sense*. The Latin translation of *conscience* would thus be of *common sense as applied to moral questions*, and so very close, as has been seen, to today's usage, both technical and popular.'[8]

On the other hand, Nietzsche drew attention to the element of individualism inherent in the Christian dogma of the immortal soul, which he reviewed as the 'extremist form of equality of rights, tied to an optical magnification of one's own importance to the point of insanity.'[9] Thus conscience, or the care of one's immortal soul, becomes the primary concern for Christians, coming before the welfare of one's people or the human race. The individual's destiny – the journey to the heavenly city – supersedes all collective destinies. Individuals are of absolute importance; the care of one's soul can never be a means or an instrument of some higher good – the flourishing of culture, the advance of knowledge, the growth of productivity, the diminution of pain, the greatest happiness of the greatest number, the construction of a classless society, world domination, or whatever.

Christian dogma has centred on the awesome drama of sin. However the phenomenon of sin is conceived to be consistent with the omnipotence of God, Christians are held to be responsible for their sins, and free to sin or not to sin. At the same time, Christianity teaches us that individuals will not be able to refrain from sinning without the mediation or redemption of Jesus. Christianity emphasizes original sin – our inherited incapacity not to sin – more than Judaism or Islam, but also pairs original sin with redemption. Moses and Mohammed pointed to the ways to avoid sin; it follows that the concept of a Redeemer seems blasphemous to Jews and Moslems because it is inconsistent with the unity of God. Christianity seems to portray humans as morally crippled so that they can find their means to walk with Jesus. Human choice may be limited to the option of accepting or rejecting redemption, but the drama and stakes of the choice are not diminished by being narrowed in their focus.

Christian conscience presents the capacity for choice as the definitive feature of human beings. Nothing is more important for Christians than moral choices; their ultimate destiny depends on avoiding those sins that will consign one to damnation. The classical rationalism of Plato and Aristotle, in which one's humanity is gauged in terms of one's reason, is superseded by a voluntarist Christian world view; conscience and will come to occupy the places of reason and nature in pagan philosophy. Plato and Aristotle thought humans unequal with respect to their capacity to reason; Christians emphasize human equality in what matters most – the propensity to sin and the capacity to accept redemption from sin.

Our examination of the history of the modern self will begin with Martin Luther at the Diet of Worms. In the minutes of the trial of Luther, Dr Johann von Eck entreated the accused: 'Lay aside your conscience, Martin; you must lay it aside because it is in error.' Luther is reported to have responded: 'My conscience is captive to the Word of God: I cannot and will not retract anything, since it is neither safe nor right to go against conscience. I cannot do otherwise, here I stand, may God help me, Amen.'[10]

This dramatic exchange seems to pit church authority against Luther's inner certainty. However, von Eck's view that one should put aside conscience if it is an *erroneous* conscience was one that Luther accepted, however much some of his contemporaries rejected the position that conscience can err. Prolonged sectarian strife was necessary before von Eck's view – that an erroneous conscience has no sanctity or inviolability – ceased to be the dominant view in the Christian world. Luther, as Jaroslav Pelikan points out, was an 'enemy of radical subjectivism'; he strongly repudiated the position of Thomas Muenzer and Andrew Carlstadt that each man is his own authority in religious matters, and he supported the bloody suppression of the peasant rebels inspired by this radical subjectivism.[11] Luther protested too much that his teachings on conscience were not anarchistic: 'Therefore the antinomians, who defend themselves with our example, deserve to be hated by all, even though it is manifest why in the beginning we taught as we did concerning the grace of God.'[12]

Luther emphasized his obedience to the Word of God and the dangers of individual conscience throwing off this anchor: 'If conscience is separated from the Word of God, it is like a ball which is kicked about the earth.' He told us that conscience cannot be sure if it 'is led by its own feeling, but only if it relies on the Word of God.'[13] He opposed the Catholic priesthood as 'instructors of conscience' in the confessional since 'no one's conscience should be instructed or corrected except by Holy Scripture.' Amidst the earthquakes of this world, 'God has ordained that our conscience must rest on solid rock.'[14] Not only instability but hysteria would result if conscience were separated from the revealed truths of the Bible. For conscience, Luther told us, is like a woman's womb, and the two testaments are testicles.[15] He portrayed conscience not as a virginal nun but as a wife lawfully wedded to the Bible, receptive to its seminal input.

Luther's emphasis on the authority of the Bible has been perceived by Protestants as distinguishing their beliefs from those of Catholics. While the dichotomy between the authority of the Bible and the authority of the church may well be misleading, it seems that medieval theologians, concerned with scholastic distinctions between *synderesis* and *conscientia*, devoted very little attention to Biblical material on conscience.[16] Thomas More thought that Luther's conscience was grounded on subjective certainty, not communicable reason; More overlooked the Bible as the ground of the certainty of Luther's beliefs.[17]

Luther sought to evade subjectivism by grounding conscience in the Bible, yet his teaching emphasizes individual interpretation of the Bible rather than canonical tradition or church authority. The meaning of the Bible, Luther declared, is self-evident:

> The book is laid into your own bosom, and it is so clear that you do not need glasses to understand Moses and the Law. Thus you are your own Bible, your own teacher, your own theologian, and your own preacher. The way He directs you, you only need one look at them to find out how the book pervades all your works and words and thoughts, your heart and body and soul. Just guide yourself by this, and you will be more wise and learned than all the skill and all the books of the lawyers.[18]

If proverbially the man who is his own lawyer has a fool for a client, Luther is celebrated for declaring every man his own priest. While deprecating Muenzer and Carlstadt for insisting that every person is his or her own ultimate authority in Biblical interpretation, Luther implies that the Bible is sufficiently transparent in meaning that each person is competent to interpret it for himself. However, he wrote to Andrew Carlstadt: 'I know full well that while it is the Spirit alone which accomplishes everything, I would surely have never flushed a covey if the languages had not helped.'[19] Learning thus is not necessarily at odds with conscience.

In Luther's celebrated stand of conscience, he declared that 'it is neither safe nor right to go against conscience.' It is not safe to go against conscience because one has to fear God's punishment: 'The poets fancied that souls were terrified by the bark of Cerberus; but real terror arises when the voice of the wrathful God is heard, that is, when it is felt by the conscience.'[20] There is no greater suffering than the pangs of conscience; yet they are not entirely negative, for they are the birth pains of a reborn life. Pangs of conscience demonstrate the existence of God and also attenuate his wrath. Just as a dog that has stolen some meat from the table knows he has a master when it puts on a hangdog expression and puts its tail between its legs to minimize the expected beating, so pangs of conscience prove to us that we have a Master who can be moved by our remorse and repentance.

If the rightness of obeying conscience derives from its safeness, how is Lutheran conscience distinct from St Thomas Aquinas's prudence? Josef Pieper wrote that according to St Thomas, for whom prudence was the highest virtue, 'conscience and prudence mean, in a certain sense, the same thing.'[21] Pieper qualified the equation with 'in a certain sense' because he knew that St Thomas defined prudence as 'wisdom in human affairs.'[22] Conscience differs from prudence in that it is not concerned with merely worldly affairs but with human affairs as they touch on the divine, or with supernatural objectives. *Prudentia*, for St Thomas, was not Aristotle's *phronesis* but rather, in Pieper's words, 'supernatural prudence.'[23] While Pieper widened the scope of prudence to equate it with conscience, he also enlarged the scope of conscience in St Thomas's thought.

According to St Thomas, conscience was not a distinct human faculty like reason and will; it was 'not a power but an act.' But *synderesis* could be said to be the first natural habit: that which inclines us to good, just as sensuality inclines us to evil. *Synderesis* is not a choice because it always inclines to good. For this reason, it is not a faculty like will; it can be ignored, unlike (St Thomas implies) the faculty of reason. St Thomas said that '*synderesis* is not a power but a habit; though some hold that it is a power higher than reason.' *Conscientia* and *synderesis* are sometimes confused; the difference between them is that the former errs while the latter never does. *Conscientia* is application of the divine and natural law to a particular case[24] and can err from ignorance of principles or circumstances, or in the process of deduction.[25] *Synderesis* is the infallible first premise of a syllogism – that good is to be done and evil avoided – while *conscientia* places the particular under the general rule and deduces a conclusion from it. The infallible first premise is too general to guide human conduct, but *conscientia* is fallible.

Luther came to drop *synderesis* as not Biblical, and not authentic Greek.[26] Thus, for him *Gewissen* (related to *Gewissheit*, subjective certainty) became the definitive quality of human beings. Although Luther intended to avoid the subjectivism of Muenzer and Carlstadt, he broke with the rationalism of St Thomas, for whom reason was the highest faculty and prudence was the highest virtue. Although in some sense conscience is supernatural prudence, St Thomas would not have agreed with Luther's statement that it is not safe to 'go against conscience.'

But would Luther have thought that the rightness of obeying conscience is a function of its safeness? Is the rectitude of one's intentions ultimately governed by a calculation of one's other-worldly interests (as I take Pieper's equation of conscience and prudence to mean)? Or is the safeness of following conscience a function of its rightness? Is it *prudent* to follow conscience because it is *right* to do so? Luther's formulation suggests that the safeness and rightness of following conscience are irreducible to each other, but that perhaps the safeness is in the hands of God and the rightness is in the hands of men – humans are responsible for the purity of their intentions, and God for the consequences of actions.

Conscience and Law

Luther opposed what he called the antinomianism of Muenzer and Carlstadt, but his position on conscience constituted a break with the Thomist tradition of natural law. Conscience plays a role in Lutheran theology comparable to the role of natural law in Thomistic theology. In his excellent study of the sources of the modern legal tradition, Harold Berman writes that the Lutheran conception of conscience helped remove ecclesiastical control from civil society by sanctifying property and contract: 'Property and contract rights ... were held to be sacred and inviolable, so long as they did not contravene conscience.'[27] That is, Thomistic natural law regulated property and contract rights. Proprietors were conceived as stewards of God's property, not owners free to use and abuse their property at will; commercial exchanges were to be regulated by the idea of a fair wage and a just price; and usury was prohibited. The natural law regulations of property and contract gave way to the Lutheran idea that individuals are free to do as their conscience directs. To be sure, Luther did not believe in economic *laissez-faire* or the abolition of all economic crimes; he believed, as Thomas did, that proprietors are the stewards of common property, and that various forms of economic acquisition are unjust, sinful, and subject to the criminal arm of the state. However, Luther's emphasis on conscience seems a modern substitute for divine and natural law.[28] Lutheran conscience played an important role at the time when natural and divine law were questioned but still retained the authority to pose moral conflict.

Since he did not want the conscience of Christians to get bogged down in worldly matters, Luther contended that government regulation should govern trade and usury, rather than conscience.[29] Although Luther seemed traditional rather than modern with respect to the natural law restrictions on unjust acquisition, his teachings on conscience seem opposed to law, or antinomian. For him, universally applicable rules were inconsistent with the variety of possible interpretations for individual cases: 'Because of the diversity of consciences, therefore, it can happen that one man sins and another does the right thing in one and the same action which, as such, is allowed.'[30] In *The Freedom of a Christian*, Luther preached against the antinomians who despised 'ceremonies, traditions and human laws'; yet he was hardly a friend to ceremonies, traditions, and laws. He opposed papal traditions and ceremonies that did not have a clear Biblical warrant. For him, conscience was separate from all external phenomena such as outward works, ceremonies, dress, and food – from the vestments of priests, monks, and nuns, from fasts and feasts, from holidays and holy places.[31] Above all, for him conscience stood apart from and opposed to law. He declared: 'The pope's laws coerce consciences under statutes, rules, and orders. This results in the loss of both the kingdom and liberty. Otherwise the Gospel permits the outward dominion of governing, if only consciences are kept free and are not fettered by human right.'[32]

Christians, Luther believed, had been set free from all laws. Laws serve 'for outward government, not for the conscience.' He lamented that the papacy manifested 'an impure conscience' in creating 'endless laws for itself, as a spider fashions its weapons.' Pointless legalism inhered in Catholic attempts to erect laws over conscience: 'One law leads to a hundred new ones, and these hundred multiply into a hundred thousand.'[33] Indeed, Luther made the unconvincing argument that the Catholics and the Anabaptists were alike in merging worldly and spiritual interests, whereas he himself left consciences free by not intruding in worldly matters: 'If I, Martin Luther, wanted to instruct princes in their function and others in their tasks, I would be a busybody bishop.' In his view, schismatics, Anabaptists, and antinomians were like the Romanists in thinking that the Gospel concerns laws and works; that is why they took up the fisted sword, not confining themselves to preaching, or the oral sword.[34]

Luther contended that Erasmus forgot that Jesus preached not peace but a sword; The Word of God indeed causes tumults, but, *contra* Erasmus and the path of peace, one must spread the Word at all times and places.[35] The purpose of law is not to spread truth, but to maintain peace. In *Concerning Worldly Government*, written in 1523 (two years before the great peasant rebellion in Germany), Luther said that Christians have no need of princes, sword, or law.[36] After the peasant war,

Luther maintained the Augustinian view that government is an evil, but a necessary evil because of original sin. However, the necessity of government is limited to coercing the body in order to maintain civil peace, and does not extend 'beyond the body to matters of conscience.' Luther asserted that one should obey secular authorities 'so long as they do not bind our conscience and so long as they give commands that pertain to external matters only, even though they deal with us as tyrants do.'[37] He urged his followers 'to obey the government, but to the extent that it commands you to do good things; for it happens that some men administer the government unjustly. A Christian distinguishes between a good and a bad command of a prince.'[38]

Like St Augustine, Luther counselled martyrdom rather than rebellion in upholding conscience in the face of unjust laws. But he added that it is the individual's own judgment, not that of the church, that decides when a human law has contravened Christ's commands.[39] It would be a violation of conscience not to resist injustice 'at least with words.'[40]

Luther maintained that 'the law exists for the sake of the conscience, not the conscience for the sake of the law.' If one cannot support both at the same time, one should support conscience at the expense of the law. Forcing people to obey the law, Luther said, sears the conscience, as is written in 1 Timothy 4:2.[41] Even if the law is universal, Luther held, one should 'respect the conscience more than the law.' Law should yield to conscience because it 'is a temporal thing which must ultimately perish, but the conscience is an eternal thing which never dies.'[42]

An example Luther often cited to illustrate the difference between his position on conscience and Roman legalism indicates the depth of his psychological insight as well as the roots of his moral theology.[43] A mother came to confess to Luther that eighteen years earlier, she had substituted herself in the bed of a servant girl to whom her young son had become erotically attached. The mother told him that she had done so in order to save the girl from sin and because she, being a widow, was the proper person to teach her son a moral lesson. However, when her son came to the servant girl's bed, the mother got carried away and did not reveal her identity to him. The result was a daughter, who was raised away from home and the son. Years later, the son again fell in love with a young woman, not knowing that his beloved was both his daughter and his sister. The mother wanted to prevent this incestuous union and asked Luther, her confessor, what she should do. Luther asked her if the two were happy; when the mother said they were, he advised her to stay out of their affairs. The marriage was not sinful because it was conducted with an innocent conscience. In this situation, Luther was raising conscience above the law against incest. He understood better than Freud that incestuous desires often originate in parents, not children. But even if Luther was superior to Freud as a moral psychologist, it is far from clear whether his conscience was governed by the clear meaning of Scripture rather than by his empirical knowledge of human nature or his shrewd common sense. Gerald Strauss described Luther's antinomian conscience: 'To judge and choose is to draw on empirical knowledge of the world, on a sense of right and wrong, on conscience. This is man's autonomy. It is also the impulse that moves Barrabas.'[44]

Luther sanctioned the bigamous marriage of Landgrave Philip of Hesse, while opposing the Anabaptist position on free love or polygamy. In doing so, he had to consider the political position of Germany – Philip was negotiating with Catholic as well as Protestant theologians with respect to his desire for an open bigamous marriage – as well as the interests of Philip's wife and children.[45] Although he found precedents for bigamy in the records of the patriarchs, here the Word of God was not the sole grounds of his judgment.

The core of Luther's teachings is this: 'I lift my voice simply on behalf of liberty and conscience, and I confidently cry: No law, whether of men or of angels, may rightfully be imposed upon Christians without their consent, for we are free of all laws.'[46] By substituting *persons* for *Christians* in the above credo, contemporary libertarians could use Luther's confident cry as their own.

Erik Erikson asserted that 'Luther's emphasis on individual conscience prepared the way for the series of concepts of equality, representation, and self-determination which became in successive secular revolutions and wars the foundation not of the dignity of some, but of the liberty of all.'[47] Erikson rightly emphasized the egalitarianism of each person being her own priest, and the autonomy and self-determination of Lutheran conscience (however heteronomous, or anchored in Scripture, Luther claimed it to be); yet I cannot see how representative government derives from Lutheran conscience, for interests can be represented, whereas consciences cannot. Furthermore, as David Warren Sabean reminded us, we must distinguish between what conscience meant to Luther and his contemporaries and what conscience means to us today. Conscience in the Reformation, Sabean wrote, 'was retroactive rather than proactive'; it 'was not a mechanism for self-control and self-direction. Conscience was still tied to grace and not yet tied to virtue.'[48] That is, conscience for Luther was more like a judge, determining guilt or innocence after the fact; it was not a Rousseauan or Kantian conscience (i.e., autonomous or self-legislating), as Erikson suggests. Moreover, Erikson left out the rule of law as a central ingredient of liberal democracy, and Luther's teachings on conscience militated against the rule of law.

I am attempting to establish in this section that the Lutheran Reformation constituted a rupture with the Thomistic tradition of natural and divine law. Georgia Christopher wrote that 'Luther denigrated reason because he associated it with the concept of law.'[49] Although Luther seems not to have known St Thomas's work very well, it would appear that he viewed the system of St Thomas as representing a version of the bureaucratic legalism against which he preached constantly. 'Jurists have nothing to do with conscience,' Luther declared. 'An eternal fight wages between jurists and theologians, just as law and grace are forever opposed to each other.' St Thomas could not have accepted the following conclusion of Luther: 'Therefore the conscience must be unaware, in fact, as dead toward the Law as a virgin is toward a man, and vice versa.'[50] Conscience and law are antithetical to each other; they are locked in a relationship of attraction and repulsion, despite numerous efforts – Kant's being the most successful – to synthesize or harmonize them. Later, we shall see that the eighteenth-century Enlightenment rejected conscience in large part because it undermined the rule of law. Enlightenment rationalism was not simply a repetition of classical rationalism or Thomist rationalism. It had to contend with the radical subjectivity unleashed (unintentionally) by Luther; it was a return to a structure of reason and law, and a retreat from the freedom of individual conscience. Enlightenment rationalism championed sceptical toleration under the slogan of freedom of conscience, but also subordinated individual subjective certainty to the rule of public opinion or social censure.

Christopher Hill asserts that the Protestant Reformation historicized conscience by liberating it from the theology of natural and divine law, and clerical authority and tradition: 'The effect of the appeal to lay consciences was to admit that standards are not eternal. Conscience changes with social attitudes and pressures when faced with new facts and problems.'[51] Whatever the effect of conscience in the seventeenth century, neither Luther nor Calvin would have admitted that what God had graven on the hearts of all mankind, as is written in Romans 2:15, was anything but eternal truth.

Calvin and Protestant Theology

Calvin, like Luther, worried about the radical subjectivism attendant on Protestant notions of conscience. He rejected what he called the antinomian view that Christian freedom absolves men from 'tribunals, or laws, or magistrates.'[52] Indeed, he went so far as to declare that 'he who builds on conscience builds on hell.'[53] But, Calvin maintained, the key aspect of Christian liberty is 'that the consciences of believers, when seeking an assurance of their justification before God, should raise themselves above the Law, and forget all righteousness of the Law.'[54] Under the pretext of Christian liberty, evil or misguided men become anarchic or licentious; Christian liberty is not licence, but rather faith and obedience to the Gospel. Calvin placed law and works in opposition to the Gospel and faith. His doctrine of the predestination of the elect reinforced the Lutheran emphasis on faith (as opposed to works) to undermine the priesthood's mediation in securing individual salvation. To him, although good works were a sign of faithful obedience, they were a manifestation of faith and not a substitute for it: 'as works respect men, so conscience regards God.'[55] Faith in Jesus frees us from the laws of the Old Testament, and from the traditions and rules of the Roman Church, and from external things such as observances, rituals, ceremonies, and dress. Calvin drew this dramatic conclusion: 'Now, since the consciences of believers, being privileged with the liberty we have described, have been delivered by the favour of Christ from all necessary obligation to the observance of those things in which the Lord has been pleased they should be set free, we conclude that they are exempt from all human authority.'[56]

Since Calvin was distressed with the antinomian Christians of his time, we may infer that in the above statement he was not condoning the form of anti-authoritarianism that his followers would display in the next century. Calvin repudiated his follower, John Knox, for spearheading the downfall of Mary, Queen of Scots, from the throne of Scotland, and he counselled nonresistance to prevailing powers.[57] Yet at the same time, he thought that it was God, and not the devil, working in man, that 'broke the sceptre of insolent kings, and overturned tyrannical governments. Let princes hear and fear.'[58]

Christians may be free of all external authority, but they are not free of God within the human soul. Christianity provides a spiritual not a carnal liberty. Conscience mediates between God and humanity; it functions as both witness and prosecutor – as a lower court judge and jury serving the divine legislator and supreme judge: 'This sentiment, therefore, which places man before the Divine tribunal, is appointed, as it were, to watch over man, to observe and examine all his secrets, that nothing may remain enveloped in darkness. Hence the old proverb, Conscience is as a thousand witnesses.'[59]

Conscience is not just a divine spy but a vigorous prosecutor or inquisitor; 'it does not suffer a man to suppress what he knows within himself, but pursues him till it brings him to conviction.'[60] It is also a severe but merciful judge that metes out noncapital punishments. Calvin wrote: 'Thus we turn away or mitigate punishments ... by inflicting punishments on ourselves of our own free will. In a word, believers forestall the judgement of God by penitence, and the only remedy by which they can obtain acquittal in the sight of God is by voluntarily condemning themselves.'[61] As we punish ourselves with guilt and atonement, conscience can diminish the gravity of our offence toward God. Conscience, then, is self-knowledge conjoined to our apprehension of the judgement of God.[62]

For Calvin, moral law combined natural law and conscience, with the latter apparently identical to equity. 'Equity, being natural, is the same to all mankind'; yet equity is the product more of supernatural revelation than of natural reason: 'conscience ... has been engraven by God on the minds of all men, the whole rule of this equity ... is prescribed in it.'[63] Conscience, like equity, serves as a standard for judging positive law.

Conscience serves the more general function of restraining the bestial side of our nature, especially when we are summoned to war: 'In time of war all humanity would be forgotten amidst the din of arms, if men were not awed by more than a common dread of punishment.'[64] Conscientious objection to war becomes a minority voice in Protestantism, whereas nationalism, assisted by the break with the universal church, trumpets the din of war. Calvin's understanding of conscientious objection to warfare was not a complete break from the Augustinian conception of a subject's duty to obey the ruler in time of war, but it prepared the way for the Leveller view that compulsion in military service was as anathema as compulsion in religion.

William Tyndale, who broke the law by translating the Bible into English, wrote in *The Obedience of a Christian Man* (1528) that 'the law is God's and not the king's. The king is but a servant to execute the law of God and not to rule after his own imagination.'[65] He was adamant that the Christian faith frees men from law: 'And thus all laws are under love, and give room to love: and love interpreteth them, yea and breaketh them at a time, though God himself command them. For love is lord over all laws.'[66]

Perhaps the most controversial aspect of Tyndale's translation of the Bible was his translation of *ekklesia* not as church but as congregation. A century later, two boys in Somerset who broke church windows while playing ball defended themselves by asserting that the church is where the congregation is assembled.[67] Sir Thomas More thought that Tyndale's translation provided a tendentious Lutheran interpretation of the Bible: his main objections were to the use of the words congregation (for church), elders (for priests), repentance (for penance), knowledge (for confession), love (for charity), and favour (for grace).[68] The translation constituted 'a pestilential heresy' because it provided plain scripture unmediated by authoritative church teaching – a heresy to be punishable by burning. Stephen Greenblatt wrote: 'More's attack seems at its most odious when he charges that Tyndale's books killed men; the killing was done by the state More served and in defense of the church More loved.'[69] More thought the Protestant conscience to be anarchic: 'And this they call the libertye of the gospell / to be discharged of all order and all lawes / and do what they lyst / whiche be it good / be it bad / is as they say nothynge but the works of god wrought in them.'[70] With reference to Tyndale, Christopher Hill writes: 'In the sixteenth century the most persistent and determined law-breakers were the godly, who – like twentieth-century conscientious objectors in wartime – claimed to be obeying a higher authority than that of the state.'[71]

In the century that followed, not only the ungodly, like Hobbes and Spinoza, but also the godly, like Blaise Pascal and Samuel Rutherford (denounced by Milton as a 'forcer of conscience' and a 'New Presbyter is but Old Priest writ large'),[72] would worry about the criminality of godly conscience.

Henry VIII, once defender of the faith from the Lutheran heresy, reformed the English church in what Catholics later portrayed as a profession of conscience (although Luther and Tyndale opposed Henry's divorce). In *The Hind and the Panther* (III.206–9), John Dryden wrote of Henry's divorce:

Though largely prov'd, and by himself profess'd
That conscience, conscience would not let him rest:
I mean, not till possess'd of her he lov'd,
And old, uncharming *Catherine* was remov'd.

Sir Thomas More died a saintly martyrdom for refusing to give his blessing to Henry's remarriage. In his *Utopia* he considered 'whether God did not desire a varied and manifold worship' and thought that perhaps something 'in the variety of religions ... delights His inscrutable will.'[73] However, in his duties as chancellor, More promoted religious uniformity and suppressed heretical dissent; he died at the hands of the state he had faithfully served, protesting that he died 'the king's good servant, but God's first.'[74]

Henry's daughter, known to Protestants as Bloody Mary for her attempts to re-establish Catholicism in England, created hundreds of Protestant martyrs. John Foxe's *The Book of Martyrs* described their fate and became, after the Bible, the most widely read book in Britain until Thomas Paine's *The Rights of Man*; in it, a caption to an illustration of a martyr burning at a stake declared: 'Better the flames, than a conscience seared.'[75]

William Baldwin's *A Treatise of Morall Philosophie* (1547) went through twenty-three editions during the Elizabethan era; the author opposed conscience to the world, its ways and seductions: 'The conscience of man is (in himselfe) a secret knowledge, a privie opener, testimonie, or witnesse, an accuser, an inward troubler or tormentor, it is also a satisfier or joyfull quieter of the minde of man in all his doings.'[76]

In 1559, in order to close the 'privie opener,' Elizabeth imposed the Act of Uniformity. While she said that she did not want a window on men's souls (i.e., she was not an inquisitor, unlike Catholic rulers), the Act of Uniformity stipulated fines for not attending church on Sundays and holidays, for hearing or saying mass. It also forbade worship except in the Book of Common Prayer and prescribed Communion three times in a year within the Church of England. The Act of Supremacy imposed on all clergy and public officials an oath of allegiance to the Crown as the head of the Church of England. Laymen were judicable in ecclesiastical courts for fornication, slander, and nonpayment of tithes.[77]

In Scotland, John Knox sounded *The First Blast of the Trumpet against the Monstrous Regiment of Women* in 1558, directed at the 'cursed Jezebel' Mary Queen of Scots (who may well have been a model for Hamlet's mother Gertrude, as we shall see in the next chapter). Knox saw himself as having a vocation as watchman 'whose eyes he doth open, and whose conscience he pricketh to admonish the ungodlie.' His calling as a watchman 'compelleth me to utter my conscience on this mater, not withstanding that the hole worlde should be offended with me for so doing.' Knox predicted that the fire of God's holy Word would devour not only the pope's laws but also 'the wicked laws of ignorant and tyrannous princes.'[78] Knox was professing to stand alone against the world (although in fact he had the Scots nobility with him against Mary). In his righteous indignation he extended the scope of antinomian conscience – to care for the souls of others, as well as one's own soul. Mary's son, James VI of Scotland and I of England, declared Presbyterian conscience to be noxious: 'Scottish Presbytery ... agreeth as well with Monarchy, as *God* and the *Devill*.' More pithily, James declared: 'No Bishop No King.'[79]

Thomas Bilson, in *The True Difference between Christian Subjection and Unchristian Rebellion* (1585), claimed that since the Bible is open to laity and clergy, 'every christian's conscience is as good as any other.'[80] Richard Hooker took the egalitarian edge off Protestant conscience by emphasizing the role of natural reason in interpreting and supplementing supernatural revelation. As Peter Lake wrote, 'Hooker would have no more truck with a view of the scripture as essentially self-authenticating than he would with one which saw it as self-interpreting.'[81]

The first half of the seventeenth century was perhaps the high water mark of writings on conscience; significant treatises on conscience were written by William Perkins, William Ames, William Chillingworth, Robert Sanderson, and Jeremy Taylor. Chillingworth's biographer, Robert Orr, asked: 'Does not the idea of human autonomy relegate God to the role of an adviser, whose advice we may freely accept or reject?'[82] To be sure, theologians did not want to demote God to a Jiminy Cricket advising an immature Pinocchio on the right thing to do. William Perkins insisted that conscience, 'in regard of authoritie and power ... is placed in the middle between man and God, so it is under God and yet above man.'[83] Ministers of God, Perkins wrote, are not judges of conscience; rather, they are messengers of reconciliation. They cannot remit sins; they can only help or minister to individuals in caring for their own salvation.[84] Perkins distinguished Protestantism, as a religion of the inner person, from Judaism and Catholicism, as religions of external observance; the latter consist 'in bodily rites, and outward ceremonies, actions, and gestures, yea in outward things, as garments, meats, drinks. And their rule was, *Touch not, tast not*; from all which we are wholly freed by Christ.'[85]

Perkins wrote that the pangs of conscience are a foretaste of the fires of hell. If they burned like hellfire itself, human freedom would be eliminated; humans would be mere puppets of God. The pangs of conscience are a merciful forewarning of hellfires; until the hour of death, they are not sufficiently painful to compel us to avoid sin.[86] It is not merely imprudent to neglect the pangs of conscience; it is monstrously ungrateful: 'If there were no iudge, no hel, nor death, yet we must be grieved because we have offended, so mercifull a God and loving father.'[87]

William Ames considered conscience 'mans judgement of himselfe, according to the judgement of God in him.' He called conscience judgment 'to show that it belongs to the Understanding, not to the Will.'[88] However, conscience for him was practical (i.e., not theoretical) judgment, directed by the revelation we have by faith. Thus an erroneous conscience was morally binding on those who sincerely erred; Christian liberty precluded individuals being judged by other men's conscience.[89] Faith being voluntary, Ames would not compel infidels into faith; but heretics – those who stubbornly refused the truth of the Bible – might be compelled to conform. Yet at the same time, the Calvinist Ames did not consider Catholics, Moslems, Anabaptists, Arminians, and Lutherans to be heretics against whom state coercion was justifiable.[90] He thought that soldiers are not bound to fight for their prince in manifestly unjust wars; but they should do so when the justice of the cause is unclear.[91] He opposed conscience to absolute rights of property; in his view, Christians were stewards of God's property, and are bound to pay just prices and fair wages, and should be prohibited from charging interest on loans.[92]

Robert Sanderson wrote: 'There cannot be imagined a higher contempt of God, than for a man to despise the power of his own conscience, which is the highest sovereignty under Heaven, as being God's most immediate deputy for the ordering of his life and ways.'[93] Bishop Sanderson distinguished *science* as theoretical understanding from *conscience* as practical understanding with respect to the degree of certainty: 'a *mathematical* certainty, which consists in *demonstration*, and cannot be false, is not to be expected in *moral* cases, by reason of the infinite variety of circumstances, and the inconstancy of human affairs.'[94] Conscience 'is placed in the middle between God and Man, as a *handmaid* to obey the One, and as a *mistress* to command the other.'[95] Conscience acts retrospectively as a witness to give testimony, or as a judge to accuse or absolve, but it acts prospectively as 'a Lawgiver, a Preceptor, an Adviser, or a Counsellor.'[96]

Jeremy Taylor in *Ductor Dubitantium* agreed with Sanderson's view that conscience deals with matters that fall short of mathematical certainty; and like Hooker and Sanderson, he thought that reason must supplement Biblical revelation if errors of conscience are to be minimized: '*Legislative Reason* is not conjoyn'd to the *Judge Conscience*' in erroneous conscience.[97] When joined to reason, conscience is a legislator: anticipating Rousseau and Kant, Taylor wrote that legislative conscience can give a law but not a privilege.[98] Conscience as prospective is distinct from prudence in that the latter is concerned solely with things of this world, and with advantage and disadvantage, not with what is honest and dishonest.[99]

As C.S. Lewis noted, during the seventeenth century conscience was elevated in status from witness, prosecuting attorney, and judge to legislator. William Ames stated that conscience is *law* in the major premise of a syllogism, a *witness* in the minor premise, and a *judge* in the conclusion.[100] As an example, the major premise asserts that adultery or divorce is wrong; the minor premise asserts that I am an adulterer (in heart if not in deed); and the conclusion is that I am a sinner. The question whether the law giver is God or man is resolved in favour of God by the theologians; conscience as legislator is the God in man commanding the worldly flesh in man.

Although Sanderson and Taylor emphasized the difficulty of establishing demonstrable truth in matters of conscience, Protestant theologians were generally reluctant to give up the category of erroneous conscience, or they were willing to espouse the later view of Pierre Bayle that 'an erroneous Conscience has the same Rights as an enlighten'd Conscience.'[101] Indeed, they stressed that God rewards diligence and sincerity in the search for salvation, as well as finding the right path; and they thought that error has some rights, and that erroneous conscience has some moral authority. On the other hand, Perkins and Ames, and even Chillingworth, Sanderson, and Taylor, thought it a sin to follow an erroneous conscience. The rights of erroneous conscience were championed more as a weapon to combat the legal disabilities imposed by the Act of Uniformity than as an acknowledgment that one's (or one's church's) conscience could err, and more outside the Church of England by Catholic recusants and Protestant dissenters than inside, however Latitudinarian some Anglicans were in a church comprising both Calvinists and Anglo-Catholics.[102] Elliot Rose pointed out that while Catholic recusants and Puritan dissenters often took the stance of conscience alone against the world, they opposed conformity as groups or members of a church, not as isolated individuals.[103]

The tradition of Protestant casuistry, or theological reflection on cases of conscience, declined in the second half of the seventeenth century. Casuistry came to connote Jesuitical reasoning, which was perceived as both overly scholastic and not morally scrupulous. Casuistry was designed for the confessional, not the pulpit; it concerned itself with what is permitted or forbidden, rather than what is morally best and spiritually inspiring. A confessor or director of conscience is more likely to be lax or indulgent with those who come to confession than a priest would be with himself, or than the standards upheld by Protestant preachers to inspire their congregations. After the late seventeenth century, casuistry came to connote self-indulgent reasoning rather than to denote moral theology. The decline of casuistry, Edmund Leites writes, 'promoted the transfer of power to the state' and came to 'even be seen as a covert way of making the state more powerful by having people control *themselves* with values that suit the state's interests.'[104] As casuistry waned in England, individual conscience replaced ecclesiastical control of civil society.

Reflection on the meaning of conscience was not confined to theologians. The Quaker George Fox asked his wife Margaret, 'You will say that Christ saith this, and the apostles say this; but what canst thou say?'[105] Mary Carey denounced the uniformity of belief as popish and unchristian; the spirit 'bloweth where it listeth,' and inspires not only men but women, not only the old but youth, 'not only superiours, but inferiours; not only those that have University-learning but those that have it not; even servants and handmaids.'[106] In the name of conscience, the Levellers opposed compulsion in religion and military service; John Lilburne, Richard Overton, and William Walwyn wrote that 'every mans Conscience being to be satisfied in the justness of that cause wherein he hazards his own life, or may destroy others.'[107] John Reeve declared: 'Whosoever hath the divine light of faith in him, that man hath no need of man's law to be his rule, but he is a law unto himself, and lives above all laws of mortal men, and yet obedient to all laws.'[108] Laurence Clarkson said that 'the censures of Scripture, Churches, Saints, and Devils, are no more to me than the cuting off of a Dogs neck'; swearing, drunkenness, adultery, and theft were no more sinful than prayer and praise if the inner light informed the soul. 'No matter what Scripture, Saints, or Churches say, if that within thee do not condemn thee, thou shall not be condemned.'[109] Reeve's colleague, Lodowick Muggleton, founder of a sect bearing his name, asserted that 'if there were no God to reward the good nor punish the evil, yet could I do no otherways than I do; for if I do well, not because I expect any reward from God, and I refrain from evil, not for fear God should see me; ... but I do well and refrain from evil to please the law written in my heart, so that I might not be accused in my own conscience.'[110]

Protestant conscience combated radical subjectivism and antinomianism from the time of Luther's break with Rome; yet by the time of the English Civil War, Luther's egalitarian conscience had become revolutionary, antinomian, and subjectivist, with individual judgment rather than God as the measure of all things.

Pierre Bayle referred to an atheist sect, founded by Matthias Knuzen in 1673, called the Conscienciaries:

> They asserted that there is no other God, no other Religion, no other lawful Magistracy, but *Conscience*, which teaches every man the three fundamental principles of the Law, *to hurt no body, to live honestly, and to give every one his due.*

The articles of the Conscienciaries creed were (quoting Bayle):

> I. There is neither a God nor a Devil. II. Magistrates are not to be valued, Churches are to be Despised, and Priests rejected. III. Instead of Magistrates and Priests, we have learning and reason, which joined to conscience teach us to live honestly, to hurt no man, and to give every one his due. IV. Matrimony does not differ from fornication. V. There is but one life, which is this, after which there are neither rewards, nor punishments. VI. The holy Scripture is inconsistent with itself.

Bayle called the Conscienciaries 'horribly impious,' 'manifestly impertinent,' and indeed 'stark mad.' However, he added, 'the impertinencies of this German shew us, that the notions of natural religion, the Ideas of the *honestum*, the impressions of reason, in a word the inward light of conscience, may continue in the mind of a man, even when the notion of the being of God, and the belief of another world are intirely rooted out.'[111]

By the middle of the seventeenth century, conscience had travelled a long way from its Pauline origins. For some, conscience continued to dictate obedience to worldly authority; but an increasing number of radical Protestants were contending that worldly authority had to obtain the assent of individual conscience. The antinomian call of conscience came to prominence in seventeenth-century Britain. While it was usually accepted that the authority of conscience derived from God, radicals denied that the efficacy of conscience depended on supernatural sanctions. Yet the sanctity of conscience persisted, and may even have been enhanced, despite the questioning of its supernatural source.

Chapter 2

Conscience Makes Cowards of Us All

Montaigne's Self-Reflectiveness and Lutheran Scruples

A conceptual analysis of the meaning of conscience in the seventeenth century might begin with an analysis of Hamlet, and particularly of the statement in his celebrated soliloquy that 'conscience makes cowards of us all.' The same proposition is advanced in *Richard III* by one of the murderers of Clarence (I.iv.134). Still later (V.iii.211), Richard exclaims, 'O coward conscience! how dost thou afflict me' when it assails him in his sleep. Just before his downfall, Richard III fortifies his resolve to continue in his criminal ambition:

> For Conscience is a word that Cowards use,
> Devis'd at first to keepe the strong in awe,
> Our strong armes be our Conscience, Swords our Law.
> March on, ioyne bravely, let us too't pell mell,
> If not to heaven, then hand in hand to Hell.

Richard is portrayed as someone lacking a conscience, or more accurately, as someone who hears the silent call of conscience only in the still of the night, when it is not being drowned out by the daily clamour of armed ambition. Could we say that Hamlet is the converse of Richard – someone with an excess of conscience and a deficiency of ambition? Could Shakespeare have been implying that conscience and worldly ambition are inversely related? Later I will try to show that Hamlet *is* ambitious, but our first and main task is to clarify the meaning of conscience.

In *The Varorium Shakespeare*, Horace Howard Furness noted that the conscience that makes a man a coward, when stated by the murderer, means moral judgment – that is, consciousness of right and wrong, or moral sense.[1] Furness also noted that when Richard speaks of cowardly conscience, he is referring to religious scruples.[2] But with reference to Hamlet, Furness noted that the conscience that makes cowards of us all is reflection, 'the pale cast of thought' that sicklies o'er 'the native hue of resolution.' Goethe certainly had Hamlet in mind when he propounded this maxim: 'The man who acts never has any conscience; no one has any conscience but the one who thinks.'[3] Furness is right to emphasize the intellectual conscience of Hamlet, as distinct from the moral-religious conscience to which Richard III and his hired assassin refer; but we would be wrong to think that Hamlet's conscience is simply intellectual reflection or philosophic consciousness and does not also include the moral judgment of the murderer or the religious scruples of Richard.

Let us associate conscience as intellectual reflection with Michel de Montaigne and conscience as moral-religious scruples with Martin Luther. It is unclear whether Shakespeare read Montaigne, but scholars have been inclined to see Hamlet's conscience as more like Montaigne's reflectiveness than Luther's self-judgment in the shadow of God's impending judgment upon us. Hamlet's profession (II.ii.245–6) that 'there is nothing good or bad, but thinking makes it so' seems to reflect Montaigne's sceptical subjectivism, not Luther's certainty.[4] If Montaigne's view that each person is an autonomous moral agent, responsible to himself alone, is a distinctly modern attitude, Hamlet's conscience could be said to embody it. Jacob Zeitlin wrote that it is 'the primacy of the individual conscience which makes the *Essays* a landmark in the history of ethical thought in Europe.'[5] Hamlet's conscience exhibits protean qualities. The reflectiveness of a contemplative does not preclude the moral-religious preoccupations of a Lutheran. Pierre Bayle described Philip Melanchthon as follows: 'I think Melanchthon was not free from doubts, and that there were many points about which he could not positively say, *It is so, and it cannot be otherwise.* He was of a mild and peaceful disposition, he had a great deal of wit, much reading, and a vast knowledge. Such a mixture of natural and acquired qualities is commonly a source of irresolution.'[6]

Melanchthon, the gentle peacemaker in warring times and staunch adherent to Lutheran conscience, was a professor of philosophy at the

University of Wittenberg, where Hamlet was educated. To a composite of Hamlet as philosopher and Lutheran, I would like to add the vanity and inner emptiness of an actor. Terry Eagleton writes: 'Hamlet has no "essence" of being whatsoever, no inner sanctum to be safeguarded; he is ... a hollow void which offers nothing to be known.'[7] Later I will return to the theme of conscience being nothing, and human beings as nothing more than their moral choices. What I wish to emphasize here is that the inner-directed Hamlet, the man of conscience and soliloquies, is also the other-oriented Hamlet, the actor aware that all eyes are upon him.

Of all Shakespeare's plays, *Hamlet* has the most soliloquies and references to conscience. As Hidekatsu Nojima asserts, 'Soliloquy is a mirror held up to the inner mind.'[8] At the same time, as Stephen Greenblatt observes, the isolation of soliloquy 'only intensifies the sense that he is addressing a large audience: the audience of the theatre.'[9] This tension at the heart of soliloquy is also at the core of conscience and the shift from the seventeenth-century individualist – whether bourgeois egoist or conscientious Puritan – toward the eighteenth-century gentleman whose conduct was governed by social esteem and censure (i.e., by audience reactions). As soliloquy was to the seventeenth century, conversation was to the eighteenth century.

In Shakespeare's time, conscience meant moral judgment, reflective consciousness, and self-consciousness. Hamlet's conscience that makes cowards of us all is a composite of Lutheran scruples about the desirability of private revenge and about the veracity of ghosts, of a contemplative's indecisiveness about what needs to be done and unending reflection on the merits of this or that, and of stage fright from the actorish awareness that all eyes, including those of Claudius and his spies, are upon him.

A problem with understanding the meaning of conscience in Shakespeare is that we are separated from the Renaissance and the Reformation by the Enlightenment. When Voltaire translated Hamlet's soliloquy into French, he used the word *scrupule* instead of *conscience*, even though the French *conscience* would have captured the Elizabethan meaning of conscience better than *scrupule* or the eighteenth-century English usage of conscience. Until 1678, when Ralph Cudworth coined the word 'consciousness' in *The True Intellectual System of the Universe*, the word 'conscience' did double-duty for both 'conscience' and 'consciousness' – for both moral judgment and a state of awareness and self-awareness.

For the cloudy, spectral, and indefinite word *conscience*, Voltaire substituted the word '*scrupule*.'[10] Poets thrive on ambiguity, on multiplicity in meaning; thinkers prefer clear, unambiguous meaning. Voltaire's translation of Hamlet's soliloquy bears Voltaire's message that Christian scruples prevent heroic action. However, the substitution of 'scruple' for 'conscience' is not without ambiguities; one can have scruples not only of conscience but also of prudence and honour. Voltaire's translation also bears his general message that conscience is as cloudy and spectral as a ghost – a gothic folly in line with the barbarity of this foreign play.

Sigmund Freud was a child of the Enlightenment, and his view of the superego as the contingent product of one's upbringing is an amplification of a central Enlightenment theme. Freud's misinterpretation of Hamlet, which has dominated twentieth-century interpretations of the play, is an integral part of his assault on Protestant notions of conscience as an innate guide and divine monitor of our conduct: 'As regards conscience God has done an uneven and careless bit of work.'[11] Freud interpreted Hamlet's conscience as signifying sexual guilt; only Hamlet's guilt over his Oedipus complex – his desire to kill his father and couple with his mother – could explain his hesitation in killing Claudius to avenge his father.[12] Even if we ignore fear of hell, which C.S. Lewis says is the meaning of conscience in Hamlet's soliloquy,[13] a prudent man would hesitate after considering the punishment for regicide. Imagine Hamlet facing a court of law, saying that he killed Claudius because a ghost told him the king was a murderer, or that he read Claudius's guilt on his face at the staged *Mousetrap*. A humane court might send him to Sigmund Freud, who on hearing that Hamlet thought a ghost told him to kill the king, would declare him nutty as a fruitcake and confine him for life in a lunatic asylum. Prudence, or Freud's reality principle – not merely hysterical guilt or the strictures of an irrational superego – might well evoke hesitation in a regicide. The Freudian superego prevents contemporary readers or auditors from understanding Hamlet's conscience.

For Shakespeare's contemporaries, conscience meant self-awareness coupled to an awareness of God's impending judgment upon oneself. We have already referred to Luther's stand of conscience at the Diet of Worms (punningly alluded to in *Hamlet*, IV.iii.22).[14] Conscience, according to the widely respected English theologian William Perkins, 'signifieth a knowledge joyned with a knowledge.' The *con* in *conscientia* (knowledge) connotes a joining of knowledge of things to self-knowledge, and a joining of an individual's judgment to God's knowledge of right and wrong, and a joining of our self-knowledge to God's knowledge of our thoughts and intentions.[15]

Shakespearian scholars have long debated Shakespeare's and Hamlet's theology. Dover Wilson thought that Hamlet was a Catholic because he believed in purgatory (from whence the ghost of his father came) and because of the importance he ascribed to Extreme Unction (a sacrament lacking at the death of King Hamlet, whose unshriven soul would be confined to purgatory – King Hamlet did not die in the apparently blessed state of Claudius, kneeling in prayer, when Hamlet might have killed but did not, wrongfully thinking Claudius's soul would ascend to heaven).[16] On the other hand, Protestants do not believe in purgatory, and thus the ghost exhorting Hamlet to revenge must come from hell.[17] Although Hamlet inclines to a Calvinist idea of God's predestining will, Roland Frye and Mark Matheson hold Hamlet on balance to be a Lutheran; Shakespeare certainly emphasized that Hamlet was a student at the great Lutheran university of Wittenberg.[18] Luther taught: 'Each must watch over his own conscience, and thus each must have the right to judge spirits and prophets; but no one has the right to take the sword for himself.'[19] Luther preached against private revenge and also counselled against trusting apparitions such as Hamlet's father. When Hamlet says in his soliloquy that no traveller returns from death (III.i.79–80), he is following Lutheran doctrine.

If there is debate about Hamlet's theology, there is also considerable debate among Hamlet scholars about the meaning of conscience. A.C. Bradley insisted that in Hamlet, conscience means 'reflection on the *consequences* of action.'[20] Even though prudential calculation is the antithesis of the Lutheran emphasis on purity of *intention*, conscience in *Hamlet* has usually been interpreted by scholars to refer to reflectiveness rather than moral purity.[21] Perhaps Shakespeare scholars insist on reflection or consciousness as the primary meaning of Hamlet's soliloquy because in English conscience no longer also means consciousness. In other words, they are alerting readers to a meaning beyond the current normal or unscholarly usage of conscience. The unscholarly meaning of conscience as moral judgment is part of the meaning of Hamlet's character, and the meaning of the play, and the meaning of the soliloquy about conscience making cowards of us all. As Eleanor Prosser wrote: 'The crux of the entire soliloquy lies in the word *conscience*. To Shakespeare and his contemporaries, the word rarely meant "consciousness," the usual editorial gloss.'[22]

Conscience, Honour, and Prudence

By substituting the word *scrupule* for conscience, Voltaire was trying to clear up the ambiguity surrounding the meaning of conscience. However, scruples can arise from honour and prudence as well as conscience. Let us now examine how conscience, honour, and prudence are conceptually related.

In *Hamlet*, honour is not a check but a goad to revenge. Laertes and Fortinbras are moved by honour. As an antithesis to Hamlet, Laertes's code of honour demands revenge; he says to Claudius (IV.v.127–32):

> To hell allegiance! vows, to the blackest devil!
> Conscience and grace, to the profoundest pit!
> I dare damnation: – to this point I stand, –
> That both the worlds I give to negligence,
> Let come what comes: only I'll be reveng'd
> Most thoroughly for my father.

Hiram Haydn referred to Laertes's code of honour: 'There is never any danger of conscience making a coward of him: in the established courtly tradition, he immediately recognizes revenge as rightful, above all authority of positive law.'[23]

It is not honour that keeps Hamlet from stabbing the kneeling Claudius in the back at prayer, so much as his concern that if he were to do so, Claudius might go to heaven. In sharp contrast, Laertes says that to revenge his father's death and dishonour, he would cut Hamlet's 'throat i' the church' (IV.vii.127). Hamlet compares his overly contemplative manner – 'Of thinking too precisely on the event, – / A thought which, quarter'd, hath but one part wisdom / And ever three parts coward' (IV.iv.39–40) – with that of Fortinbras, who is prone 'greatly to find quarrel in a straw / When honour's at the stake' (IV.iv. 55–6).

In 1550 the Catholic theologian Juan de Valdes wrote that bestial outrages are inhibited chiefly and most strongly by '*honour*, inasmuch as pertains to this present life, and *conscience* for the life to come.' Curiously, Valdes thought pagans generally more moral than Christians because men are counselled 'more resolutely and more virtuously in a business, than when they put it in a case of *honour*, than when they put it in a case of conscience.' (One has soliloquies about matters of conscience, but one takes counsel about affairs of honour.) 'Whereupon considering, that of these chains with which men stand bound, the strongest is the honour of the world; inasmuch as a man doth more easily cast his conscience behind, than his honour.'[24]

Laertes, Hamlet's opposite, upholds the code of honour even while planning with Claudius to apply poison to the foils in his fencing match with Hamlet. When Hamlet begs Laertes's forgiveness for the death of his father and sister, Laertes says he will withhold forgiveness until he takes counsel on the code of honour (V.ii. 259–61): 'Till by some elder masters of known honour / I have voice and precedent of peace / To keep my name ungor'd.'

In contrast to Valdes, Montaigne insisted on the 'this-worldly' nature of conscience. Montaigne thought it disastrous to maintain that religious belief is essential to justice. Socrates was a just man 'not because his soul is immortal, but because he is mortal.' Conscience has 'the means of sustaining itself without other aid,' such as otherworldly rewards and punishments. 'Use enables us to see the enormous difference there is between devoutness and conscience.'[25]

Montaigne rejected Valdes's distinction between worldly honour and otherworldly conscience, and as a result tended to merge the concepts of honour and conscience. In 'On Glory,' he wrote: 'Every person of honour will rather choose to lose his honour than to injure his conscience.'[26] This paradoxical way of writing suggests two senses of honour: the social sense of honour exhibited by Fortinbras and Laertes, and the personal sense of honour, which merges with conscience in men like Hamlet. However, whereas Lutheran conscience is democratic (i.e., possessed by everyone), Montaigne's personal sense of honour is aristocratic (i.e., possessed by those who think themselves to be princes). Montaigne blended the aristocratic and social ideas of honour and glory with the democratic and individualist language of conscience: 'The shortest way to arrive at glory would be to do for the sake of conscience what we do for the sake of glory.'[27] In merging conscience with honour or glory, Montaigne seems to be fusing character and reputation, the internal and the external. While Montaigne's proposition that we will get more glory if we are governed by conscience can be questioned on both logical and empirical grounds, we also note that Hamlet plays a more glorious part than either Fortinbras or Laertes.

If scruples of honour are not a factor for Hamlet, perhaps there are scruples of prudence as well as scruples of conscience. Can we consider 'conscience makes cowards of us all' to be a poetic translation of Montaigne's thought: 'An over-circumspect and wary prudence is a mortal enemy to high exploits'?[28] Catholic and Enlightenment thinkers tended to draw conscience and prudence closely together; Protestant and romantic thinkers tended to distance conscience from prudence. Josef Pieper stated that for St Thomas Aquinas and his Catholic followers, conscience and prudence were synonymous.[29] He argued that Catholic rationalism has resisted Protestant divisions between reason and faith, between prudential calculation of consequences and purity of motive. The Lutheran separation of conscience and prudence has generated the irrationalist and voluntarist doctrines of existentialism, and has left conscience bereft of counsel and an expert tradition of moral reasoning (casuistry). The Catholic church, as the director of consciences, will ward off the tendency of natural prudence to isolate itself from supernatural charity. Thus Pieper's identity of conscience and prudence rests on a notion of 'supernatural prudence.'[30]

Let us now consider a Hamlet who is unconcerned with his eternal welfare and is governed solely by natural prudence, that is, by calculations of his worldly interests. Let us, as a thought experiment, follow Shôhei Ooka's *Hamlet's Diary* and see the Prince of Denmark as a Machiavellian hero, for whom prudence is the highest virtue and success in seizing power the chief goal. Textual support for Hamlet as a man without conscience (or goodness of heart, *ryo shin*) can be found in his brutal treatment of Ophelia, his remorseless murder of Polonius, the killing of his childhood friends Guildenstern and Rosencrantz (whose deaths 'are not near my conscience'); V.ii.58, and his vulgar competition with Laertes on the grave of Ophelia. Textual support for Hamlet's ambition to be king, and for Claudius thwarting that ambition, is found in Act V, and only after Hamlet has public proof of Claudius's wrongdoing – namely, Claudius's letter ordering the death of Hamlet. (There is no evidence of Claudius's guilt in killing Hamlet's father, except for the expressions of bad conscience in Claudius's soliloquies. Perhaps the play would be more dramatic if we eliminated Claudius's conscience, just as Voltaire eliminated Hamlet's, so that the audience was not privy to knowledge that Hamlet lacks.) Hamlet says to Horatio:

He that kill'd my king and whor'd my mother
Popp'd in between the election and my hopes;
Thrown out his angle for my proper life,
And with such cozenage, – is it not perfect conscience
To quit him with this arm?

Both Rosencrantz (II.ii.247) and Guildenstern (II.ii.251) think that Hamlet's melancholy arises from thwarted ambition. In Act III (i.24), Hamlet confesses his sins: 'I am very proud, revengeful, ambitious.' Later, when Rosencrantz asks him to explain his melancholy, he responds, 'I lack advancement.' When Rosencrantz replies that Claudius has given his word that Hamlet will succeed him, Hamlet responds ambiguously: 'Ay, but while the grass grows' (III.ii.323–26). When Claudius asks, 'How fares our cousin Hamlet?' Hamlet responds, 'I eat the air, promise-crammed' (III.ii.88–9). Thwarted ambition, not morbid character, could well have caused his melancholy.

Most of the literature (including Goethe and Hegel on Hamlet's 'beautiful soul,' and Freud on the hysteric's sexual guilt) emphasizes Hamlet's character to explain his delay in avenging his father, destroying the usurper Claudius, and asserting his rightful claim to the throne of Denmark. Ophelia, on the other hand, is usually portrayed as a victim of circumstances, torn between love and filial duty in a patriarchal society. But perhaps external circumstance rather than inner character explains Hamlet's delay in avenging his father and asserting his right to the throne. That is, perhaps a Machiavellian Hamlet (guided by prudence) would act no differently from a Lutheran Hamlet (stricken by conscience).

Saxo Grammaticus's story presented Hamlet as being in danger of his life after his father was killed; only Hamlet's successful feigning of madness prevented the king and his elaborate spy system from disposing of him.[31] In Shakespeare's story, Polonius, Rosencrantz, and Guildenstern spy on Hamlet at the behest of Claudius, and Ophelia is commissioned to spy on Hamlet by her father. But is Hamlet's life in danger? Claudius forces Hamlet to stay at Elsinore, overriding Hamlet's wish to return to Wittenberg. In Acts III and IV, Claudius says he would dispose of Hamlet if the prince were not so loved by his mother and the general populace.

Hamlet's mother is the hinge or joint on which the play turns. Claudius refers to Gertrude as 'the imperial jointress of this warlike state.' (I.ii.9). A jointress is a widow who enjoys a jointure, or an estate settled on a wife. Gertrude's joining with Claudius may well have been occasioned by the threat of young Fortinbras, who, on the death of Hamlet's father, thought 'our state to be disjoint and out of frame' (I.ii.20). At the end of Act I, after the ghost urges Hamlet to avenge his death, Hamlet laments: 'The time is out of joint: – O cursed spite / That ever I was born to set it right!'

Dover Wilson and Roland Frye assert that Elizabethan audiences would have considered the marriage of Claudius and Gertrude to be as taboo as Oedipus's with his mother Jocasta.[32] I think the parallel misleading, because no one knew at the time of Oedipus and Jocasta's marriage that it was incestuous, whereas Claudius and Gertrude's marriage obtained the blessing or consent of the Danish court and aristocracy. The Book of Leviticus (18:16, 20:21) prohibits marriage between a widow and her brother-in-law unless the previous marriage had been without children (Deuteronomy 25:5–10), as was the case when Henry VIII married his dead brother's widow, Katherine of Aragon; but was clearly not the case with Hamlet's father and Gertrude. While marriages between brother and sister-in-law were considered incestuous – although not to the degree of those between son and mother – the Danish court that accepted the marriage was fully aware of their relationship. Thus it would seem that *raison d'état* legitimated the joining of Gertrude and Claudius; that is, the imminent threat from the Norwegian Fortinbras to the state of Denmark, and political instability arising from the uncertainty of succession to Hamlet's father, made the incestuous marriage acceptable.

We might think 'the imperial jointress' held her position as Queen rather like Mary Queen of Scots, who reigned in Scotland after the death of her first husband, and shortly after her second husband, Darnley (James I's father), was murdered by Mary's lover, Bothwell. James I did not immediately succeed his father on the throne of Scotland. Instead, after Mary and Bothwell were deposed a regency was installed, which ruled until James came to maturity at the age of twenty-one. James apparently overcame his Oedipus complex and did not avenge his mother's death at the hands of Elizabeth I. As a reward for his circumspection, he was promised the throne of England, which he obtained with Elizabeth's dying breath in 1603, the year Hamlet was first performed. Gertrude exhibits none of the qualities of the Machiavellian virgin queen – qualities that enabled her to rule independently in England from 1558 to 1603.

If Hamlet, like James, was not automatically entitled to the throne on the death of his father – the Danish crown was styled an elective monarchy (V.ii.65; V.ii.342) – we might ask why Gertrude (and the Danish court) chose Claudius rather than Hamlet to succeed Hamlet's father. Perhaps Hamlet was too moody, contemplative, and unwarlike to be an effective king; Hamlet says that Claudius is 'no more like my father / Than I to Hercules' (I.ii.150–1) and thus seems to be conceding that he is incapable of heroic deeds.[33] Or perhaps Hamlet, like James, was too young to be king, and thus Gertrude chose Claudius as regent. Against this interpretation are the repeated statements of the gravedigger in Act V that Hamlet is thirty years old – the exact number of years to the day that Hamlet's father slew Fortinbras's father. Most scholars take this ascription with a grain of salt;[34] thirty years might just mean a generation, or a span of time. Or perhaps the thirty years refers more to the age an actor must have attained in order to take on this demanding role (the first Hamlet, Richard Burbage, was in his mid-thirties in 1603). The First Quarto states that Yorick has been buried for twelve years (rather than the twenty-three noted years in the Second Quarto), that is, the same number of years that have passed since Hamlet's father slew Fortinbras (rather than the thirty years of the Second Quarto).[35]

What difference does Hamlet's age make? A.C. Bradley, a strong supporter of Hamlet as thirty, wrote: 'It matters little here whether Hamlet's age was twenty or thirty: in either case his mother was a matron of mature years.'[36] Are mature matrons as sexually active as Gertrude apparently is? If Hamlet were twenty or younger, Gertrude would still be capable of reproduction as well as sex. Our hypothetical Machiavellian Hamlet would have an interest, as heir to the throne, in keeping Gertrude from Claudius's embrace – as much so as a Freudian Hamlet who has an unseemly interest in his mother's sex life, or the Christian Hamlet who thinks sex with a fratricide is wrong.

Let us assume for a moment that Hamlet is a young man, blocked from the throne of Denmark by his age and military inexperience. (Shakespeare's contemporaries went to university in their mid-teens; Francis Bacon, for example, graduated from Cambridge at the age of fifteen.) As a prudent Machiavellian – one whose greatest wish is to assume power – what would he do that a man of conscience would not? Hamlet, as a competitor to the throne of Denmark, is a threat to Claudius, and any sign of vengeance or even self-assertion on Hamlet's part would be deemed treason by the king. A prudent Hamlet would be reluctant to kill the king, out of fear of punishment for regicide or attempted regicide; a conscientious Hamlet would be slow to avenge his father, because of his need to be absolutely certain of Claudius's guilt so that he did not deserve punishment on earth and renewed punishment in hell. In Shakespeare's time, theologians were unanimous that it is sinful to act when one doubts the action is right.[37] A prudent Hamlet would be aware of the ghastly punishment meted out to regicides; he would also know that such painful torture was a mere dress rehearsal for even greater punishment in the hereafter. It is reported that Jacques Clément, hacked to death by courtiers, died with a smile on his face after killing Henri III in 1589 because he knew he had just avoided the tortures awaiting him.[38] The misguided Guy Fawkes, who attempted to kill James I in Parliament in 1606, was tortured in the Tower of London; the cries of the incredibly brave Fawkes were heard miles away in Westminster. Japanese productions of *Hamlet* are less likely than Western productions to ignore Claudius's assertion that a divinity hedges around a king and that it is treason to oppose him (IV.iv.123–4).[39] Only in the fantasy world of the psychoanalytic couch and the Western theatre can one ignore obstacles, besides Hamlet's character, to his revenge.

Francis Bacon, in his essay 'Of Revenge,' asserted: 'The most tolerable sort of revenge is for those wrongs which there is no law to remedy; but then let a man take heed the revenge be such as there is no law to punish; else a man's enemy is still beforehand, and it is two for one.' Bacon's concern that revenge may be imprudent does not seem to reflect Lutheran scruples of conscience. But in his preference for public rather than private revenge, Bacon seems to be uniting prudence and conscience: 'Public revenges are for the most part fortunate ... But in private revenges it is not so. Nay rather, vindictive persons live the lives of witches; who, as they are mischievous, so end they unfortunate.'[40] Hamlet would have to worry not only about punishment but also about what sort of person he was to heed ghostly advice to exact hellish revenge.

Peter Mercer makes an interesting distinction between being *in* the play and being *at* the play: 'As an audience we can scarcely have any doubt at all what we see is in fact the ghost of Hamlet's father [but] a revenge ghost is something that belongs only in a play.'[41] That is, Freud and most members of Western audiences do not believe in ghosts, yet they do believe that the ghost is telling the truth and is rightly urging Hamlet to seek prompt revenge. (To be sure, those gulled by Lacan into seeing the ghost as a phallus – not the real thing but still more impressive and nauseating than any actual penis – have no problem cutting down the primal signifier.)[42] Yet neither our Machiavellian Hamlet nor our Lutheran Hamlet (who are *in* the play and not merely *at* the play) believes in truth-telling ghosts. Prudence would counsel Hamlet not to avenge himself without a publicly acceptable warrant, and conscience would bar private revenge and would urge Hamlet, as a minister of justice, to bring Claudius before the law. The reference (II.ii.554–5) to fatting kites on Claudius's offal may indicate Hamlet's wish to see Claudius hanging on a gibbet to feed birds of prey. Certainly, law plays an important role in *Hamlet* – for the Machiavellian as an ideological veil covering up sheer power or conquest (as when Hamlet's father killed Fortinbras's father in combat, winning lands in Denmark 'by a sealed compact, / Well ratified by law and heraldry' [I.i.86–7]; or at the conclusion of the play when Fortinbras has won back the kingdom of Denmark by force of arms and claims the throne by right of descent, Hamlet's 'dying voice' having earlier voted for Fortinbras's election [V.ii.342]). The lawfulness of Hamlet's retribution should not be ignored by those who wonder why Hamlet does not exact speedy revenge.

In the accounts by Saxo Grammaticus and François de Belleforest, Hamlet (Amlethus, Hamblet) had to persuade the Danish people that the king he killed was a tyrant and a fratricide, and that his revenge was therefore just.[43] The Hamlet legend was a Nordic version of the story of Brutus, who sullied his flesh in the dirt and spoke like a lunatic until he could revenge himself on Tarquin.[44] But the second Brutus – 'the noblest Roman of them all' – who killed a tyrant, died unhappily. Regicide, as Hobbes was to point out, is not a prudent business.

If both prudence and conscience oppose private revenge and support public justice, Hamlet has no choice but to delay his revenge. The play within the play enables Hamlet to play at revenge; it also gives him an added subjective certainty – Horatio, Hamlet's eyes on Claudius's guilt, is noncommittal after the play. Hamlet has exposed himself to Claudius, who plans Hamlet's death in England at the hands of Rosencrantz and Guildenstern. But Hamlet turns the tables on Claudius's agents and returns confidently as 'Hamlet the Dane,' the rightful king, with public evidence of Claudius's guilt – namely, Claudius's letter ordering Hamlet's death – and now has 'perfect conscience' to avenge himself as minister of public justice. The prudent Machiavellian Hamlet would do much as the conscientious Lutheran Hamlet would do – at least until the duel with Laertes, who from the outset of the play seems to be a competitor for the throne. A foxy or prudent Hamlet would have avoided the duel as Horatio urged, or at least would have examined the foils with which they fought; Claudius knew that Hamlet 'being remiss, / Most generous, and free from all contriving, / Will not peruse the foils' (IV.vii.134–6).

A Machiavellian Hamlet might have fought the duel with Laertes to rid himself of a hated rival and establish an uncontested claim to the throne of Denmark. Machiavellian grandeur might have led Hamlet to overlook the foils, thinking that his enemies would be displaying their unworthiness for the throne by resorting to such underhanded tactics. However, it was certainly not foxy of Hamlet, who had clear proof that Claudius wanted him dead, not to examine the weapons before the duel. Our thought experiment that the man of conscience is really a man of prudence has come to an end; it overstrains credibility to portray Hamlet, who is 'free from all contriving,' as primarily a prudent man. However, perhaps it is more Hamlet's sense of honour than his conscience that did him in, or was responsible for his failure to examine the foils.

The Machiavellian Hamlet whose conscience is merely calculation of consequences is not really tenable; Hamlet is more concerned with doing what is right than with doing what is prudent, more concerned with the purity of his intentions than with the felicity of results, more concerned with his preparedness for the afterlife than with his power and profit in this life, more concerned with the unsullied mind than with the all-too-solid flesh. Ultimately, our present-day fascination with Hamlet lies more in his character (as a contemplative, indecisive, self-critical young man who grows from cowardice and doubt to confidence and serenity) than in his situation (of a prince robbed of the throne by a person he suspects killed his father and dishonoured his mother). Hamlet is more interesting than Laertes or Fortinbras; conscience is more interesting and more opaque than honour. *Hamlet* stands out from the source stories and contemporary revenge plays, in which honour is the dominant motif. Shakespeare's play interests us because it is about conscience. As Montaigne wrote, conscience is more important than Socratic wisdom; it 'alone truly denotes us for what we are.'[45] Serena Jourdan wrote that for Montaigne and Shakespeare, 'conscience may be said to create the self [but] may also be said to destroy the self' in order to protect the self's integrity.[46] But since Montaigne and Shakespeare did not completely differentiate conscience from honour – Hamlet, like Laertes and Fortinbras, has a sense of honour (of his social place and reputation) as well as a conscience – one could argue that Hamlet's sense of honour, more than his conscience, led to his undoing.

Conscience, Consciousness, and Self-Consciousness

The conscience that makes cowards of us all is what sixteenth- and seventeenth-century theologians called 'a doubting conscience'; the 'perfect conscience' of Act V is what theologians referred to as a certain or assured conscience (or what we would now call a good conscience). One who follows an assured conscience has no need to worry about consequences; he knows that what he is doing is right. For this reason, as we shall see in the next chapter, conscience can make heroes of us all. In its lofty flight over consequences, Milton's conscience is imprudent.

The conscience that Hamlet exhibits in his soliloquies and in his conversations with Horatio does not mean just reflectiveness (the typical academic's 'on the one hand ... on the other hand' – the reflection that never comes to a conclusion, let alone a decision); it also means self-critical moral judgment (the willingness to consider whether one's desire for revenge is of hellish origin, the ability to weigh one's own ambitions against the welfare of the state). Conscience combines reflective consciousness with moral judgment; it also suggests both the soliloquy's internal mirror (seeing oneself as God sees one) and its opposite (being seen in the eyes of others as an actor before an audience).

To be self-conscious means to be shy or timid, to imagine that others are watching. Conscience and self-consciousness suggest interiority and subjectivity or Hamlet's inner life, yet they also suggest Hamlet's actorish quality – his vain awareness of all eyes being upon him, of playing to an audience. His life is not just his own and God's, but that of his audience. Hamlet, the inner-directed man of conscience, is also an actor, vain and other-oriented as actors are, whose concern at his death is that Horatio not kill himself but live 'to tell my story.' Otherwise, 'what a wounded name, / Things standing thus unknown, shall live behind me!' (V.ii.231–2, 236). Hamlet's beautiful soul encompasses a Protestant conscience, a philosophic consciousness, and an actor's vain awareness that the spotlight is on him.

In a way that foreshadows the movement in Hegel's *Phenomenology of Mind* away from conscience as subjective certainty toward intersubjectivity or the recognition of others, Hamlet's inner life or subjectivity must be confirmed by others in order to partake of eternity in audience reactions. Hamlet's conscience/consciousness emphasizes the seventeenth-century individual, alone and living in the eyes of God;

but it also anticipates the eighteenth-century individual, social and living in the eyes of others. Adam Smith would later equate the Protestant conscience with an 'impartial spectator'; conscience, during the eighteenth-century Enlightenment, was perceived as deriving from a spectator's sympathetic identification with an actor, and an actor playing to spectators and courting their applause. Montaigne's conscience – the self-defining quality in man as distinct from the God in man – professes conscience to obtain glory; true inner character and false outer show come together in Hamlet. If it is the case that 'every person of honour will choose to lose his honour than to injure his conscience,' the decision to give up worldly honour is governed by the prospect of gaining enduring glory.

Chapter 3

Conscience Makes Heroes of Us All

Conscience and Individual Self-Assertion

At the beginning of the seventeenth century, Shakespeare seemed to be saying that conscience inhibits decisive and heroic action; toward the end of the century, John Dryden asserted that professions of conscience were incompatible with those of humility.[1] Bishop Stillingfleet referred Dryden to a work by Thomas Allen, rector of Kittering in Northhamptonshire, that praised both conscience and humility. The obscurity of both the author and the work seemed to Dryden more to verify than to falsify his claim that conscience and humility were incompatible. Dryden expressed a Catholic scepticism about Protestant claims that conscience was a counterpart to an infallible pope. In his preface to *The Hind and the Panther*, he wrote that 'conscience is the Royalty and Prerogative of every Private man. He is absolute in his own Breast, and accountable to no Earthly Power for that which passes only betwixt God and Him.' Dryden stated clearly that individuals abuse Scripture for their private ends:

> No help from Fathers or traditions train
> Those ancient guides she taught us to disdain ...
> And, after all her winding ways are tried,
> If doubts arise, she slips herself aside
> And leaves the private conscience for the guide.
> If then that conscience set the offender free,
> It bars her claim to Church auctority.[2]

Samuel Butler in *Hudibras* also attacked the Puritan conscience, but with ironic lightness rather than the heaviness of Catholic tradition.

Recognizing that conscience should be the supreme court in the land, he asked:

> Why should not conscience have vacation
> As well as other courts of the nation;
> Have equal power to adjourn
> Appoint appearances and return ...?[3]

A.L. Rowse agreed with Dryden that Milton's conscience was devoid of humility, and with Butler that it was priggish and unremitting. Milton's conscience, Rowse wrote, was 'self-righteous and self-satisfied, self-confident and self-laudatory, arrogant and aggressive.'[4] In this description, Milton's conscience seems to be the opposite of Hamlet's conscience: the latter is self-absorbed, self-doubting, and unassertive. While self-doubting and self-confident men of conscience appear to be opposites, they are both self-centred. Conscience and self were coupled in the seventeenth century, as distinct from the coupling of opinion and society in the eighteenth century. The self-doubting or self-confident individual came to be dissolved in the sociable individual of the eighteenth century; the inner compass gave way to the radar of public opinion, of social approval or disapproval.

In *Paradise Lost* (III.194–7), Milton has God place a divine lighthouse within the human soul that can illuminate the way to safe harbour and emit sounds to warn us of dangerous rocks. The inner light calls out to mortals; the call of conscience illuminates our way:

> And I will place within them as a guide
> My Umpire *Conscience*, whom if they will hear,
> Light after light well us'd they shall attain
> And to the end persisting, safe arrive.

Milton's Abdiel, an angel invented by Milton whose name signifies servant of God, is the prototype of the man of conscience:

> Among the faithless, faithful only he;
> Among innumerable false, unmoved
> Unshaken, unseduced, unterrified
> His loyalty he kept, his love, his zeal;
> Nor number, nor example with his wrought
> To swerve from truth, or change his constant mind
> Though single. (*PL*,V.897–903)

In the face of such poetic power, which to me is unequalled in English, one would require the self-confidence of A.L. Rowse to respond, 'Bah, humbug!' It is possible to analyse the thought conveyed through Milton's Abdiel without dismissing Milton as 'self-righteous and self-satisfied, self-confident and self-laudatory, arrogant and aggressive.' The posture of the individual alone against a hostile world is a trait seen in Hamlet and men of conscience generally. Gordon Rupp wrote of Martin Luther: 'With courage and constancy, having begun to fight for what he believed, single-handed and alone, he stood his ground and fought manfully to the end.'[5] I do not mean to deprecate Luther's courage when I point out that he had the support of many Germans in his fight with Rome, and the support of the German nobility in his battle with the antinomians. John Knox declared that his vocation as a watchman 'compelleth me to utter my conscience in this mater, not withstanding that the hole worlde shuld be offended with me for so doing.'[6] Knox of course had the support of the Scottish nobility in his assault on Mary Queen of Scots. Milton's Abdiel portrays the stance of conscience against what the eighteenth-century Enlightenment took to be the powerful force of social censure or public opinion:

> And for the testimony of truth has borne
> Universal reproach, far worse to bear
> Than violence: for this was all thy care
> To stand approved in sight of God, though worlds
> Judge thee perverse. (*PL*.VI.33–7)

If the stance of conscience is extremely individualistic – that of the individual alone against the world – it seems to merge with the totally conscienceless man, the merchant Barterville, in Thomas Dekker's *If This Be Not a Good Play, the Devil Is in It*. Barterville says:

> Nature sent man into the world, (alone,)
> Without all company, but to care for one,
> And that ile doe.[7]

The devil Lurchall responds: 'True Citie doctrine sir.'

We shall see that most eighteenth-century thinkers rejected the premise of natural individuality, both in the form of the egoism of Barterville (Hobbes, Spinoza, Locke, and Mandeville) and in the form of the Presbyterian conscience. Or rather, eighteenth-century thinkers tended to merge self-love and conscience within a social psychology in which the two were harmonized (and perhaps governed) by a desire for social approval and an aversion to social censure. In his *Essay on Man* Alexander Pope seemed to capture the banner of the eighteenth century: 'Thus God and nature linked the general frame / And bade self-love and social be the same' (III.317–18).

Seventeenth-century soliloquy gave way to eighteenth-century conversation. According to Samuel Johnson, solitude is 'one of the greatest obstacles to pleasure and improvement.'[8] Public opinion replaced the moral soliloquizing of conscience. Moreover, conscience, to eighteenth-century British thinkers, became identified with the disorder and violence of 'the Puritan revolution.'

Milton and Antinomianism

Christopher Milton, John's younger brother, was a royalist, a Catholic, and a lawyer, and was appointed a judge during the reign of James II. John Milton's conscience was the antithesis of the conservative legalism of his brother; it proclaimed republicanism and revolution.

In Chapter 1, we examined the antinomian character of Protestant conscience, particularly as it was expressed at the time of the English Civil War. John Milton was not unambiguously antinomian. Indeed, in *Paradise Lost* (V.160) he characterized the forces of Satan as anarchistic; Satan claims that it is unjust to bind with law. Christian liberty, as celebrated in Milton's poems and prose, is not undisciplined, nor is it mere licence. Northrop Frye wrote: 'Liberty for Milton is not something that starts with man: it starts with God. It is not something that man naturally wants for himself, but something that God is determined he shall have; man cannot want it unless he is in a regenerate state, prepared to accept the discipline and responsibility that go with it. Hence, as Milton says, none can love freedom but good men; the rest want not freedom but licence.'[9]

Milton's freedom of conscience is not, then, Satanic licence. Yet both seem to be antinomian in character. Milton wrote: 'CHRISTIAN LIBERTY means that CHRIST OUR LIBERATOR FREES US FROM ... THE RULE OF THE LAW AND OF MEN, AS IF WE WERE EMANCIPATED SLAVES.'[10] In *The Doctrine and Discipline of Divorce*, Milton opposes conscience and law. He wrote that 'the matter of divorce is not to be try'd by law, but by conscience, as many other sins are.' Sins and crimes are not coextensive: 'To make a regularity of sin by law, either the law must straiten sin into no sin, or sin must crook the law into no law.'[11] Law is always coercive; it regulates others' conduct through legally enforced sanctions. Conscience is always free; it judges only one's own conduct, not that of others: 'But if any man shall pretend, that the scripture judges to his conscience for other men, he makes himself greater not only then the church, but also too high for any mortal.'[12] Conscience exceeds its office when it judges others as well as oneself. Northrop Frye rightly observed that 'the desire to persecute has its origin, not in zeal, but in the deification of some human form of understanding: its root is not "You must believe in God," but "You must believe in what I mean by God."'[13] The criminalization of sin, as well as the persecution of sin and heresy, is based on disbelief in the efficacy of conscience.

Milton insisted that 'no man, no synod, no session of men, though called the church, can judge definitively the sense of scripture to another mans conscience, which is well known to be a general maxim of the Protestant religion' and a reason why no crime of heresy exists within Protestantism.[14] 'No visible church, then, let alone any magistrate, has the right to impose its own interpretations upon the consciences of men as matters of legal obligation, thus demanding implicit faith.'[15] To those who think that freedom of conscience should not scandalize believers, Milton boldly declared: 'As for scandals, if any man be offended of the conscientious liberty of another, it is a taken scandal not a given.'[16] To these uplifting words, Milton added that the magistrate cannot curtail liberty of conscience because it 'is the certain and sacred gift of God, neither to be touched by him, nor parted with by us.' But although he sanctified conscience, Milton did not universalize freedom of conscience or provide clear guidelines for distinguishing conscientious liberty from criminal licence.

Milton believed that Presbyterian government of the church was 'the hedge, and Bulwarke of Religion.'[17] Thus, religions with different structures of church authority were not to be tolerated under the principle of freedom of conscience. Papacy and prelacy were linked in servile conjunction with monarchy. In the early 1640s Milton seemed to want to shape the discipline and government of the Church of England into a national Presbyterian church; later, however, he became a staunch supporter of the independence of congregations from a national church directed by Parliament. Roger Williams had described religious persecution as 'soul rape'; in a similar vein, Milton famously denounced 'the new forcers of Conscience under the Long

Parliament' that had dared to 'adjure the Civil Sword / To force our Consciences that Christ set free' and concluded that *'New* Presbyter is but Old Priest Writ large.'[18] But did Milton's conscience forbid coercion in matters of religion, as Roger Williams' conscience did? Or did Milton think – as his antagonist Samuel Rutherford did – that coercion is legitimate in the service of the godly over the ungodly, and illegitimate only when used by the godless against the god-fearing? Furthermore, if coercion and conscience are incompatible, how could Milton justify a politics of regicide and revolutionary violence?

For Milton, freedom of conscience did not mean merely religious toleration; religious toleration and political liberty were inextricably intertwined. Nor is freedom of conscience freedom of thought as distinct from freedom of action; free expression of thought in speech and writing cannot in practice be separated from the type of regime hospitable to critical thought and the political activity necessary to overthrow inhospitable regimes. Milton's celebrated words in *Areopagitica* – 'Give me the liberty to know, to utter, and to argue according to conscience, above all liberties' – were not the slogan of a debating society. Milton's celebration of freedom of conscience was not the same as the enlightened dicta of Jeremy Bentham and Immanuel Kant, who commended us to speak freely while obeying punctually.[19] Indeed, one might assert that for Milton, freedom of conscience meant the opposite of enlightened conformism coupled to free speech. Denis Diderot wrote: 'We must speak out against senseless laws until they're reformed and, in the meanwhile, abide by them. Anyone who on the strength of his own personal authority violates a bad law thereby authorizes everyone else to violate the good. Less harm is suffered in being mad among madmen than in being wise on one's own.'[20] Milton's conscience was not an enlightened prudence and genteel conformism: 'I fear yet this iron yoke of outward conformity hath left a slavish print upon our necks; the ghost of a linnen decency yet haunts us.'[21]

In *The Communist Manifesto*, Marx and Engels wrote that freedom of conscience is the appropriate ideology for the capitalist marketplace, in that it applies the principle of free competition to religious goods and services.[22] Milton in *Areopagitica* indeed argued for free trade in the knowledge business: 'Truth and understanding are not such wares as to be monopoliz'd and traded in by tickets and statutes, and standards.'[23] It would be best to leave printing entirely to conscience, trusting to the strength of truth and its victory in the competition of ideas, 'were it not the chief strong hold of our hypocrisie to be ever judging one another.' Monopoly is to Catholicism what competition is to Protestantism. Limitations to the free competition of ideas had their historical source in the Catholic inquisition but were 'catcht up by our Prelates, and hath caught some of our Presbyters.' Milton contended that because Catholicism is intolerant, publications promoting it should be suppressed.[24] Freedom of conscience was not, for Milton, unlimited toleration. Note here that Milton's intolerant anti-Catholicism had a strong political motive; his Protestant conscience dictated revolutionary republicanism.

Conscience, for Milton, was the divine light within – a guide to conduct, and not merely faith or belief. The God within not only forbids but also commands. Conscience is not a timid nay-sayer – not Hamlet's conscience that makes cowards of us all; rather, it is the clarion call of the spirited warrior. Conscience does not merely proscribe murder; it also prescribes the death of tyrants and their minions. In his regicidal *Eikonoklastes*, Milton denounced King Charles's reluctance to agree to the execution of Strafford: 'And this also we may take for truth, that he whose conscience thinks it sin to put to death a capital Offender, will as oft think it meritorious to kill a righteous person.'[25] The conscience of those active in politics cannot shrink from the taking of life if it serves the cause of popular liberty.

What is the source of Milton's certainty, which does not appear to be based on a weighing of probabilities? Milton thought that political and moral matters were to be disputed and proved on the basis of Scripture; only opinions provable by scriptural evidence are as unshakeable as the angel Abdiel.[26] However, the scriptures are merely external authority: 'The pre-eminent and supreme authority, however, is the authority of the Spirit, which is internal, and the individual possession of each man.'[27] Thus, each person must judge for himself what to believe and what to do: 'Each believer is entitled to interpret the scriptures ... for himself. He has the Spirit, who guides truth, and he has the mind of Christ. Indeed, no one else can usefully interpret them for him, unless that person's interpretation coincides with the one he makes for himself and his own conscience.'[28]

Milton's antagonist, Samuel Rutherford, a 'New Presbyter' who 'is but Old Priest writ large,' referred to 'that athesticall [sic] plague of liberty of conscience.' Conscience, for men like Milton, would be 'made every mans rule, umpire, judge, Bible, and his *God*, which if he follow, he is but at the worst, a godly, pious, holy Hereticke, who feareth his conscience more than his *Creator*, and is to be judged by you a saint.'[29] Rutherford thought it a foul and fatal error to follow erroneous conscience, and contended that to champion the rights of erroneous conscience, as Roger Williams did, was to promote godless libertinism.[30]

Milton, however, did *not* champion the rights of erroneous conscience. Moreover, the anarchism of the right of conscience or individual judgment of right and wrong is mediated in Milton by an aristocracy of virtue. In *Paradise Lost*, Milton declared: 'God and Nature bid the same, / When he who rules is worthiest, and excels / Them whom he governs' (VI.172–4).

Jackie Disalvo wrote: 'Like Locke, Milton argued that the poor were fated to be ruled, rather than rule, by their inferior rationality.'[31] In *A Second Defence of the English People*, Milton wrote that 'nothing is more natural, nothing more just, nothing more useful or more advantageous to the human race than that the lesser obey the greater, not the lesser number the greater number, but the lesser virtue the greater virtue, the lesser wisdom the greater wisdom.'[32] Thus, although Milton justified the right of conscientious judgment, he was in fact justifying the judgment of men like himself, not the inner light as it appeared to uneducated men, or Mary Carey's 'servants and handmaids.' Christopher Hill wrote: 'For Milton the Bible is not to be interpreted according to any individual conscience, however vulgar and ignorant. There must be objective definitions of man's good in society, definitions which are "reasonable," written by nature on the hearts of educated men; and these can be used to test the Bible, and as a check on individual interpretation.'[33] Thus the egalitarianism of Milton's view that each person must judge the Scriptures by his own in-dwelling spirit coexisted with an adherence to an aristocracy of reason and learning, rather than of birth or social status.

Although Milton would have rejected Samuel Rutherford's contention that he followed his conscience rather than the Bible or God, he thought that to follow one's conscience does not mean servile dependence on scripture but rather a liberal interpretation of it. Milton interpreted Christ's words (Luke 14:16) 'Compel them to come in,' traditionally interpreted to mean that force is justified in the case of heretics, to mean 'draws ... by the inward persuasive motions of his Spirit and by his ministers; not by the outward compulsions of a magistrate and his officers.'[34] Milton interpreted St Paul's counsel in Romans 13, to submit oneself to worldly powers and not resist them because these powers are divinely ordained, to mean that 'Christ set up his laws not to subvert the general form of government but to give it a firmer foundation.'[35] Milton found a Biblical warrant for divorce and usury, and indeed compared them as both subjects of conscience, not law.[36] Milton's contention that divorce and usury are matters of conscience rather than law anticipated the contemporary libertarian stance that the state has no business in the bedrooms and boardrooms of the nation and that anything is morally permissible between consenting adults.

Conscience and the Law of Divorce

The tension in conscience between revelation and reason, heteronomy and autonomy, dependence on Scripture and freedom of interpretation, can be seen in Locke's and Milton's advocacy of divorce. Locke shared Milton's view that marriage is a contract, dissolvable at will, and not an indissoluble sacrament that can be voided only by the adultery of one of the parties.[37] Milton cited Moses divorcing Zipporah for hardness of heart.[38] While the Bible does not mention Zipporah's hardness of heart, it does mention one dramatic incident that took place before Moses divorced her and married a Cushite (Numbers 12:1). Zipporah, apparently understanding that God intended to kill Moses for being remiss in the matter of circumcision, picked up a sharp rock, circumcised their son, Gershom, and spread the blood on Moses' thigh (Exodus 4:24–6). Zipporah's quick-wittedness saved Moses' life and perpetuated the Jewish race. The next and last mention of Zipporah is when Moses divorced her. Milton did not speculate that a reason why Jesus thought the only grounds for divorce to be adultery (Matthew 5:32; 19:19) was that women are vulnerable to the dominant will of men. Milton's appeal in *The Doctrine and Discipline of Divorce, Tetrachordon,* and *Colasterion,* to 'the higher Session of Conscience' – above all judicial courts – is not easily distinguished from the will of the husband. To Jesus' rule that adultery is the sole grounds for divorce, Milton added 'frigidity' and 'disproportion, contrarity or numnesse of minde.' Thus, character faults of women were the grounds Milton alleged for divorce. Indeed, 'it is absolutely certain that the word *fornication* means not so much adultery as the wife's constant contrariness, faithlessness and disobedience, which all show that her mind is not her husband's even if her body is.'[39] There can be little doubt that Milton is 'absolutely certain,' but it is far from clear that Jesus used words with such poetic licence, or shared Milton's view that women's minds and bodies belong to men. 'What could be more just?' Milton asked rhetorically in his argument for divorce, if a master has given a slave a wife, and the slave is freed after seven years, than that 'the wife and her children shall be the master's.'[40]

The burning eroticism of Adam's fall from grace through love of Eve in *Paradise Lost* is present in Milton's divorce pamphlets. I find it impossible to agree with A.L. Rowse's judgment that Milton was not interested in sex; indeed, I am inclined to C.S. Lewis's contrary view that Milton's work is more sexually charged than that of any other English poet.[41] Inverting the Pauline maxim that it is better to marry than burn, Milton stated that it is better to divorce than burn: 'If the woman be naturally so of disposition, as will not help to remove, but help to encrease that same God-forbidd'n loneliness,' then divorce is preferable to 'visiting the stews, or stepping to his neighbors bed.' If Christian mercy does not supersede the law against divorce, the alternative, Milton added, is 'to grind in the mill of an undelighted and servil copulation, must be the only forc't work of a Christian marriage, oft times with such a yokefellow, from whom both love and peace, both nature and Religion mourns to be separated.'[42]

Whatever the merits of Milton's arguments in favour of divorce, we see the inner-directedness of conscience, as distinct from considerate attentiveness to the needs and perspectives of others. The situation of a young wife from a royalist family introduced into a Puritan household during the English Civil War did not influence his contention that the obstinacy and disobedience of the wife was grounds for divorce. Thus, when he referred to the horror of grinding in the mill of an undelighted and servile copulation, he did not entertain the situation of his own wife, who, after her royalist family was beggared in the Civil War, returned to him on her knees and bore him children before dying after the fourth child. Milton's conscience did not make him more sensitive than other men to the feelings of wives, for all that he championed love in marriage and freedom of divorce.

On matters of love and hate, freedom of conscience opposes coercive law. For Milton, Protestant conscience justified freedom of divorce, whatever Jesus said on the subject. To bolster his argument for polygamy, instead of citing the precedent of Luther's support for Philip of Hesse's bigamous marriage, Milton resorted to the authority of the Old Testament.[43]

Antinomian Conscience and Intolerance of Catholics

That Milton's conscience is antinomian is evident partly in its militant intolerance of Catholics. As Charles Geisst points out, Milton's intolerance of Catholics inheres in his championship of conscience.[44] Papists are opposed to political liberty; they are intolerant; they consult priests and superstitious traditions rather than the Bible; they are heretics, for a heretic is 'he who follows the Church against his conscience and persuasion grounded on scripture.'[45] Milton pointed out that the literal meaning of heresy is *choice*, before putting this rhetorical question: 'What is freedom but choice?'[46] Christopher Hill wrote: 'A man may be a heretic in the truth, if he takes over at second hand a doctrine which he has not made his own: conversely, a man cannot be a heretic if he follows his conscience sincerely – even "though against any point of doctrine by the whole church received." The heretic is "he who follows the church against his conscience and persuasion grounded on the scripture."'[47]

Catholics, Milton thought, lack a conscience in that they do not make judgments for themselves. Thus, Robert Catesby and the Gunpowder Plotters were not acting from conscience, not because regicide is wrong but rather because the plotters did not express independent judgment. According to Milton, the Gunpowder Plotters were pawns of the Jesuits.[48] Protestants put conscience above the Church; papists put the Church above conscience.[49] In *Paradise Lost*, Milton inveighed against the Roman merger of spiritual and secular power, which violates conscience: 'and from that pretense / Spiritual Lawes by carnal power shall force / On every conscience' (XII.521–3). For him, the Catholic church was guilty of sacrilege: 'for on Earth / Who against Faith and Conscience can be heard / Infallible' (XII.528–30).

Milton's view of the universal Christian Church differs from that of orthodox Roman Catholicism: 'The Christian Church is universal; not ti'd to nation, dioces or parish, but consisting of many particular churches complete in themselves; gatherd, not by the compulsion or the accident of dwelling nigh together, but by the free consent chusing both their particular church and their church officers.'[50] Catholicism is a priestly despotism, not a Christian federated republic of free, self-disciplined men.

Conscience dictates that the Roman Catholic church be destroyed and Catholic practices suppressed: 'If they say that by denouncing their idols we violate their Consciences, we have no warrant to regard

Conscience which is not grounded in Scripture.'[51] Thus, for Milton, liberty of conscience means that 'no true Protestant can persecute, or not tolerate his fellow Protestant, though dissenting from him in some opinions.'[52] For Milton, freedom of conscience certainly did not mean toleration for Catholics. Perez Zagorin found Milton's views on freedom of conscience absurd: 'Why wasn't the Catholic conscience as much entitled to freedom as the Protestant?'[53] Milton perhaps would have replied that just as thought is a condition of freedom of thought, so the exercise of conscience is a condition of its liberty. Milton's denial of freedom of conscience to Catholics is similar to Locke's position in *Letters concerning Toleration*, but is based on more sustained argument. Milton viewed Catholicism, with its confession, penance, easy absolution, and indulgences, as lacking the self-command he thought essential to Christian liberty.[54] The rights of conscience correspond to its duties. The Catholic church has failed in its prime duty to create conditions for the exercise of conscience or independent judgment. Catholics have flabby moral muscles or improperly developed consciences. For Milton, freedom of conscience meant freedom for those who have developed a conscience.

Milton's conscience was a martial banner precisely because it was partisan or antinomian. His republicanism was fiercely anti-Catholic. Anti-Catholicism provided a focus for his republican partisanship, that is, an enemy against which Protestant sectarians might find common cause. With the notable exception of Roger Williams and some Levellers and Quakers, commitment to the republican cause was equivalent to anti-Catholic bigotry. The individualism of Milton's championship of the rights of conscience became, through intolerant anti-popery, partisan collectivism.[55] Individual conscience became partisan class consciousness.

Although Milton was not as egalitarian as the radical antinomians of the civil war years, he asserted in *The Tenure of Kings and Magistrates* that 'no man who knows ought, can be so stupid as to deny that all men naturally were borne free, being the image and resemblance of God himself.'[56] Milton supported an aristocratic republic of virtue, not an aristocracy of birth; but he seemed democratic with respect to the right of revolution. He rejected Salmasius's view that judges of kings as tyrants should be 'wise, learned, of pre-eminent worth or birth'; for him, all those who had 'felt the weight of slavery's yoke' were competent judges of the tyrant Charles and his minions, Strafford and Laud.[57] Thomas Hobbes stood aloof from the controversy between Claude

Salmasius in his defence of the king and Milton in his defence of the English people; Milton's defence of regicide was written with as good Latin and ill reason as Salmasius's opposition to it.[58]

In Milton's writings we see how conscience has become heroic or revolutionary. Despite Milton's occasional praise of humility, John Dryden was not wrong in linking conscience with self-confidence. The voice of conscience replaced both custom and traditional authority; individual interpretation of Scripture empowered the weak to challenge their superiors in the social hierarchy. The dictates of conscience engendered zeal, discipline, and the duty to overthrow popery and prelacy. Liberty of conscience meant political as well as religious liberty; it mandated a political regime permitting and even encouraging experimentation in thought and deed. Conscience dictated the violent overthrow and repression of those who would deny freedom of conscience. Milton's antinomian and partisan conscience was the banner of revolutionary republicanism. As Milton's sonnet 16 implored: 'Helpe us to save free Conscience from the paw / Of hireling wolves whose Gospel is their maw.'[59]

Milton would have agreed with Montaigne's posing of alternatives: 'We should either wholly submit to our ecclesiastical government or altogether dispense with it.' But he disagreed with the anti-Protestant conclusion Montaigne drew from this alternative: 'It is not for us to determine what degree of obedience we owe to it.'[60] Milton's conscience entailed the private judgment of right and wrong and the right of revolution; Montaigne's conscience prescribed the maintenance of tradition. However different their politics, Montaigne and Milton shared the central insight that the judgments of conscience define human existence, that conscience judges what is appropriate to oneself not others, and thus that the measure of each individual is to be found within himself or herself.

Chapter 4

Hobbes on Conscience outside and inside the Law

Sceptical Toleration and the Certainty of Conscience

W.K. Jordan and Gordon Schochet have distinguished freedom of conscience, which is a principle mandating separation of church and state, from religious toleration, which is a pragmatic state policy aiming to secure civil peace between warring sects.[1] Freedom of conscience is an entitlement, whereas toleration is a privilege granted by the state (which has the authority to permit or suppress dissenting sects and thus favours a dominant religion, whether or not it is officially established). Immanuel Kant praised Frederick the Great for renouncing 'the haughty name of tolerance' in favour of genuine freedom of conscience.[2] Freedom of conscience is claimed to be a human or prepolitical right; whereas toleration is a civil arrangement, and thus a consequence of politics. In distinguishing freedom of conscience from tolerance, Schochet does not mention the unbending character of men of principle, or the general intolerance exhibited by champions of conscience and its freedom. W.K. Jordan wrote that the Puritan's glorious defence of the rights of conscience 'compensates for the generally bigoted and intolerant character of his moral philosophy.'[3]

Men of conscience such as John Milton, Pierre Jurieu, and John Locke could be as intolerant of Catholics as Cardinal Richelieu and Bishop Bossuet were of Huguenots. In France, those who did not participate in the war purportedly between Christ and the Antichrist were known as 'politiques.' Among these the most notable was the theorist of state sovereignty, Jean Bodin. Thomas Hobbes is the English *philosophe politique*.

Bodin argued that the sovereign authority of the prince exceeds that of all ecclesiastical authorities.[4] Although the sovereign is subject to natural and divine law, he is not subject to any laws of his predecessors or himself, or to any earthly judge.[5] According to Bodin, the greatest tyranny is less miserable than anarchy; and it is tyrannical for a prince to forbid his subjects the private exercise of their religion, although it is prudent to forbid public debate of a religion generally received and established.[6]

Michel de Montaigne was also sceptical of the Protestant conscience. He thought there was 'much more danger than profit' in the project of translating the Bible into the vernacular, since the Bible 'is not for everyone to study.' He piously professed to have submitted his ideas to 'the judgement of those to whom it belongs to direct not only my actions and my writings, but my thoughts as well.'[7] Peter Burke linked Montaigne's scepticism to his deference to authority: 'Montaigne here gave his public assent to the Church's right to thought control, and to the attitude of mind recommended by St. Ignatius in his *Spiritual Exercises* (1548): "I will believe that the white object I see is black if that should be the decision of the hierarchical Church." After all, sceptics knew that senses could not be trusted.'[8]

Sceptical toleration is not the same as championing the rights of conscience. It does not betray a sceptical disposition to maintain that it is a fundamental violation of human dignity for the state to limit access to the saving truths of the Bible, or that it is soul-rape to force conscience and prescribe what is essential for salvation (which is properly a matter for an individual's own judgment). Hobbes was the most philosophic spokesman for the tradition that combined religious scepticism with the Erastian supremacy of the state in matters of conscience. Let us call this attitude enlightened tolerance, to distinguish it from the certainties of Protestant conscience; there is a world of difference between on the one hand affirming that the Protestant conscience is so sacrosanct that the most fundamental human rights are violated when the state interferes with it, and on the other hand being sceptical of all religious opinions, tolerating equally those which do not disturb the public peace. Voltaire voiced the defining creed of the Enlightenment: 'What is tolerance? It is an adjunct of humanity. We are formed of weaknesses and errors; let us forgive one another our follies – that is the first law of nature.'[9]

In this chapter I place Hobbes at the apex of that tradition of thought known as the Enlightenment. I do so even though contemporary writers such as Isaac Kramnick and Stuart Brown omit Hobbes from their catalogue of Enlightenment thinkers.[10] Eighteenth-century *philosophes* recognized Bacon and Locke, but not Hobbes, as their spiritual forebears. As Norman Hampson wrote: 'Everyone found Hobbes an embarrassing ally.'[11] Yet Hume, Voltaire, and Diderot shared Hobbes's scepticism about the claims of conscience, and combined religious scepticism with support for an established church. In *La Voix du sage et du peuple*, Voltaire declared: 'Reason informs us that the prince must be absolute master of all ecclesiastical policy (*Police*), without any restriction whatsoever.'[12] Hobbes's mighty Leviathan can be understood as the philosophic statement of the politics of sceptical tolerance.

Thus we may distinguish Hobbesian tolerance from Milton's or Locke's rights of conscience: the former is born of scepticism, the latter of subjective certainty. Hobbes's scepticism of Protestant conscience led him to advocate the decriminalization of heresy, as well as religious toleration under the aegis of an established and latitudinarian Church of England. Liberty of conscience means the separation of church and state; freedom for all religious sects that hold religion to be a matter of interiority and privacy, not of public profession; and intolerance for those not graced by a Protestant form of communion.

Law and Conscience

In this chapter I wish to demonstrate that Hobbes feared the anarchic and antinomian tendencies of Protestant conscience, described in Chapters 1 and 3; and that a key aim of his politics was, as R.E. Ewin writes, to overcome the opposition between law and conscience.[13] If Hamlet were right that conscience makes cowards of us all, then Hobbes would have been a friend of conscience. In Hobbes's view, it was the Protestant conscience, by empowering the lower orders to challenge ecclesiastical and civil authorities, that brought about bloody civil war – that state of nature in which life is 'solitary, poor, nasty, brutish and short.' Even so, Hobbes was not completely opposed to the claims of conscience; rather, he found a place for them within the law, in the process of trial by jury. For Hobbes, conscience is housed within the rights of defendants and of jurors. Homeless, conscience is disruptive, even revolutionary. However, subjective (not demonstrative) certainty, when housed within the law, has an important civic role to play in verdicts beyond reasonable doubt.

Oliver St John, when presenting a Bill of Attainder against Strafford at the beginning of the English Civil War, told fellow parliamentarians that to pass the Bill 'private satisfaction to each man's conscience is sufficient, although no evidence has been given at all.'[14] The monstrous injustice to Charles I's chief of staff in his parliamentary trial strongly suggests to us why Hobbes opposed the politics of conscience. As Hobbes's contemporary Benjamin Whichcote stated: 'Conscience, without judgment, is superstition.'[15] A verdict according to conscience, rather than according to the evidence, might well reveal the irrationality of conscience and the reasons why enlightened reason repudiates the claims of conscience. However, as we shall see, Hobbes's jurors have a right to make a verdict according to their consciences, despite the instructions of judges as to the law and the evidence. Irreducible subjectivity is integral to trial by jury. According to Hobbes's theory, the injustice to the Earl of Strafford had at its centre the denial of the right of the accused to reject all jurors he suspected of prejudice or bias.

William Godwin shared Hobbes's secularism and egalitarianism but his anarchist views were antithetical to Hobbes's philosophic anti-anarchism. Godwin, a strong supporter of revolutionary republicanism, thought the parliamentarians were right in executing Strafford because he would have provided the ablest military leadership for the royalist side in the coming civil war. But if the parliamentary verdict had been just as well as prudent, it would have been, for Godwin, a higher justice than merely legal justice. Sounding Lutheran in his opposition of conscience to law with respect to the verdict against Strafford, Godwin wrote: 'Law is made for man; and not man for the law.'[16]

Hobbes on Protestant Egalitarianism and Antinomianism

Mark Whitaker has pointed to Hobbes's ambivalence about the Protestant Reformation: Hobbes both commended reading the Bible and warned that doing so might be a source of strife.[17] Margaret Samson portrayed Hobbes as a Protestant casuist, one who thought that the meaning of Scripture was plainly set down in the Bible, but who also thought that erroneous interpretations had to be cleared away, and true interpretations preached in the pulpits; only then could the meaning of Scripture become evident to Christians.[18] Joseph Cropsey, although he understood Hobbes to be a monarchical absolutist and legal positivist, stated that Hobbes desired a Reformation in law; that is, Hobbes advocated universal and immediate access to the statutes (as

Protestants had copies of the Bible) so that individuals could interpret laws by themselves, unmediated by a priesthood of lawyers.[19]

Hobbes wrote in *Behemoth* that the chief cause of the English Civil War was Presbyterian distemper arising from the translation of the Bible into the vulgar tongue:

> For after Bible was translated into English, every man, nay every boy and wench, that could read English, thought they spoke with God Almighty, and understood what He said, when by a certain number of chapters a day they had read the Scriptures once or twice over. The reverence and obedience due to the Reformed Church here, and to the bishops and pastors therein, was cast off, and every man became a judge of religion, and an interpreter of the Scriptures to himself.[20]

The Protestant conscience empowered the poor and ignorant to challenge their betters in the social order. Hobbes recognized that the nobility and the gentry in the royalist cause lacked the morale of the lower orders in the parliamentary cause. The power of the Protestant conscience was, for Hobbes, precisely the danger: 'If it be lawful then for subjects to resist the king, when he commands anything that is against the Scripture, that is, contrary to the command of God, and to be judge of the meaning of Scripture, it is impossible that the life of any King, or the peace of any Christian kingdom, can be long secure.'[21]

John Dunn declared Hobbes's views on the rights of conscience to be 'great but alarming,'[22] although it is not clear whether he shared the alarm of those critical of Hobbes's deficient respect for the rights of conscience. On the other hand, Richard Tuck asserted that Hobbes *defended* conscience in that he 'mistrusted any privileged body of intellectuals who might come to have some kind of independent ideological authority over their fellow citizens.'[23] I wish to extend Tuck's view to encompass a Protestant conscience within Hobbes's account of due process of law; and to suggest that Hobbes's attack on common lawyers, such as Sir Edward Coke, exemplifies a Reformation in law.[24] In doing so, I wish also to suggest that Hobbes's command theory of law includes a role for jurors in the interpretation of law. While Hobbes is well known for his view that a subject's liberty depends on the sovereign's silence – that a subject is free to do whatever the sovereign does not forbid in law – I wish to emphasize the freedoms that subjects enjoy *within* the law, as defendants subject to due process of trial by jury. Also, while Hobbes is celebrated or reviled as the father of legal positivism – law as the will of the sovereign – he not only defended jurors' rights to be independent of both bench and government, but also asserted that jurors decided not only fact (whether or not an accused stole some property, met with other Quakers, or uttered a view critical of government) but also law (whether the theft was a capital felony, whether the meeting constituted unlawful assembly, whether the utterance constituted seditious libel). In this light, jury verdicts according to conscience are the appropriate institutional mode for the kind of judgment that is so dangerous outside an institutional forum.

Hobbes objected to the unwarranted certitude of those men of conscience who paraded their opinions as something beyond question. Conscience vacillates between opinion and knowledge, between revelation and reason, and between individual inwardness and sectarian collectivism. Hobbes asserted that 'men, vehemently in love with their own new opinions, though never so absurd, and obstinately bent to maintain them, gave those their opinions also that reverenced name of conscience, as if they would have it seem unlawful, to change or speak against them; and so pretend to know they are true, when they know at most, but that they think so.'[25]

Conscience, for Hobbes, moves back and forth between the poles of individuality and collectivity,[26] and between those of dubious opinion and certain knowledge. W.K. Jordan argued that by emphasizing the complete subjectivity of faith, 'Hobbes had destroyed the possibility both of persecution and of sectarian resistance. An icy toleration, the toleration of spiritual death, emerges from this masterly and amazing logic.'[27] Hobbes thought that the subjective certainty of men of conscience is recognized and reinforced by fellow communicants; Protestant inwardness becomes politically dangerous in group sectarianism. Hobbes's fellow traveller, Benedict de Spinoza, wrote:

> Not that I wish to charge the wretched sectaries with impiety for adapting the words of Scripture to their own opinions; for since Scripture was originally adapted to the understanding of the masses, everyone is free to adapt it to his own opinions if he sees that he can thereby obey God with greater conviction in matters of justice and charity ... The reason why I accuse them is that they refuse to allow this same liberty to others, and persecute everyone who disagrees with them.[28]

Hobbes also thought that upholding the rights of conscience was tantamount to imposing on others the sovereignty of one's own opinions.[29] If Hobbes was worried about individuals claiming a sanctity to their private opinions under the name of conscience, he succeeded in diminishing the extent to which Biblical citation was used to undergird political opinions. W.K. Jordan wrote: 'Following the publication of the *Leviathan* the Bible speedily disappeared as the prime source of political theory.'[30]

Hobbes wrote: 'It is either *science* or *opinion* which we commonly mean by the word *conscience*; for men say that such and such is true in or upon their conscience; which they *never* do, when they think it is *doubtful*, and therefore they know, or think they know it to be true.'[31] In Hobbes's view, conscience is opinion parading as knowledge, an unwarranted certainty justifying private judgment of right and wrong, a pretence to judge the sovereign will declared in law:

> Another doctrine repugnant to civil society, is, that *whatsoever a man does against his conscience, is sin*; and it dependeth on the presumption of making himself judge of good and evil. For a man's conscience, and his judgement is the same thing, and as the judgement, so also the conscience may be erroneous. Therefore, though he that is subject to no civil law, sinneth in all he does against his conscience, because he has no other rule to follow but his own reason; yet it is not so with him that lives in a commonwealth; because the law is the public conscience, by which he hath already undertaken to be guided. Otherwise in such diversity, as there is of private consciences, which are but private opinions, the commonwealth must needs be distracted, and no man dare to obey the sovereign power, further than it shall seem good in his own eyes.[32]

It would seem that conscience plays no role in the mighty Leviathan. The Hobbesian science of justice appears to take the 'con' out of conscience, to supersede the right of private judgment of good and evil. The greatest error of the universities, Hobbes asserted, was to teach 'that men shall judge of what is lawful and unlawful, not by the law itself, but by their own consciences; that is to say, by their own private judgments.'[33] Yet individual conscience is upheld and safeguarded in 'public conscience' or the rule of law.

The inner realm of conscience is sacrosanct in that individuals can be tried and punished only for their deeds, not for their thoughts, and only on the basis of public evidence, not on their private intentions.

One is not obliged to testify against oneself or to swear on oath. Information extracted through torture can never be used against one in a court of law. Hobbes robustly repudiated the attempt to pass laws over the conscience, and he denounced the Romano-canonical procedures of inquisition, torture, and confession prevalent in the Kingdom of Darkness.

> There is another error in their civil philosophy, which they never learned of Aristotle, nor Cicero, nor any other of the heathen, to extend the power of law, which is the rule of actions only, to the very thoughts and consciences of men, by examination, and *inquisition* of what they hold, notwithstanding the conformity of their speech and actions. By which, men are either punished for answering the truth of their thoughts, or constrained to answer an untruth for fear of punishment. It is true, that the civil magistrate, intending to employ a minister in the charge of teaching, may inquire of him, if he be content to preach such and such doctrines; and in case of refusal, may deny him the employment. But to force him to accuse himself of opinions, when his actions are not by law forbidden, is against the law of nature; and especially in them, who teach, that a man shall be damned to eternal and extreme torments, if he die in a false opinion concerning an article of the Christian faith. For who is there, that knowing there is so great danger in an error, whom the natural care of himself, compelleth not to hazard his soul upon his own judgment, rather than that of any other man that is unconcerned in his damnation?[34]

According to Montaigne, torture was falsely thought to facilitate the power of conscience: 'For in the guilty man conscience seems to assist the rack to make him confess his misdeed and to weaken him; while, on the other hand, it fortifies the innocent man against the torture.'[35] Evidence extracted through torture is excluded when an immunity is recognized with respect to self-incrimination, or when confession is not held to be the best evidence of guilt. Hobbes insisted that 'accusations upon torture, are not to be reputed as testimonies' – an aspect of a defendant's immunity from self-incrimination.[36] 'A covenant to accuse oneself, without assurance of pardon, is likewise invalid.'[37] Hobbes maintained that 'whatsoever hurt a man is made to suffer by bonds, or restraint, before his cause be heard, over and above that which is necessary to assure his custody, is against the law of nature.'[38] Torture, while against the law of nature in Hobbesian theory, was practised in England until 1640, and persisted throughout the eighteenth century in continental Europe.[39] Jean Calas, the Huguenot accused of murder and tortured to death without confessing (thus saving his family from similarly meeting a grisly end), was championed by Voltaire; the Huguenot minister Rochette, and the Protestant Greniers accused of attempting to free him from prison, were tortured to death at the same time without any defenders among *les lumières*. While Voltaire did not think Rochette should be executed simply for conducting Protestant services, he thought the Greniers might be participants in a Protestant rebellion and thus did not object to the use of torture to bring 'the rebellion' to light.[40] The Enlightenment's aversion to torture was moderated by a Hobbesian aversion to rebellion.

The Hobbesian sovereign cannot punish subjects without a public trial[41] based on precedent law[42]. Hobbes made clear in Chapter 28 of *Leviathan* that to do so is to wage war on subjects; it is an act of hostility, not of punishment, and reintroduces the state of war that sovereignty served to supersede. Punishment of the innocent is thus contrary to the law of nature. However, Hobbes also made it clear that the sovereign is not bound by civil laws. The sovereign can choose to proceed against subjects within the terms of existing law or outside the law, by virtue of his power. If the sovereign acts through law, the subject can take the sovereign to court: 'For seeing the sovereign demandeth by force of a former law, and not by virtue of his power; he declareth thereby, that he requireth no more, than shall appear to be due by that law.'[43] To take a current example (although sovereignty in Canada is divided between the Canadian people and the people in the various provinces), the Canadian or Quebec people could expropriate native lands by virtue of their power, or could litigate with members of the Cree nation with respect to treaty rights. If the sovereign lays claim to something by virtue of its power, it is an act of hostility to the Cree, and reinstitutes a state of nature with respect to them. A prudent sovereign (one who does not want to turn Canada into Yugoslavia) would then proceed against subjects by existing law, and meet these subjects in court rather than on the battlefield. In such a situation, the subject 'hath the same liberty to sue for his right, as if it were against a subject; and before such judges, as are appointed by the sovereign.'[44]

A problem arises here, because two chapters later, in Chapter 23 of *Leviathan*, Hobbes insisted that suits between two subjects 'ought in equity to be judged by men agreed on by consent of both,'[45] whereas in a suit of a subject against a sovereign, the sovereign chooses the judge. Hobbes continued in Chapter 23 to insist that if one is going to be judged by men not God (as in trial by combat, ordeal, or oath), justice requires that one be able to reject one's judges in equity courts, and jurors in common law courts. Thus, 'if the defendant be allowed to except against such of his judges, whose interest maketh him suspect them, (for as the complainant he hath already chosen his own judge), those which he excepteth not against, are judges he himself agrees on.'[46] Whether equity judges or jurors, the authority and finality of a verdict depends on the fact that 'the defendant is judged by his own judges'[47]; as he said in *Dialogue of the Common Laws*, 'every man is bound to acquiesce in the sentence of the judges he chooses.' If Hobbes were consistent, the subject who takes her sovereign to court would have the choice of which of the Crown-appointed judges she would prefer to hear the suit against the sovereign.

Hobbes's principle seems to be that the authority of human justice (as distinct from God's impending judgment on us all) depends on a defendant's ability to choose his judges or jurors, and reject those he suspects of bias. In trial by jury, the defendant 'might make his exceptions, till at last twelve men without exception being agreed on, they were judged by those twelve. So that having his own judges, there could be nothing alleged by the party, why the sentence should not be final.'[48]

In his *Dialogue of the Common Laws*, Hobbes seemed to exalt equity courts at the expense of common law courts. The central feature of common law procedure is trial by jury, which, as James R. Stoner, Jr, pointed out, Hobbes never derogated. In Hobbes's time, equity or prerogative courts accepted written depositions of witnesses and thus favoured the poor (since claimants and witnesses did not have to take a long time off work to face the accused in a jury trial). Hobbes asserted: 'Nor is a Jury more capable of duly examining Witnesses than a Lord Chancellor.'[49] We might note that the seventeenth-century jury took a more activist role than contemporary juries in examining witnesses and defendants. Nor did Hobbes state, in his *Dialogue* or in Chapter 26 of *Leviathan* (which discusses the abilities of a judge), that jurors are incompetent to decide points of law. Indeed, he looked on juries as preferable in difficult treason trials, such as the one that decided Henry Garnett's role in the Gunpowder Plot: 'the proof, when it is doubtful, is to be judged by a jury of twelve lawful men.'[50] Verdicts according to jurors' consciences are desirable when guilt or innocence is not demonstrable; subjective certainty has a role when one needs a verdict beyond reasonable doubt. Furthermore, jury verdicts complement the command theory of law in that they demonstrate public acceptance of the sovereign's will in particular cases, and inspire public confidence that right has been done, and instil the conviction that law, as the sovereign's command, rests on consent rather than coercion.

The theoretical opposition in the *Dialogue of the Common Laws* is between Sir Edward Coke's position that jurors decide facts whereas common law judges decide law, and Hobbes's position that judges and jurors interpret law, as the sovereign's will, on the basis of equity. 'In the courts of common law all trials are by twelve men, who are judges of the fact; and the fact known and proved, the judges are to pronounce the law; but in the spiritual court, the Admiralty, and in all the courts of Equity, there is but one judge, both of fact and law; this is all the difference.'[51] Hobbes's position is not that jury trial should be suspended in favour of judges in equity courts, but rather that jurors should decide both law and fact. The jury decides 'whether the fact laid before them, be burglary, robbery, theft or other felony. For this is to give a leading judgment to the jury, who ought not to consider any private lawyers Institutes, but the statutes themselves pleaded before them for direction.'[52] We can perhaps glimpse why Hobbes thought that jurors' equitable interpretations of law are consistent with his command theory of law: jurors displace common lawyers as those who give leading judgments of statute law.

The key requirement of a judge or juror, as distinct from an advocate who needs to be learned in the laws, is equity.[53] In Kantian jargon, jury verdicts are reflective rather than determinative judgments. That is, they do not merely subsume a particular case under a general law:

> In the ordinary trials of right, twelve men of the common people, are the judges, and give sentence, not only of the fact, but of the right; and pronounce simply for the complainant, or for the defendant; that is to say, are judges not only of the fact, but of the right; and in a question of crime, not only determine whether done, or not done; but also whether it be *murder, homicide, felony, assault,* and the like, which are determinations of law; but because they are not supposed to know the law themselves, there is one that hath authority to inform them of it, in the particular case they are to judge of. But yet if they judge not according to that he tells them, they are not subject to any penalty; unless it be made appear, that they did it against their own consciences, or had been corrupted by reward.[54]

There are many notable things in this magnificent passage. *First*, the verdict according to conscience is inviolable, contrary to the practices of the day, when jurors could be punished for not following the directions of the bench. For example, in 1665, Chief Justice Hyde told a split jury to agree: 'And as for you, that say you cannot in conscience find him guilty, if you say so again, without giving reasons for it, I shall take an order against you.'[55] But for Hobbes, the only ground for punishing a juror is for accepting bribes, and the only ground for not accepting a jury verdict is if it is coerced. Hobbes clearly opposed directed verdicts; for him, the judge's knowledge of the law was not binding on the consciences of jurors. *Second*, Hobbes opposed Sir Edward Coke's position that juries are only competent to determine fact, while judges determine law. Hobbes's position that jurors are judges of law as well as fact was, and still is, extremely radical; it is the position the leveller John Lilburne took in his sedition charges,[56] and it was unacceptable to both Crown and common lawyers, who wished to confine the jurors to judgments of fact (e.g., whether or not Levellers or Quakers met at a particular location but not whether such meetings constituted unlawful assembly, and whether or not an abortion had been performed but not whether abortion is criminal, and whether or not a theft took place but not whether the theft constituted a capital felony or a misdemeanour). One might think Hobbes would have been opposed to the anarchic and antinomian tendencies of the Levellers; yet he shared with them a democratic trust in the conscience of the common people, *insofar as conscience is institutionalized within the law in the form of jury verdicts.*

Thomas Green states that there were two alternatives to the formal or official view of Coke that jurors decide fact, not right: the less radical view that jurors had the discretion to adjust a verdict mercifully (either to acquit or to mitigate the verdict from a felony to a misdemeanour), and the more radical view that jurors had the right to nullify unjust laws.[57] The more common view in Hobbes's time was the former.[58] If, as is likely, Hobbes had the less radical view in mind in supporting verdicts according to conscience, the logic of his position is consistent with the radically democratic position of the Levellers. The more radical position – that jurors are the finders or makers of law – seems inconsistent with Hobbes's legal positivism, namely, that law is the command of the sovereign, whether it be Crown, Parliament or people.

Specific jury verdicts may conflict with the will of the sovereign. How can one square the circle of legal positivism and the equitable discretion or conscience of jurors? Jurors are immune from punishment. However, Hobbes asserted that the Crown can annul a jury verdict, while a judge cannot; although in the context of the king's prerogative of pardon, it appears that Hobbes had in mind the overturning of guilty verdicts.[59] The conflict between juror interpretation of law and Hobbes's command theory would be resolved if the experience of jury service could educate jurors to see the reasoning behind the sovereign's command in law, whether the jurors come to the reason for law by themselves, or instructed by Crown-appointed judges. Alternatively, the Crown would have to defer to the consciences of jurors. Since the sovereign cannot rely on 'terror of legal punishment,'[60] but only on subjects' convictions that laws are just, a prudent sovereign would not impose laws that would not be supported at jury trial. As Stephen Holmes indicates, for Hobbes, sovereign 'authority is excessive when it is self-defeating, when it undermines itself by alienating potential co-operators.'[61] Hobbes wrote: 'A law may be conceived to be good, when it is for the benefit of the sovereign; though it be not necessary for the people; but it is not so. For the good of the sovereign and people cannot be separated.'[62] Since the sovereign's duty is to make the need for law 'perspicuous' to the people, the jury system will educate both jurors and the general public to see the sovereign will. A good law is one that secures obedience through consent. The jury system can be seen as part of a command theory of law, in that the jury verdict is a litmus test of whether the law will be obeyed, enforced, and confirmed in the convictions of the people.

A command theory of law does not mean the arbitrary rule of an absolute monarch. The sovereign 'commands the people in general never but by a precedent law, and as a politic, not a natural person.'[63] As a natural person, the king may find his command blocked by jury verdicts; but as a politic person, the sovereign will understand that its edicts, when not upheld by juries – one might think of James II and the Seven Bishops, which led to the Glorious Revolution, or the Morgentaler case in Canada, which decriminalized abortion – do not have the force of law. To the extent that the Crown accepts the counsel of jurors, the jurors' law-finding or interpretative role is not necessarily in conflict with the sovereign's law-making function. Commands are not effective unless they are actually obeyed. The jury system, by mediating the relationship between ruler and ruled, makes law as command effective, and facilitates the sovereign's ability to rule with sword in sheath.

If I may jump from Hobbes's thought to the two thinkers who reintroduced conscience into political philosophy, following the post-Lockean rejection of conscience as an innate practical principle, I would like to say that Rousseau and Kant could have profited from Hobbes's views on jury verdicts. Kant's principle that positive law is legitimate insofar as citizens could have passed the law, and Rousseau's view that people are only free when they are obeying laws they have legislated, can be compared with the radical interpretation of Hobbes's view – that is, that jurors are judges of law as well as fact. Perhaps the great continental champions of conscience or moral autonomy could have learned from Hobbes's reflections on the most democratic institution in the English tradition. In the radical interpretation that makes jurors judges of law, jurors nullify laws that do not accord with their sense of equity or fairness, or they indirectly make law through their deliberations on specific cases. For Hobbes, the discretion, prerogative, sanctity, and inviolability of the jury verdict is the appropriate sphere of conscience. Like Hegel, Hobbes thought that the definitive mark of modernity – namely, subjectivity – must be housed within institutions. Outside institutional settings, subjective certainty is lunatic. Homeless, conscience is dangerous. The two great modern political philosophers found an appropriate home for Protestant conscience.

Reason and Conscience as Judge and Jury

In his third *Letter concerning Toleration*, Locke referred three times to responsible individuals 'following the light of their own reason and the dictates of their own conscience.'[64] Locke did not elucidate the relationship between reason, which enlightens, and conscience, which dictates. This chapter has attempted to clarify the meaning of conscience by examining Hobbes's views of the judge–jury relationship.[65] Reason, as an upper-class and learned judge, enlightens lower-class and ignorant jurors on matters of law, but untutored conscience, as juror, dictates the outcome of the trial. William Walwyn in *Juries Justified* wrote that 'understanding is in great reputation ... but yet nothing is so precious as a true conscience' and that 'consciences ... have been as frequently found under Felt Hats and Worsted stockings, as with People of a finer stuff.'[66] The relationship between reason and conscience is similar to but still different from the Hobbesian relationship between sapience or science and prudence or natural judgment. Conscience, like prudence, is not learned; it arises naturally from experience, not artificially from books or rational method. But conscience is a judgment of right, whereas prudence is a judgment of interest.

The theoretical model that compares conscience (the 'juror') to reason (the 'judge') may seem invalid. For surely the distinctive feature of conscience is that it prescribes judgments for oneself, whereas jurors judge the conduct of others. (My conscience judges what is right for *me* to do in *these* circumstances; the inner light does not extend to determining what is right for *others* to do in similar circumstances.) Thus Hobbes's views on the jury system are consistent with his opposition to the subjective certainty of those who are judge in their own cause. Hobbes generally confined the right of private judgment to that which is necessary for self-preservation. However, if we exclude the metaphor of conscience as a juror on the grounds that a juror judges others rather than himself, other common forensic metaphors for conscience, such as a witness or a judge, might also be excluded on the same ground. One is a witness on behalf of others, rather than oneself, or one judges others, rather than oneself.

The aspects of conscience I would like to highlight are these: *first*, untutored judgment as distinct from enlightened reason (whether of scientists or lawyers); *second*, subjective certainty, more than an estimate of probabilities; *third*, judgment of right, not merely prudential reason; and *fourth* and finally, immunity or sanctity of judgment. Hobbes opposed the antinomian tendencies of Protestant conscience, but he also recognized the irreducibility of conscience in the modern world. Conscience, like equity, is bound in relationships of attraction and repulsion to law; like equity, it stands outside the law but is bound to the law it judges. By institutionalizing subjective certainty within the law – within the rights of defendants and jurors – Hobbes hoped to tame the potentially anarchic and revolutionary character of the Protestant conscience.

It is useful to compare the relationship between reason and conscience with the relationship between judge and juror. In the sixteenth and seventeenth centuries, judges and juries contended for supremacy as interpreters of law. Hobbes's juror is inviolable; his judgement, however fallible, is final. Thus for Hobbes, conscience is both fallible (relative to demonstrable science) and inviolable (relative to prudential judgments). Verdicts according to conscience are autonomous, in that they are independent of the bench and the government and are not subject to the heteronomy of prudential calculation of the means to satisfy one's dominant passion. In the strongest interpretation of the role of the Hobbesian juror, conscience resides between judge (after the fact) and legislator (before the fact); it interprets law and thus participates in the construction of new law (rather than merely meting out guilt and punishment). Finally, conscience is innate or untutored; it is the self-reliant judgment of the common man, who confirms or rejects the rules and rulings of his wisers and betters. Conscience is plebeian certainty opposed to the learned reason of the upper-class judge. Like equity, conscience resides between the poles of autonomy and heteronomy – between free, creative judgment and subordination to existing rules. In the Hobbesian account of verdicts according to conscience, the invisible becomes visible; the God within is institutionalized in jurors' decisions beyond reasonable doubt.

Chapter 5

Enlightened Reason versus Protestant Conscience in John Locke

The Deprecation of Conscience in An Essay concerning Human Understanding

The Cambridge Companion to Locke asserts: 'John Locke is the most influential philosopher of modern times.'[1] Certainly Locke's writings were widely read and admired in the eighteenth century. Benjamin Franklin stated that he read and digested Locke's *Essay concerning Human Understanding* before he was sixteen years old.[2] Franklin's claim is more credible than if he had claimed to have read Plato, Aristotle, Augustine, Thomas, Descartes, Hobbes, Spinoza, or Leibniz at that age. Locke's writings are popular philosophy. Nathan Tarkov wrote: 'Americans can say that Locke is *our* political philosopher.' David Wootton universalized Tarkov's assertion: 'Almost all of us can now say that Locke is *our* political philosopher.'[3] It is a telling commentary on the English-speaking world that we have owned Locke as our political philosopher when, as Wootton observes, the inconsistencies in Locke's doctrine are so glaring that we have reason to doubt that his works were written by a single author.[4] Could it be that Locke is our political philosopher because he is not overly demanding of sustained thought and because we all can use some of his inconsistent teaching for our own purposes? In this chapter I will examine Locke's inconsistent teachings on conscience and its rights.

Locke's friend Isaac Newton thought *An Essay concerning Human Understanding* written by a Hobbist.[5] Locke's student, the third Earl of Shaftesbury, also thought Locke a Hobbist for undermining the natural basis of morality: ''Twas Mr. Locke that struck at all fundamentals, threw all order and virtue out of the world, and made the very ideas of these (which are the same as those of God) *unnatural*, and without foundation in our minds.'[6] Whatever the grounds for Newton and Shaftesbury thinking that only an atheist and hedonist could have written Locke's *Essay*, Locke scholars have been hard pressed to reconcile his philosophy, which seems to repudiate both natural law and the rights of conscience, with his *Two Treatises of Government* and *Letters concerning Toleration*, which are based on natural law and the rights of conscience.

Locke's *Essay* asserts that human beings have an innate desire for happiness and aversion to misery (I.iii.3), or desire pleasure as good and repudiate pain as evil (II.xx.2; II.xxi.42); but at the same time they have no innate ideas or practical principles of good and evil. Conscience is not 'written on their Hearts' but rather is produced 'from their Education, Company, and Customs of their Country.' Conscience 'is nothing else, but our own Opinion or Judgment of the Moral Rectitude or Pravity of our own Actions' (I.iii.8). Locke goes on to say that men will do any evil when 'at Liberty from Punishment and Censure' (I.iii.9). Locke denied that there are innate principles or natural laws regulating our conduct (I.iii.13). Later, he omitted natural law in his typology of law: divine law, concerned with sins and duties; civil law, concerned with criminality and innocence; and the law of opinion or reputation, concerned with virtues and vices. In the first edition of his *Essay*, Locke divided law into the Divine Law, the Civil Law, and 'The Philosophical Law, if I may so call it.'[7] Philosophic law is the rule of public opinion, under which people are governed not by conscience but by social approval and censure.

Locke elaborated this philosophic law: 'Vertue and Vice are names pretended and supposed every where to stand for actions in their own Nature, Right and Wrong.' In reality, however, they 'are constantly attributed only to such actions, as in each Country and Society are in reputation or discredit.' Therefore, the real measure of what 'is every where called and esteemed Vertue and Vice, is this approbation or dislike, praise or blame ... according to the Judgment, Maxims, or Fashions of that Place.'[8] The internal monitor is replaced by external censure in philosophic law. Locke wrote:

> I think, I may say, that he, who imagines Commendation and Disgrace, not to be strong Motives on Men, to accommodate themselves to the Opinions and Rules of those with whom they converse, seems little skill'd in the Nature, or History of Mankind, the greatest part whereof, he shall

find to govern themselves chiefly, if not solely, by this Law of Fashion; and so they do that, which keeps them in Reputation with their Company, little regard the Laws of God, or the Magistrate.⁹

To be sure, Locke did not definitely ally himself with 'the greatest part' who follow fashion or public opinion rather than divine or civil law. However, he equated the law of philosophers with the law of fashion. Fifteen years earlier, in 'Philanthropy, or The Christian Philosophers,' Locke wrote:

The first question every man ought to ask in all things he doth, or undertakes, is: How is this acceptable to God? But the first question most men ask is: How will this render me to my company, and those whose esteem I value? He that asks neither of those questions is a melancholy rogue, and always of the most dangerous and worst of men.¹⁰

Locke extended Hobbes's insight that love of virtue derives from love of praise. Since human beings are in large part products of their education, the true secret of education or socialization is to teach children to love approbation and hate disapprobation: 'Esteem and disgrace are, of all others, the most powerful incentives of the mind, when once it is brought to relish them.'¹¹ In this respect, Locke advanced beyond Hobbesian individualism toward the rise of 'society' in the eighteenth century: social order does not simply depend on the sword of the mighty Leviathan but on the network of social expectations. Since the dissolution of government is not the dissolution of society (a reversion to the state of nature or, in Hobbes's view, to an anarchic state of war), Lockean politics can be more liberal, even revolutionary, than those of his philosophic predecessor.

The eighteenth-century Enlightenment espoused Locke's replacement of conscience or the God within by public opinion or fashion; but *les philosophes* saw themselves as setting fashions or leading public opinion rather than simply following these, as Locke saw 'the greatest part' of mankind did. Locke taught the eighteenth century that social censure is a more effective monitor of human conduct than individual conscience: 'But no man scapes the Punishment of their Censure and Dislike, who offends against the Fashion and Opinion of the Company he keeps, and would recommend himself to. Nor is there one of ten thousand, who is stiff and insensible enough, to bear up under the constant Dislike, and Condemnation of his own Club.'¹²

Here Locke seems to be pointing away from the archetypical seventeenth-century inner-directed, stiff-necked individualist toward the other-oriented, clubbable gentleman of the eighteenth century. What the Enlightenment picked up from Locke was not Locke the revolutionary and man of Protestant conscience, but rather the man who in his rejection of innate ideas was suggesting that human beings are both malleable and open to being educated – who was repudiating original sin and the fixedness of human experience. As Locke concluded his *Some Thoughts concerning Education*, young people are to be 'considered only as white Paper, or Wax, to be moulded and fashioned as one pleases.'[13] Through education and social approbation, men can be enlightened to virtue.

Regarding the question of why the eighteenth-century English did not have an Enlightenment as the Scots, French, Germans, and Americans did, J.G.A. Pocock and Roy Porter contended that after the Glorious Revolution, there was no longer any need to 'écrasez l'infâme.'[14] To this view, Knud Haakonssen adds that the Glorious Revolution inaugurated a regime where 'public opinion was so significant that it drew in educated minds as opinion-makers and-seekers and diverted them from becoming a secluded and potentially oppositional elite of philosophers.'[15] Locke linked public opinion with philosophic law and thus anticipated the enlightened non-Enlightenment of eighteenth-century England.

Gilbert Ryle related a conversation with Bertrand Russell that might have occurred two centuries before, if one could be sure where the irony began and ended. Russell asserted, '"Locke was the spokesman of Common Sense." Almost without thinking I retorted impatiently, "I think Locke invented Common Sense." To which Russell rejoined, "By God, Ryle, I believe you are right. No one ever had had Common Sense before John Locke – and no one but Englishmen have ever had it since."'[16] Locke helped bring English philosophy and the common sense of an enlightened public opinion close together.

Besides the philosophic law or the law of fashion, Locke referred to reason and revelation as guides to conduct. Although Scriptural revelation is a useful guide to life beyond the grave, reason must judge whether the revelation truly comes from God. Revelation without reason is enthusiasm; enthusiasts, who do not exercise their God-given reason, are apt to dictate to others (IV.xix.3) and engender dangerous sectarian strife (IV.xx.17–18). It is enlightened reason, not irrational conscience, that promotes civic tolerance: '*Reason* is the proper Judge;

and *Revelation*, though it may in consenting with it, confirm its Dictates, yet cannot in such cases, invalidate its Decrees' (IV.xviii.6). Locke's central teaching is this: '*Reason* must be our last Judge and Guide in every Thing' (IV.xix.14).

Neal Wood wrote that it is 'highly probable [that] Locke's notion of the self-directed man was largely influenced by the Puritan idea of the individual conscience as the divinely inspired guide and director of life.'[17] James Tully refers to '*the* Lockean belief about the modern, post-Reformation individual: that the civic person is constituted by moral sovereignty over one's core beliefs and practice that cannot be alienated.'[18] However, Locke's *Essay* championed rational autonomy and deprecated conscience as irrational.

Whereas Michel de Montaigne asserted that conscience constitutes personal identity or makes individuals what they are, Locke in his *Essay* (II.i.11; II.xxvii.16–17) asserted that consciousness (a newly coined term) constitutes selfhood or personal identity. Locke borrowed the term from Ralph Cudworth's *The True Intellectual System of the Universe* (1678).[19] Christian Wolff in his translation of Locke's *Essay* coined the German word *Bewusstsein* (consciousness) to distinguish consciousness from *Gewissen* (conscience). Pierre Coste's translation of Locke's *Essay* distinguished *Conscientia* as inner conviction from *Scientia* as common knowledge shared by all, and used *conscience* for conscience and *con-science* for consciousness.[20] Contemporary English translations of the French *conscience* used conscience, consciousness, or self-consciousness depending on the context.[21] Self-consciousness, Coste thought, could not be translated into French. Jean Le Clerc agreed with Coste that consciousness 'is more commodious than the French word' (*conscience*). Leibniz suggested that the French adopt *consciosité* for the English 'consciousness'; when the French rejected his suggestion, he coined *aperception* for 'self-consciousness.'[22] Diderot and D'Alembert's *Encylopédie* lamented that 'what the English express by the word *consciousness* can only be rendered in French by periphrasis.'[23]

Locke's championship of rational consciousness over irrational conscience resonated immediately in continental Europe. One might speculate that the word 'consciousness' was welcome as a tool for differentiating human understanding from conscience as 'the God within.' Locke in his *Essay* (III.ix.3) distinguished the civil from the philosophic use of words; the former serves common use, while the latter serves 'to convey the precise Notions of Things, and to express, in general Propositions, certain and undoubted truths.' *Consciousness* appears to be

Locke's philosophic word; *conscience* appears to be an unphilosophic word, but one that plays an important role in his civic thought: in his *Two Treatises of Government* and his *Letters concerning Toleration*.

Conscience, in Locke's *Essay*, does not appear as a human faculty or ability, as do reason or consciousness, but as the content of consciousness; it is not the ability to make moral choices, or the capacity to make independent moral judgments; rather, it is the set of moral opinions arising from a determinate experience and environment. The egalitarianism of Protestant conscience seems to be jeopardized by Locke's championship of reason over conscience. Locke asserted that 'the greatest part of Mankind, who are given up to Labour' are unalterably captives to 'invincible ignorance' (IV.xx.2). Indeed, there are greater differences between the understandings of human beings than there are between those of some men and the beasts (IV.xx.5). Locke espoused Hobbesian nominalism without the philosopher's humanity or egalitarianism. Humanity, or the human species, Locke held, is a social construct or human artifact (III.vi.35–7). Indeed, Locke believed that some women had conceived children by mandrills, just as he had personally witnessed the offspring of a cat and a rat (III.vi.23). If Locke appeared credulous in thinking that the boundaries to the human species are made up by men, his nominalism undermined the reality of humanity and may have played a part in legitimating the slave trade.[24] To be sure, one has no warrant to assert that Locke's participation in the slave trade was directly connected to his repudiation of conscience as an innate practical principle; but one may consider whether Locke's rejection of conscience in his *Essay* is integrally related to his nominalism. Locke thought that both the contours of conscience and the boundaries of the human are human artefacts. However, his participation in the slave trade was prior to, and probably independent of, his philosophic elaboration of empiricism and nominalism.

Nevertheless, Locke's championship of reason above conscience in his *Essay* may constitute an inegalitarian strand in the texture of his thought; reason seems to be the privilege of an enlightened few. Outside his philosophic works, conscience seems the allotment of the unenlightened many. In 1698, Locke wrote in his commonplace book that 'a ploughman that cannot read, is not so ignorant but he has a conscience, and knows in those few cases which can concern his own actions, what is right and what is wrong.'[25]

In *The Reasonableness of Christianity*, Locke argued that the Christian gospel is particularly well suited to poor labourers, and seemed to champion Christian conscience over philosophic reason. Christian gospels 'reward the pains and hardships of those who stuck firm to their duties, and suffered for the testimony of a good conscience.' Christian conscience offers men assistance in overcoming worldly temptations. The ancient 'philosophers who spoke from reason' demonstrated 'the beauty of virtue' but 'leaving her unendowed, very few were willing to espouse her.' Christianity endowed virtue with a heavenly reward and thus made her more attractive: 'Interest is come about to her; and virtue now is visibly the most enriching purchase and by much the best bargain.'[26]

Christian conscience, however well suited to labourers, is not limited to them. In *An Essay* (II.xxi.59), Locke wrote that 'if there be no Prospect beyond the Grave, the inference is certainly right, *Let us eat and drink*, let us enjoy what we delight in, *for to morrow* we shall die.' Since a rational calculator must consider our prospect beyond the grave, 'our greatest interest,' Locke concluded, is 'the Condition of our eternal Estate' (IV.xii.11).

In his *Letters concerning Toleration*, Locke three times referred to morally enlightened individuals 'following the light of their own reason, and the dictates of their own consciences.'[27] Locke did not elaborate on the conceptual relationship between enlightening reason and dictatorial conscience. However, he defined conscience as the care of souls.[28] Care for one's soul, Locke asserted, is our fundamental priority and more important than the public peace.[29] Let us, then, provisionally distinguish between Hobbesian prudence, or care for the self, and Lockean conscience, or care for one's soul. Is Lockean reason, which enlightens, the same as Hobbesian prudence but different from conscience, which dictates that one concern oneself first with one's immortal soul?

Locke did not clarify the relationship between reason and conscience, and even seemed to use one when the other would have been warranted. For example, in his *First Treatise of Government* Locke referred to the internal voice of God as reason, not conscience: 'For the desire, strong desire of Preserving his Life and Being having been Planted in him, as a Principle of Action by God himself, Reason, *which was the Voice of God in him*, could not but teach him and assure him, that pursuing his natural Inclination he had to preserve his Being, he followed the Will of his Maker' (1.86, emphasis in original). Prudent self-preservation, however Locke dresses up reason in clerical garb, is normally distinguished from conscience. Michael Rabieh writes that 'by reinterpreting God as supporting his rational law of nature, Locke has left him in our conscience, but it is a conscience which sees little tension between self-interest and morality.'[30] Rabieh does not distinguish between the care of self and the care of soul, between prudential calculation of worldly interests and concern for our eternal welfare. John Marshall asserts that 'at some moments for Locke "reason" was little more than calculation of interest, although celestially-focussed interest.'[31] If Lockean reason is prudence, whether worldly or supernatural prudence, we can understand why Shaftesbury thought Locke had overthrown a natural basis for moral virtue.

Religion and Politics: The Reluctant Path to Toleration

Locke consistently distrusted the conscience of the common man. In his early political writings he tended to fear the anarchic and antinomian character of conscience. In his *First Tract on Government* (1660) he held that the duty of the civil magistrate is to secure civil peace by legislating uniformity of religious worship. Social peace 'is committed to his care open to be torn and rent in pieces by everyone that could pretend to conscience and draw a sword.'[32] In his *Second Tract on Government* he argued that conscience is a highly flammable idea that appeals to the ignorant masses. Indeed, political freedom and liberty of conscience are 'two slogans which people are extraordinarily quick to rally around.' Indeed, the burning zeal of those who discover how to legitimate the rashness and ignorance of the multitude by appealing to conscience often 'ignites a fire capable of devastating everything.' Indeed, if each followed his own conscience, 'each individual would become his own law-giver, and his own God.' Clearly, Locke lacked sympathy with the proponents of conscience: 'They claim the sacred freedom of their consciences must not be violated in any respect by religious rites and regulations. They claim that liberty of conscience is sacred at all times, and is answerable only to God.'[33]

In *An Essay concerning Toleration* (1667), Locke continued to consider 'the question of liberty of conscience which has for some years been so much bandied amongst us.'[34] This essay justifies the governmental repression of 'papists and fanatics.' It is notable not only because Locke justifies intolerance toward Protestant dissenters ('fanatics'), particularly the Quakers, who disrupt social hierarchy through their practice of keeping on their hats;[35] but also because he provides the fullest account of why toleration cannot be granted to Catholics, and why extending toleration to Protestant sectarians would be a prudent means to win them over to the Whig cause. The most consistent principle of Locke's political thought is his insistence that Catholicism is 'absolutely destructive of human society'[36] because foreign priests can absolve Catholics for any breach of faith with their fellow British subjects: 'Nor can they be thought to be punished merely for their consciences who own themselves at the same time subjects of a foreign power.' Suppressing Catholicism is not violating conscience because Catholics lack a conscience; 'they owe a blind obedience to any infallible pope who hath the keys of their consciences tied to his girdle.'[37] Because Protestants have a conscience, persecution of Protestant dissenters is ineffective; indeed, Protestantism flourishes with persecution and wanes without it. If Protestant dissenters are tolerated 'and persecution and force does not drive them together, they are apt to divide and subdivide into so many little bodies' such that 'the public can have no apprehension of them as long as they have their equal share of common justice and protection.'[38] In contrast, toleration will not make Catholics divide of themselves: 'Add to this that popery having been brought in upon the ignorant and zealous world by the art and industry of the clergy, and kept up by the same artifice backed by power and force, it is the most likely of any religion to decay where the secular power handles them severely.'[39] The interest of the clergy, as distinct from the laity, is more highly exalted in Catholicism than in Protestantism. A policy of suppressing Catholics 'knits all the Protestant party firmer to our assistance and defense.' A policy of tolerating 'fanatics' will enable Whigs to make use of them against Catholics at home and abroad, and may even 'bring them over to our profession.'[40]

The *Tracts on Government* and *An Essay concerning Toleration* exhibited a Hobbesian fear of the anarchic character of claims to freedom of conscience; they supported the magistrate's duty to crush Catholicism, and to suppress religious sects if these posed a danger to civil peace; and they anticipated the objective of the *Letters concerning Toleration* – namely, toleration for all Protestant sects. Moreover, *An Essay concerning Toleration* is more comprehensive than the *Letters* in that it presents prudential reasons for the differential toleration of Catholics and Protestants.

In his *Letters concerning Toleration*, Locke asserted that 'the Romish religion ... is not ... a true religion.'[41] In his postscript to the first *Letter*, he averred that Protestants and Catholics do not share the same religion, since the former 'acknowledge nothing but the Holy Scriptures to be the rule and foundation of their religion,' while the latter 'take in also traditions and decrees of popes.'[42] Like Milton, Locke thought Protestant conscience firmly grounded in Scripture; but also like Milton, he freely or liberally interpreted the Bible.

In his first *Letter concerning Toleration*, Locke seemed to repudiate his aversion to liberty of conscience, which was so manifest in his earlier *Tracts on Government* and in *An Essay concerning Toleration*. Locke contended that seditious assemblies and sectarian strife would vanish if all churches would teach 'that liberty of conscience is every man's natural right, equally belonging to all dissenters as to themselves; and that nobody ought to be compelled in matters of religion, either by law or by force.'[43] Force is ineffective against Protestant dissenters; 'men cannot be saved whether they will or no. And therefore, when all is done, they must be left to their own consciences.'[44]

One might consider whether Locke's argument that conscience cannot be 'forced' is similar to that of a contemporary pamphlet: 'As to the uniting therefore of mens minds into one Religion, it is impossible; it is as impossible to make all mens consciences of the same extent and latitude, as to make all mens shooes of the same size.'[45] Locke's argument seems to lack the element of moral impermissibility we encounter in Roger Williams's view that forcing conscience is 'soul-rape' – that is, something that can happen but ought not to happen, or happens only with a violation of humanity. Nor did Locke's *Letters* maintain the spirit of *The Hireling Ministry* where Roger Williams wrote: 'I desire not that liberty to myself, which I would not freely and impartially weigh out to all the consciences of the world beside.'[46] Locke did not apply the Golden Rule to show the inconsistency of persecution and Christianity, as did Richard Hubberthorn, Samuel Fisher, and Francis Howgill: 'But every man is willing to have the LIBERTY of his OWN CONSCIENCE, therefore ought to ALLOW it to another.'[47]

As Jeremy Waldron points out, Locke's argument that the state ought not, because it cannot, force conscience is inconsistent with his fear of the spread of state-supported Catholicism in continental Europe, and with his advocacy of state sanctions against Catholics and atheists.[48] One might also wonder whether Locke's intolerance of atheists is consistent with his deprecation of conscience in *An Essay*, and with his view that public opinion or social censure can regulate conduct effectively; atheists, after all, are moved by social approbation and disapprobation just as much as theists. In his first *Letter concerning Tolera-*

tion, Locke asserted that if governments could prescribe religion, then only atheists 'could, with a safe conscience, obey their several decrees.'[49] David Wootton asserts that Waldron has missed the core of Locke's argument for toleration; it is not so much the ineffectiveness of persecution but the irrationality of allowing others to make decisions on our behalf that is the ultimate ground for Locke's late championship of freedom of conscience.[50] To be sure, Wootton's argument does not encompass Locke's intolerance of Catholics and atheists.

John Marshall points out that 'for Locke the intrinsic harmlessness of religion properly defined and the desirability of a liberty of conscience compatible with peace and justice remained conceptually and motivationally foundational to Locke's case.'[51] Liberty of conscience is harmless insofar as men are Protestants but doff their caps to their social superiors. An antithetical view to the harmlessness or unimportance of conscience is expressed by John Dunn: 'The right to freedom of conscience in Locke's eyes is fundamentally a right to worship God in the way one judges God requires: a right which follows from and is barely intelligible without a duty to do just that.'[52] Dunn's view seems to me a more comprehensive account of Locke's *Letters* than the partial insights of Waldron, Wootton, and Marshall. Moreover, it captures the spirit of Locke's life-long hatred of Catholics, who learn their religion, Locke averred, 'from the Instructions which are given them, than from the Reading of Books.' Although they do not think of themselves as such, they are truly heretics because the 'receiv'd Doctrine of their Masters are the only Rule that they follow'; Catholics know nothing, and instead blindly follow an authoritarian tradition.[53]

Later liberals have judged Locke's Protestant conscience intolerant. Thomas Jefferson thought Locke wrong to limit toleration so that it excluded Catholics and atheists: 'Perhaps the single thing and which may be required to others before toleration to them would be an oath that they would allow toleration to others.'[54] Contemporary liberals have offered partial support for Locke's intolerance to Catholics around the theme that one cannot tolerate the intolerant.[55] Locke and his supporters seem to have overlooked the experience of Holland and colonial Maryland, where no harm came to Protestants after toleration was extended to Catholics.[56] Locke's intransigent intolerance of Catholics, and specifically of the Catholicism of James II, was integral to his revolutionary commitment – born in the Exclusion Crisis of 1679–81, through the Rye House Plot and Monmouth Rebellion – to the Glorious Revolution. I can see no evidence for James Tully's assertion that

'Locke was willing to tolerate Catholics if they would relinquish their political obedience to the Pope but the various efforts for this failed.'[57] Rather, as Mark Goldie has written, 'Locke was always deeply hostile to catholicism and utterly inflexible in the face of it, but this was not true of all whigs.'[58] Goldie has demonstrated that many Whigs, including friends of Locke, supported James II's Declaration of Indulgence in 1687–8, whereas Locke's intransigent anti-Catholicism allied him with the Anglican establishment (that wished to preserve the Test Act for holding public office) in their effort to depose James II. William Penn and other Quakers supported what they saw as James II's attempt to extend toleration to dissenting Protestants as well as Catholics; Penn stated that James II was the only person at court during the Whig ministry of the mid-1670s to listen to his pleas for toleration.[59]

Nevertheless, the general rule was that liberalism and anti-Catholic bigotry belonged together. J.R. Jones writes: 'Almost without exception those who acted consciously in the defense of constitutional liberties and the rule of law showed themselves to be oppressors of the Catholic minority.'[60] Daniel Defoe expressed a common Whig position; before the Glorious Revolution, he wrote that James II's professed concern for liberty of conscience was fraudulent. James was like Julian the Apostate, who killed Christians 'to reinforce *Paganism* by Liberty of Conscience.' Depriving Catholics of liberty is not restricting conscience because Catholics lack judgment independent of the pope and his church. Popery is a frozen adder that, when warmed, will sting. Defoe thought that while 'some *professed* Protestants whose Consciences are governed by their *Interest*' supported James, the truly conscientious did not.[61] After the Glorious Revolution, Defoe supported compulsory conformity as consistent with freedom of conscience and held that the Church did 'nothing but what she ought to have done; Defend her Liberty and Religion by Force, against unjust Invasion and Tyranny.'[62] The Glorious Revolution dramatically inverted the principle, formulated at the Peace of Augsburg (1555), of *cujus regio, ejus religio* – the ruler determines the religion of his subjects.

Locke's *Letters concerning Toleration* did not match Pierre Bayle's comprehensive tolerance, which was based on a philosophic understanding of conscience and its rights. There is nothing in Locke comparable to Bayle's view that conscience is 'the eternal Law and Rule antecedent to all Religions of positive institution' and that 'what care soever God takes to give us General Rules, whether by natural Light or by his reveal'd Word; still each of us stand in need of a particular

Rule, which is Conscience, by the favor of which we give the Lye, who without it might tell us there was no certainty in any thing.'[63] In Miltonian fashion, Bayle declared conscience to be the touchstone of moral conduct; 'the interior perception of this Conscience, and its full and intire Conviction, is the final Criterion of that Conduct which everyone ought to keep.'[64]

Freedom of conscience, for Locke, seems more of a slogan for religious liberty for Protestants than a philosophic analysis of conscience. Perhaps Locke was too enlightened to have any truck with Bayle's idea of an in-dwelling God Who limits the legitimate sway of ecclesiastical policy. Perhaps the legacy of Locke is that he deconstructed conscience (as the contingent product of one's upbringing and the company one keeps) and simultaneously championed its freedom, or perhaps even disassociated freedom of conscience from the suspect concept of conscience. Perhaps freedom of conscience means no more than 'the values of a market society,' as David Wootton has it, or free competition and consumer sovereignty in the religion business; in other words, one chooses one's religion as one chooses one's shoes.[65]

Rather than the comprehensive toleration of Bayle's *Commentaire philosophique*, Locke's *Letters* match the bigoted Protestant conscience of Bayle's adversary, Pierre Jurieu, who considered Bayle's universal toleration tantamount to indifference to religion.[66] In the Glorious Revolution, Locke and Jurieu were partisan supporters of William of Orange and intransigent opponents of James II's attempt to extend toleration to Catholics as well as Protestant dissenters. After the Edict of Nantes was revoked, Catholicism was equated with violations of liberty and property, and Protestant conscience became an ideological weapon. Jurieu asserted: 'Our goods and our lives are attached to our consciences.'[67]

Conscience, as a Whig slogan, is evident in Francis Semple's 1683 verse *A Discourse Between Law and Conscience When they were both Banished from Parliament*:

> With lustie words both high and bigg
> They swore that Conscience was a whigg,
> For him they have no veneration
> Cause banisht him out of the Nation ...
> If Noble Conscience leave the Land,
> Who then will Popery withstand,
> For Law will prove a broken Reed,
> When Conscience goes in Pilgrim weed (19–22, 91–4)

92   Conscience and Its Critics

Although conscience was banished from Locke's philosophy, it had the role Semple laid out in Locke's Whig ideology.

Conscience and Revolution

While Locke was always intolerant of Catholics, his political position moved from a Hobbesian fear of the anarchic consequences of the doctrine of liberty of conscience in the 1660s, to a commitment to revolution, based on Protestant conscience, in the 1680s. For Hobbes, doctrines of conscience and an absolute right to property (a justification for the reluctance to pay taxes) were prime causes of revolution. For Locke, revolution was justified when the rights of property and conscience were not secure. Property, conscience, and revolution are interrelated elements in Hobbesian philosophy and Lockean doctrine.[68]

Hobbes and Locke both recognized that liberty of conscience and civil peace stand in inverse relationship to each other. While Locke's early writings seem Hobbesian in that he vests in the civil magistrate the duty of limiting the claims of conscience in the name of social peace, by the time of his *Letters concerning Toleration* he seems to have inverted the priority between conscience and public peace: 'the principal and chief care of every one ought to be of his own soul first, and, in the next place, of the public peace.'[69] Hobbes championed law as 'public conscience' over the claims of private conscience; Locke in his *Letters* asserted that 'obedience is due in the first place to God, and afterwards to the laws.'[70] Hobbes thought that civil law and higher (natural or divine) law do not conflict, to the extent that government decree accords with the form of law (no *ex post facto* laws, no punishment without precedent law, trial by jury, etc.); Locke asserted, in his *Second Treatise of Government* (2.12), that 'a great part of the Municipal Laws of Countries ... are only so far right, as they are founded on the Law of Nature, by which they are to be regulated and interpreted.' In Locke's political doctrine, the task of interpreting and regulating natural law gives conscience an important role. Locke's early political writings and his mature philosophy seemed to share Hobbes's distaste for those godly psychopaths who let their conscience be their guides or who follow the inspired inner light; yet he seems to have later moved away from a Hobbesian fear of civil war, toward the view that governmental oppression is the *summum malum*. Locke's revolutionary commitment arose from his Protestant conscience.

Perhaps because scholars have been reluctant to accept that there is a disjunction between Locke's philosophy and his political doctrine (in the *Letters* and *Two Treatises of Government*), the role of conscience in Locke's mature theory has been underemphasized. John Yolton writes of conscience: 'This is not a term used very often by Locke, but it is important in reminding us of a concept frequently used by writers contemporary with and just earlier than Locke. The term appears in some of his earliest writings, some that he never published. After 1690, it fades out of use.'[71]

Yolton is not accurate if one includes Locke's theological writings written after 1690; even so, he has captured a tendency in Locke's philosophical work. Yolton writes: 'The "inner legislator" of *Two Tracts* tends in the *Essay* to be reason, not conscience.'[72] However, our concern here is the place of conscience in Locke's *Second Treatise of Government*. Peter Laslett argues that while conscience is often mentioned in *The First Treatise*, there are only three references to that word in *The Second Treatise* (secs. 8, 21, and 209) and 'little is added by them; conscience is neither defined nor discussed in this book.'[73] Indeed, Laslett asserts, 'Locke brushes aside the question of conscience and political obligation, which had worried him as a young man as it had worried all his predecessors and contemporaries.'[74]

However, Laslett overlooks section 122, where Locke asserts that foreigners – and by extension nonvoting subjects – 'are bound, even in Conscience, to submit to' the government instituted by full members of society. Some of Locke's readers wish he had defined or systematically discussed the central notion of consent to government; but few have thought that, simply because the idea of popular consent lacks precise definition, consent plays a negligible role in Lockean doctrine. Locke's failure to define conscience may not have been a shortcoming on his part. Perhaps conscience is definitionally indefinite, inherently protean.

The rights of conscience do not seem to be the central theme of *The Two Treatises*, as they are of *Letters concerning Toleration*; however, in *The Second Treatise* conscience plays a vital role with respect to the private judgment and execution of the laws of nature, both before and after the social contract authorizing the majority principle; and in determining whether the legislative and executive powers of government conform to the law of nature, and in judging the conditions constituting a dissolution of trust (i.e., when individuals have the right to resist government with the force of arms). Section 8 links reason and conscience in the right of private retribution against offenders of the law of nature, and sections 21 and 209 assert that conscience decides when armed resistance to government is warranted. The role for individual judgment of right, not superseded by the principle of majority rule, is precisely the place of conscience in *The Second Treatise*, which seems to be free of the anti-Catholic bigotry that animated the Glorious Revolution and that is evident in Locke's writings on religious toleration. However, section 209 alludes to the anti-Catholicism of the Whig cause; revolution is justified, Locke argues, when the people 'are persuaded in their consciences, that their Laws and with them their Estates, Liberties and Lives are in danger, and perhaps their Religion too.'

Let us now follow the Lockean conscience through his account of the right of revolution in *The Second Treatise*. In Locke's state of nature, self-governing individuals have the right to judge privately the laws of nature (perhaps they entrust this right to the legislative power in civil society), and to execute privately the laws of nature (perhaps they in part entrust this right to the executive power in civil society). When they enter into civil society, Lockean individuals both do and do not renounce the right of private judgment and execution. The social contract authorizes the principle of majority rule (2.95–9), and this would seem to override the right of private judgment. If individuals could veto the decision of the majority, 'this would make the mighty Leviathan of a shorter duration, than the feeblest Creatures.' Locke's argument for the principle of majority rule has been held to be collectivist, and to supersede private judgment and the right of conscientious dissent; but A.J. Simmons has contested this position, in my view, successfully.[75]

Locke was quite clear that the principle of majority rule does not trump the rights of conscience. Individuals must judge for themselves whether the government has abused its trust, and if an individual thinks it has, he may 'appeal to heaven' – that is, resist the government with force of arms and initiate a violent revolution. To be sure, Locke insisted that the government always initiates rebellion by violating the laws of nature. However, the dozens of times Locke refers to 'endeavours' or 'designs' of the legislature or executive branches of government to invade the liberties and properties of subjects (2.168, 221–30), coupled to his view that it would be a mistake to wait too late to remedy anticipated governmental oppression (2.220, 240), makes it clear that Locke thought that the best defence is a good offence. The assessment of the degree of anticipated governmental oppression devolves on the conscience of individuals: 'And where the Body of the People, or any Single Man, is deprived of their Right, or is under the Exercise of a power without right, and have no Appeal on Earth, there they have a liberty to appeal to Heaven, whenever they judge the Cause of sufficient moment' (2.168). Revolution is not legitimate if subjects can appeal to the courts, or to Parliament against the Crown, or to the Crown against Parliament. But if individuals mistrust the government, they have recourse to the higher court of conscience in order to legitimate revolution. James Tully states that when Locke asserts that the people will judge when the government has abused its trust, he means that each man is judge for himself; however, Tully elsewhere says that Locke probably thought that judgment of government should reside in a 'representative constituent assembly.'[76] It is not clear how a tyrannical government would allow such an assembly to meet for the purpose of judging whether it should be overthrown. Gordon Schochet writes: 'Locke's "any single man" was not to be taken literally – and certainly did not include Col. Thomas Rainborough's "the poorest he that is in England" – but his defense of the right of revolution came to rest in the "people," whose socio-economic status Locke left somewhat ill-defined.'[77] Locke's revolutionary cohort could hardly be said to be a majority of the British population. Tully writes that 'Locke had to justify armed resistance on behalf of an oppressed minority by those not immediately affected (since Dissent made up barely 10% of the population).'[78] Added to the fraction of the Dissenters who were revolutionary were the other interests in the Whig constituency: the large landed proprietors and the mercantile and banking interests of the chartered corporations. If we are to credit Richard Ashcraft and Martin Hughes, there was also an artisanal and working-class component among the Whigs.[79] These strange bedfellows, united by anti-Catholicism from the Exclusion controversy of 1679 until the Declaration of Indulgence of 1687, when the established church and gentry felt threatened by James II, were Locke's allies in the Glorious Revolution.

This amorphous and changing constituency may explain why Locke insisted that it was individual conscience, rather than the majority principle, that provided the ultimate justification for revolution. Mark Goldie asserts that 'it cannot be presumed that whigs necessarily inclined toward a more democratic franchise. Whiggism and populism were not always the same thing.'[80] Indeed, if revolutionaries were morally bound to await the authorization of a majority, no legitimate revolution would ever take place. Locke asserted that individuals

> have, by a Law antecedent and paramount to all positive Laws of men, reserv'd that ultimate Determination to themselves, which belongs to all Mankind, where there lies no Appeal on Earth, viz. to judge whether they have just cause to make their Appeal to Heaven. And this Judgment they cannot part with, it being out of a Man's power to submit himself to another, as to give him a liberty to destroy him. (2.168)

For Locke, this right of private judgment was not anarchistic because, although an individual can be justified in taking up arms against government, exercising this right would be imprudent until a majority, or at least a substantial minority, was on side (2.168; 2.208–9; 2.230). Conscience is necessary to Locke's doctrine of revolution precisely because it can never be determined to any certainty when revolution is warranted. So, when is armed revolution justifiable? Locke's answer: 'Of that I myself can only be Judge in my own Conscience, as I will answer it at the great Day, to the Supreme Judge of all Men' (2.21). Thus I am at a loss to understand why Laslett considers conscience incidental to *The Second Treatise*, since it is so integral to the right of revolution. John Dunn is right to base Locke's theological and political individualism on the Protestant conscience.[81] Locke's conception of conscience is not limited to matters of faith and religious worship, where 'every one is ... judge for himself, what is right.'[82] Conscience, the right of private judgment, pervades *The Second Treatise of Government*. Protestant conscience, for Locke as for Milton, was what justified the commitment to revolution.

The Conscience of Jurors and of Revolutionaries

Hobbes thought that the safest place for moral decisions, which are inherently subjective, was in the judgments of jurors; outside of an institutional setting, conscience is anarchic or revolutionary. In his early political writings and late philosophy, Locke exhibited a Hobbesian fear of anarchy and sectarian strife, which he associated with the freedom of Miltonian conscience; later, however, through the patronage of the first Earl of Shaftesbury and through his strong involvement with the Whig cause, he came to see governmental oppression as a greater evil than revolution.

One might speculate why Locke did not write about juries mediating the relationship of government to governed. This inattention is surprising when one considers the importance of jury verdicts in Locke's political life during the Exclusion Crisis, the Tory reaction to the Whig-fabricated Popish Plot, and the Whig reaction to James II's reign. The grand jury that refused to convict Locke's patron, Shaftesbury, of treason, and the jury that refused to convict the Seven Bishops for their refusal to read James II's Declaration of Indulgence in their churches, gave great impetus to the Glorious Revolution.[83] Perhaps he was sceptical of the independence of juries from governmental dominance. The jurors who convicted Catholics during the Whig-fabricated papal plot of 1679–81 were selected by Whig sheriffs, as were the grand jurors who acquitted Shaftesbury. After Tories won the elections in 1681, Locke fled England, fearing that Tory sheriffs would pack juries to convict Whig plotters.[84] Locke never wrote of jurors as independent of government; moreover, in his frequent use of the term 'the civil magistrate' he tended to merge the legislative and judicial branches of government – perhaps understandable, when Parliament is the highest court as well as the source of legislation. Locke defined the civil magistrate as he who has sovereign power 'or the right of final judgement in legal cases, to sentence to death.'[85] Locke seemed to ignore the role of juries in making final judgments in criminal cases; he also insisted that it is judges, not juries, who interpret law and who affix a punishment when legislators have not determined the punishment.[86]

Alternatively, one might interpret Locke's silence on the subject of juries to mean that he took the jury system for granted as something so basic to English liberty that it needed no overt support from him, or that the abuse of jury packing was too obvious an injustice to warrant a philosopher's attention. One might hypothesize that autonomous juries are a necessary buffer to oppressive governments and are not essential to liberal regimes. According to this hypothesis, rather than defending a bulwark against government oppression, Locke aimed to overthrow the oppressive government.[87] In Locke's writings, I can find only two references to juries. In his *Report to the Board of Trade* he advocates that grand juries support justices of the peace in meting out summary justice to the idle poor; and in *The Fundamental Constitutions of Carolina* he advocated that grand jurors be required to hold three hundred acres freehold, while trial jurors must hold fifty acres freehold.[88] Since jurors interpret criminal law as well as administer legislation, the most democratic of English institutions must be liberally balanced. We are perhaps to bear in mind the cardinal principle: 'For it is as bad as a state of war for men that are in want to have the making of laws over men that have estates.'[89] Locke also recommended that jury verdicts be made by a majority vote, and that the requirement of unanimity for convictions be ended.[90] Adam Smith was later to say that the convention of unanimity in jury verdicts prevents gentlemen from taking part in juries and leaves 'only meaner sorts of people' in jury service.[91] Locke did not specify why he advocated a majority rather than unanimity in jury verdicts, but his other remarks are consistent with Smith's reasons. Locke also advocated that lawyers be barred from courtrooms – a surprising recommendation in the context of a discussion of criminal law, insofar as lawyers in the seventeenth century appeared in court only in civil cases. Here, Locke seemed to be anticipating the eighteenth-century practice – and rejecting it in advance.

In sum, Locke's few references to juries suggest that they play a role more in prosecuting crimes against property than in defending individual liberties. Locke inclined toward the prosecution; Hobbes inclined towards the defence. Hobbes supported jury verdicts according to conscience; Locke seemed to worry about the irrationality of the verdicts of lower-class jurors. The point I wish to make is that in Hobbes's political philosophy, conscience is placed within the rule of law, and specifically within trial by jury; while in revolutionary Whig doctrine, it is placed outside the law. Hobbes thought that judgment, being inherently subjective, was reliably placed in the conscience of the common man as juror; while Locke vested the right of subjective certainty in the revolutionary's conscience. The Hobbesian takes his sovereign to court; the Lockean makes the appeal to heaven, to the force of arms.

Chapter 6

Aristocratic Honour, Bourgeois Interest, and Anglican Conscience

Honour and Moral Sense

After the Restoration of 1660, the hegemony of the language of conscience and its rights was contested by a political vocabulary of interests.[1] Yet Jonathan Swift wrote in 1720 that 'there is no word more frequently in the Mouths of Men, than that of *Conscience*,' a word that was 'generally understood' but often abused by partisan interests.[2] Swift went on to argue that moral conduct, based on conscience guided by religion, cannot be replaced by a morality based on reputation and public credit. For him, the other false principle was honour: 'This is usually the Stile of Military men; of Persons with Titles; and of others who pretend to Birth and Quality.'[3] He asserted that heathens exceeded Christians in virtue because they were strict in the education of their children and instilled patriotism, and generally based their educational systems on a belief in rewards and punishments after death, rather than on a code of honour.[4]

This chapter will examine a three-cornered debate between Locke's student, the third Earl of Shaftesbury, Bernard Mandeville, and two philosophic churchmen, Bishops Berkeley and Butler. Both Berkeley and Butler provided sustained criticisms of the ideas of Shaftesbury and Mandeville. Mandeville recognized that his *Fable of the Bees* and the principles of Lord Shaftesbury were diametrically opposed. Shaftesbury, 'the sociable enthusiast,' opposed both a morality of self-interest and doctrines of a supernatural destiny that undermine a natural basis for virtue. As we saw in the last chapter, Shaftesbury thought that Locke had subverted all order and virtue through his hedonistic calculus that weighed otherworldly as well as worldly pleasures and pains.

Shaftesbury, like Locke, was widely read and admired by thinkers of the European Enlightenment. Denis Diderot's first work was a translation of Shaftesbury's *An Inquiry concerning Virtue and Merit*. In this work, Shaftesbury distinguished *natural* conscience, or the natural prudence all sensible creatures have in concerning themselves with their own interest or happiness, from *moral* conscience, or the self-consciousness of beings who know instinctively that unjust conduct is 'naturally odious and ill-deserving,' and *religious* conscience, or a fear of God. In this scheme of things, religious conscience is not properly speaking *moral* conscience, unless it is based on what Shaftesbury called humanity's 'natural moral sense.'[5]

> For to have awe and terror of the Deity does not, of itself, imply conscience ... Nor does the fear of hell or a thousand terrors of the Deity imply conscience, unless where there is an apprehension of what is wrong, odious, morally deformed, and ill-deserving ...
>
> And thus religious conscience supposes moral or natural conscience. And though the former be understood to carry with it the fear of divine punishment, it has its force however from the apprehending moral deformity and odiousness of any act with respect purely to the Divine Presence, and the natural veneration due to such a supposed being.[6]

Shaftesbury thought that a free or liberal individual is moved not by the desire for advantage or the fear of pain or loss, but rather by the moral beauty or deformity of an action. The free man's conscience is a personal sense of honour.[7]

Clearly, Shaftesbury's morality is of greater nobility than that of Locke, who did not treat God as a peer but instead looked up to Him, Who has the superior power to punish or reward His inferiors. Shaftesbury did not expect any special favours from God, Who rewards and punishes in accord with moral conscience or the natural moral sense. For him, God was more like a fellow peer – one who is absent from the House of Lords but who can be expected to vote like a gentleman when the time comes. Thus, conscience is freed from religion, from the 'celestially focussed self-interest' of Lockean doctrine.

The sociable affections, Shaftesbury felt, are the best antidote to a dismal devotion. He thought that republican virtue is quite distinct from a prudent fear of supernatural punishment; the former can only arise from a *'Sense of Partnership* with Human Kind.'[8] Association with others is natural to humankind. Those who seem to deny human sociability, such as Hobbes, are not so unsociable as to fail to communicate their apprehension about human nature to make us aware of the vulnerability of society.[9] Locke's doctrine that virtue requires supernatural support presents self-interest and the public interest as antitheses; actually, they are naturally united in the instinct of human gregariousness.[10] In addition to enjoying our goods, we share in others' enjoyments through communication. Through sympathetic identification with others, we share by reflection in their participation in the goods of life; through benevolence, we enhance our own pleasure by diminishing the pains of others; and through acting justly, we obtain *'the actual Love, merited Esteem or Approbation of others.'*[11] The reward of virtue, as Hobbes and Locke pointed out before Shaftesbury and *les philosophes* after him, is the consciousness of meriting the esteem of others. Indeed, the motive of social esteem and censure seems so powerful that the mighty Leviathan might rule with sword in sheath; in Shaftesbury's teaching, public hangings are symbols of public disapprobation:

> For in the publick Executions of the greatest Villains, we see generally that the Infamy and Odiousness of their Crime, and the Shame of it before Mankind, contribute more to their misery than all besides: and that it is not the immediate Pain, or Death it-self which raises so much Horrour either in the Sufferers or Spectators, as that ignominious kind of Death which is inflicted for publick Crimes, and Violations of Justice and Humanity.[12]

Christians might assert against Hobbes that the pangs of conscience outweigh the prospect of a painful hanging; in contrast, Shaftesbury seems to inaugurate the Enlightenment belief that the desire for social approbation is the most powerful of human motivations. Indeed, the core of Shaftesbury's thought is that belief in a God, and in supernatural rewards and punishments, is ignoble and fosters self-interest rather than the social affections.[13] The moral sense, or 'the natural sense of right and wrong,' is based on the fear of being condemned by observers of one's actions: 'So that the Offender must needs be conscious to himself of being liable to such Treatment from every one, as if he had in some degree offended All.'[14] It is illiberal to expect favour or disfavour from a divine spectator; but it is liberal to expect approval or disapproval from human onlookers. Moral conscience is the inner consciousness that one merits the approval of disinterested spectators of one's actions. Even if no one is present to witness one's behaviour, one's moral sense is offended by base or unjust actions.[15]

Paul Henri Thiry, Baron D'Holbach, elaborated Shaftesbury's line of thought: 'Conscience is the internal testimony, which we bear to ourselves, of having acted so as to merit the esteem or blame of the beings, with whom we live.' D'Holbach went on to ask whether an atheist would be motivated to abstain from crimes and vices beyond the reach of the law and the scrutiny of society: 'As for secret crimes, he will abstain from them, for fear that he shall be forced to blush at himself, from whom he cannot fly. If he has any reason, he will know the value of the esteem which an honest man ought to have for himself. He will see that unforeseen circumstances may unveil the conduct which he feels interested in concealing from others.'[16]

Shaftesbury opposed Locke's rejection of innate ideas, but also thought that innate ideas should be called natural moral sense or instinctive moral taste.[17] He did not oppose natural instinct to social construction of moral sensibility because humans are naturally social creatures and the moral sense is based on emotions directed toward fellows, whether of love, compassion, or benevolence.[18] The moral sense, based on natural social affections, can be impaired by 'contrary Habit or Custom' or by doctrines of otherworldly rewards and punishments. To lack conscience or innate moral sense is to be the most miserable of creatures.

Shaftesbury taught the eighteenth century that the important business of life was the cultivation of taste in moral and aesthetic matters. As Claude Adrien Helvétius asserted: 'Taste [is] the knowledge of what merits the esteem of mankind.'[19] Before Shaftesbury, philosophers viewed matters of taste as falling outside the range of philosophic inquiry; after him, most thinkers of the eighteenth century wrote about taste without questioning that taste is both natural and cultivated.[20] Shaftesbury wrote that the 'principal end' of his writings was 'to assert the Reality of a BEAUTY and CHARM in *Moral* as well as *Natural* Subjects; and to demonstrate the Reasonableness of a *proportionate* TASTE, and *determinate* CHOICE, in *Life* and *Manners*.'[21] He claimed to have found the standard of taste in nature itself, but also asserted that his main aim was to correct manners and taste. He thought that in poetic and moral matters, 'in the very nature of things there must of necessity be the foundation of a right or wrong Taste.' What we most need is models of moral taste, to apply just as we do Raphael as a model of artistic taste.[22] He declared that moral philosophy is aesthetic cultivation: 'To philosophise, in a just signification, is but to carry good-breeding a step further. For the accomplishment of breeding is, to learn whatever is decent in company of beautiful in arts: and the sum of philosophy is, to learn what is just in society and beautiful in Nature and the order of the World.'[23]

Moral philosophy requires breeding; taste must be learned. Shaftesbury stated that a great amount of labour is essential for the formation and correction of taste, but 'the great Work of *reforming* ... TASTE' should proceed according to 'the just *Standard* of *Nature*.' However, 'if a natural *good* TASTE be not already form'd in us; why shou'd not we endeavour to form it, and become *natural*?' At the same time, it is not nature but '*We our-selves* that make our TASTE.'[24] Shaftesbury's aim was to create *Virtuosi* or refined and cultivated gentlemen – what William Blake later called 'the Cunning-sures & aim-at-yours.'[25] Taste and genius, or the consumption and production of works of art, were not invariably in harmony.

The Man-Devil

Bernard Mandeville wrote that the principles of *The Fable of the Bees* and those of Lord Shaftesbury weve diametrically opposed; 'two systems cannot be more opposite than his Lordship's than mine.'[26] According to Mandeville, Shaftesbury's view was that man is made for society and that virtue is that which is done for the public regard, not for self-interest. Shaftesbury's ideas are 'a high compliment to humankind,' 'inspiring,' 'noble,' 'generous and refined.' 'What a pity it is that they are not true!'[27] As distinct from Mandeville's view that the vices of greed, vanity, and luxury are what produce public benefits, Shaftesbury advanced the hypocritical notion 'that men may be virtuous without self-denial.' Vice, or 'what we call evil in this world, moral as well as natural, is the grand principle that makes us sociable creatures, the solid basis, the life and support of all trades and employments without exception.'[28] To be sure, Shaftesbury's writings are useless to all those employed in trade.[29] Echoing Locke and professing to be more pious than Shaftesbury, Mandeville asked: 'If the vulgar are to be excluded from the social virtues, what rule or instruction shall the labouring poor, which are by far the greatest part of the nation, have left them to walk by, when *The Characteristics* have made a jest of all revealed religion, especially the Christian?'[30]

Religion and a code of honour make opposed demands on human beings, and their reconciliation 'must be left to wiser heads than mine.'[31] If honour and religion are opposed, both are quite distinct from trade, which is the principal concern of every nation: 'Religion is one Thing, and Trade is another.'[32] Self-interested exchange, not religion or a code of honour, is the basis of social relationships.

In *Arete-logia or, an Enquiry into the Original of Moral Virtue*, Mandeville stated that Shaftesbury's ethics are grounded on the love of esteem. Love of esteem was compatible with his own ethics based on self-love: 'our natural Desire of Society, (which directly springs from our natural Principle of Self-love) there is necessarily connected a natural desire of Esteem, or of being lik'd and regarded by those other rational agents.'[33] Indeed, 'it is much more impossible for the Desire of Esteem, to be separated from the Desire of Society, than for the Light and Heat of the Sun to be parted from one another.'[34] John Gay followed Mandeville in asserting that moral 'approbations and affections are not innate or implanted in us by way of instinct'; rather, they are socially constructed by changing standards of social approval and disapproval.[35]

Mandeville perceived a class bias in Shaftesbury's (and the later Enlightenment's) view that honourable conduct can be governed by the provision or withholding of esteem. Since the servile classes are not considered members of society any more than dogs or horses, the esteem of them does not matter.[36] To get the esteem or honour that all men pursue – a desire that might be called the vice of pride – one must flatter others: '*Moral Virtues* are the *Political Off-Spring, which Flattery begot upon Pride.*'[37]

Mandeville professed to be a better Christian than Shaftesbury, but he was no friend of the clergy. Religion, reason, humanity, indeed 'almost every thing in Nature pleads for Tolleration, except the National Clergy in every Country.'[38] Mandeville emphasized the close connection between trade and religious toleration – a connection noted by Spinoza but not stressed in English literature until the 1660s. In the 1690s, Locke indignantly responded to Jonas Proast's view that his *Letters concerning Toleration* were driven by considerations of trade, not religion.[39] Mandeville gloried in his contention that religious consciences are governed by the imperatives of trade. Since trade is the main thing in every nation, 'the multitude must be awed, no man's conscience forced, and the clergy allowed no greater share in public affairs than our saviour has bequeathed them in his testament.'[40] Bigotry will kill trade and commerce; we will become happy only when we have 'conquer'd the great Concern we have for other Men's Consciences.'[41] But care for one's own conscience is by no means a universal phenomenon: the lower classes prefer a ceremonial religion, public monuments, and common rituals, rather than Protestant interiority and privacy; having little of their own, working people attach themselves to what is common.[42]

Mandeville's thought followed the path of sceptical toleration (not the rights of conscience) from Hobbes to *les philosophes*.[43] Like Hobbes, Hume, Voltaire, and Diderot, Mandeville favoured an established church: 'A good Government in all Countries pays a deference to the National Church, and no Liberty of Conscience ought to interfere with her just Rights.'[44] The Church of England was less likely to persecute dissenters than Catholics and Protestant sectarians. When clergy preach liberty of conscience, 'the first and mildest Punishment they can expect, is to be silenc'd.' If they appealed to the multitude in their claims of conscience, they were to be punished as criminals.[45] 'But the greatest Argument for Tolleration is, that differences in Opinion can do no hurt, if all Clergy-men are kept in awe, and no more independent of the State than the Laity; whereas the Calamities that may attend Persecution are endless.'[46] The people must recognize the government as the supreme authority on earth, and Catholics and nonjurors will not do so voluntarily. For this reason, Mandeville favoured laws against both Catholics and nonjurors.[47] Freedom of conscience is not an intrinsic good, whereas toleration is a means for promoting trade and diminishing persecution. Mandeville asserted that 'the Audaciousness of fiery Pulpiteers should be restrained'; and with consummate cheek, he advocated that 'Prophaneness and Irreligion above all should be severely punish'd,' no matter how witty the profane or irreligious utterance should be.[48]

Anglican Philosophy

In George Berkeley's *Alciphron*, Shaftesbury and Mandeville are paired as unbelievers, with Shaftesbury's sentimentalism represented in Alciphron and Mandeville's materialism represented in Lysicles. Mandeville is wrong to think 'that all stings of conscience and sense of guilt are prejudices and errors of education.'[49] Shaftesbury is wrong to separate morality from religion; 'conscience always supposeth the being of a God.'[50] Rather than resting on the certainty and specificity of religious conscience, Shaftesbury relies on the *je ne sais quoi* of moral sense.[51] Without the fear of God, morality becomes manners, outward formality, and pretence. William Law agreed with Berkeley that to understand morality as taste is 'to recommend morals on the same foot with manners.'[52]

Alciphron says that men without religion are men of honour and hence of virtue, but his interlocutors respond that whatever virtue men of honour have 'is owing to fashion (being of the reputable kind) or forgotten religious upbringing.'[53] Without religion, the man of honour is 'a specious character,' 'no better than a meteor or painted cloud.' Indeed the code of honour enables men to debauch others' wives, gamble, duel, get drunk, sell votes, and refuse debts to tradesmen. Indeed, the aristocratic code prescribes this immoral conduct as the careless gallantry of an élite.[54]

In *An Essay toward Preventing the Ruin of Great Britain*, Berkeley took aim, through Mandeville and Shaftesbury, at John Locke. Berkeley insisted that it is 'impossible that a nation should thrive and flourish without virtue, or that virtue should subsist without conscience, or conscience without religion.'[55] Against Locke's rejection of innate ideas, Berkeley insisted that conscience is 'stamped on the mind,' 'engraven on the tables of the heart' or 'eternal rules of reason'; 'they are ever to be esteemed the fixed unalterable standards of good and evil; no private interest, no love of friends, no regard to the public good, should make us depart from them.'[56] Conscience is different from Mandevillean or Lockean calculation and from the sentimental benevolence of Shaftesbury. Natural reason can ascertain what is right or what is the will of God:

> But neither is the use of our reason, the only natural means, for discovering the will of God, the same being also suggested by a natural conscience, and inward feeling implanted in the soul of every man, previous to all deductions of reason, there being nothing more natural to our minds, than that distaste, disquiet, and remorse attending evil actions, and on the other hand, that joy and satisfaction which is the constant encouragement and reward of good ones.[57]

Conscience prescribes what is right prior to the calculations of reason; and conscientious action, although rewarded by pleasure, is not motivated by anticipated pleasure.

Bishop Berkeley, contrary to Milton and Locke, thought that conscience enjoins obedience to government; armed resistance is therefore damnable.[58] William Law shared Berkeley's view that conscience, rather than comfortable self-preservation, is the basis of loyalty to governments. Law wrote that a worldly epicure 'is very loyal, and as soon as ever he likes any wine he drinks the king's health with all his heart. Nothing could put rebellious thoughts into his head, unless he should live to see a proclamation against eating pheasants' eggs.'[59] If Berkeley's idealism opposes comfortable self-preservation as the aim of life, his opposition to materialism is also expressed in his call for a high-wage economy.[60] If the bourgeois materialism of Locke and Mandeville was based on a low-wage economy, Berkeley's idealism was consistent with his advocacy of high wages to stimulate the Irish economy. As William Butler Yeats wrote in 'The Seven Sages,' the Bishop of Cloyne joined Jonathan Swift and five other Irish sages in their shared hatred of Whiggery. In Yeats's view, a tory, or Irish thief, is always preferable to a whig, or a Scots drover of cattle.

Bishop Butler's moral philosophy was similar to that of Bishop Berkeley. Whereas the latter is primarily known for his epistemology, the former is better known as a moral philosopher. Butler commanded the respect of Immanuel Kant and Cardinal Newman and continues to enjoy philosophic attention.[61] Butler, like Berkeley, attacked egoist psychology from Hobbes to Mandeville and thought that the psychological rewards of a good conscience were the effect rather than the cause of moral actions. Butler tended to use Hobbes and Shaftesbury as buoys or markers of the shoals of self-love and benevolence; through these, he could steer the path of conscience. Self-love and benevolence are both natural principles; the former aims at one's own good, and the latter at the good of society. Butler differed from Hobbes and Mandeville in that he did not consider the latter reducible to the former. Butler was a man of the eighteenth century in that he thought 'we were made for society.'[62] Goodness of heart, kindness, and compassion are natural to humans, but social affections must cede pride of place to the 'superior principle of reflection or conscience in every man.'[63] Indeed, because benevolence is sometimes indiscriminate and compassion irrational, conscience seems closer to prudence or rational self-love than to benevolence: 'Reasonable self-love and conscience are the chief or superior principles ... Conscience and self-love, if we understand our true happiness, always lead in the same way. – Duty and interest are perfectly co-incident; for the most part in this world, but entirely, and in every instance, if we take in the future, and the whole.'[64] However, conscience is not a calculation of results but a reflex approval of good actions and disapproval of evil actions, whether of oneself or others. Prudence, our 'due concern about our own happiness and interest,' runs a parallel course with conscience in combating passion, impulsiveness, and immediate appetite; but conscience diverges from prudence in that it is not calculative. As David McNaughton writes: 'Judgments of conscience, unlike those of self-love, are thus not hostages to fortune; we do not have to see how things turn out in order to determine whether our moral judgment was correct.'[65]

According to Butler's *Sermons*, Lord Shaftesbury's mistake was to think it 'sufficient to abstain from gross wickedness, and to be humane and kind to such as happen to come in their way.' In reality, Butler thought, 'the very constitution of our nature' requires that our conduct be brought before the supreme court of conscience, 'as it is absolutely the whole business of a moral agent, to conform ourselves to it. This is the true meaning of that ancient precept, *Reverence thyself*.'[66] In *The Analogy of Religion*, Butler stated that Shaftesbury's error was to think that virtue flows from natural social affections, not from supernatural rewards and punishments. The core of Butler's moral theology is that God governs the world by reward and punishment, that He has given us conscience to apprehend good and evil, and that this moral discernment 'carries in it authority and a right of direction; authority in such a sense, as that we cannot depart from it without being self-condemned.'[67] While the internal guide is 'by nature a rule to us,' the dictates of conscience are also laws of God.[68] Butler thought his argument for the existence of God from the design of conscience to be valid for non-Christians as well as Christians.[69] He seemed to think his arguments hold for all but stubborn and unreasoning atheists; 'the apprehension that religion may be true, does as really lay men under obligations, as a full conviction that it is true.'[70]

For Butler as for most Protestant thinkers, conscience hovers between God and man; our experience of conscience is proof that God is attending to our welfare, whether we ask Him to or not. Conscience is both natural and supernatural. Our conscientious self-judgment is a dress rehearsal for our final judgment, but at the same time is Shaftesbury's moral sense, or the moral sense coupled to divine reason. What is crucial to Butler's thought is that conscience is the supreme human authority and the definitive attribute of human nature. In *Of Personal Identity*, Butler distanced himself from Locke in affirming that it is conscience, not consciousness or memory, that constitutes human identity.[71]

Butler's ethics centred on his idea that conscience is the supreme human authority. Conscience's judgment may lack papal infallibility, but it overrides all human competitors.[72] Some Catholic thinkers, such as G.E.M. Anscombe, have thought that Butler ignored the fact that conscience has told individuals to do the vilest things; but as Brian Hebblethwaite argues, Anscombe wants to locate 'authority in morals in the divine law over against us rather than in some principle of our human nature.'[73] Butler's conscience located the divine law within us. Man's conscience 'is, *in the strictest and most proper sense, a law to himself*. He hath the rule of right within: what is wanting is only that he honestly attend to it.'[74]

Butler would probably have agreed with Anscombe that human judgment is fallible compared with divine wisdom; but he insisted that divine wisdom is within and that individuals are the best judges of whether they intend good or evil. Also, he would have agreed with Anscombe that a moral agent is more properly a law finder than a law maker. Established clerics shared the conservative Enlightenment's hostility to conscience as autonomous or law making. In 1750, Laurence Sterne voiced this conservative apprehension of autonomous conscience as anarchic:

> And in your own Case remember this plain Distinction, a Mistake, in which, has ruin'd Thousands. – That your Conscience is not a Law; – no, – God and Reason made the Law, and has placed Conscience within you to determine, – not like an Asiatic Cadi, according to the Ebbs and Flows of his own Passions: – But like a *British Judge* in this Land of Liberty, who makes no new Law, – but faithfully declares that glorious Law which he finds already written.[75]

Butler may have shied away from a conception of conscience as autonomous, but he did assert that conscience 'claims the direction of other principles.' Conscience thus seems to occupy a more exalted place in Butler's thought than it does in Sterne, and in most Enlightenment and Catholic thinkers. In Butler's scheme of things, conscience, Lockean or Mandevillian self-interest, Shaftesbury's benevolence, an aristocratic code of honour, custom or habit, love of one's own, Christian charity, and other principles may all vie for command of one's soul, but conscience is conclusive, whereas all other principles are merely factors to be weighed in a moral decision.[76] Even reason, the candle of one's soul, is insufficient to move humans to act morally. Conscience provides a motive as well as a direction. We can act against self-interest, against compassion, even against reason and not be 'self-condemned,' not violate 'the very constitution of our nature.' But when we act against conscience we are undermining our status as moral agents in a way that acting imprudently or antisocially does not.

In championing conscience, Butler was not elevating revelation above reason: 'Reason can, and it ought to judge, not only the meaning, but also of the morality and the evidence, of revelation ... It is the province of reason to judge of the morality of the Scripture; *i.e.*, ... whether it contains things plainly contradictory to wisdom, justice, or goodness.'[77] However, Butler did not specify cases of Scriptural injunctions that seem to conflict with goodness or justice; he was not troubled, as Kierkegaard and Dostoyevsky were later, by the apparent irrationality of God's demands, such as the demand that Abraham sacrifice Isaac. Butler's championship of conscience did not involve a romantic or existential depreciation of reason.

Conscience, in Butler, has a more expansive scope than in Milton and some of the antinomian Protestants examined in Chapter 1; for Butler, the verdicts of conscience encompass not only my own actions but also those of others. As Terence Penelhum wrote:

> We do not, in common speech, talk of my conscience as judging anyone's actions but my own. In ordinary speech you cannot violate my conscience, or be troubled by promptings of anyone's conscience but your own. Yet, as Kant was later to remind us so powerfully, it is integral to my moral judgments of my own actions, if I make them sincerely, that I apply the same standards to them that I would apply to those of other agents. So conscience, in the narrower sense, is a special application to oneself of a power that we can and do exercise in relation to others.[78]

Butler used conscience the way other thinkers used reason. If conscience prescribes only for oneself, while reason prescribes for others as well as oneself, then Butler's use of conscience seems to merge with practical reason. Also, conscience, for Butler, seems identical to reason insofar as the dictates of conscience do not depend on divine revelation. Rather, Christian revelation confirms what unassisted conscience dictates. Butler then attempted to unite religion and secular philosophy.

While Butler elevated conscience as the supreme and defining attribute of humans, his views on freedom of conscience are remarkably similar to those of Hobbes, Mandeville, and Hume. Butler wrote: 'A religious establishment, without a toleration of such as think they cannot, in conscience, conform to it, is itself a general tyranny ... On the other hand, a constitution of civil government without any religious establishment, is a chimerical project, of which there is no example.' Without the guide and instruction of an established church, the generality will lapse into irreligion, 'superstition and the gloom of enthusiasm; which last, ought surely to be diverted and checked, as far as can be done without force.'[79] Although Butler held that popery was a 'manifest open usurpation of all human and divine authority,' he thought Catholics were right to emphasize 'the importance of external religion,' the public ceremonies and rituals, the holidays and processions (i.e., those things which Mandeville thought the common people cling to, having nothing private of their own). A religion based on individual conscience and interiority is cheaper than one based on clerical ceremonies. Butler lamented: 'In the present turn of the age, one may observe a wonderful frugality in every thing which has respect to religion, and extravagance in every thing else.'[80] To be sure, Mandeville thought that churchmen had an interest in the ceremonial side of religion.

Mandeville, Shaftesbury, and Berkeley in Pope and Sterne

What Butler attempted in his philosophy, Alexander Pope aimed at in his *Essay on Man* – namely, 'steering betwixt the extremes of doctrine seemingly opposite ... and in forming a temperate yet not inconsistent ... system of ethics.'[81] In his verse, Pope appeared to synthesize Mandeville, Shaftesbury, and Berkeley:

> Thus God and nature linked the general frame
> And bade self-love and social be the same.(III. 317–18)
> Self-love thus pushed to social, to divine
> Gives thee to make thy neighbour's blessing thine. (IV. 353–4)
> That reason, passion, answer one great aim,
> That true self-love and social are the same,
> That virtue only makes our bliss below;
> And all our knowledge is, ourselves to know. (IV. 395–8)

Mandeville's challenge to the eighteenth century was to assert that society is based on self-interested exchanges and that what Shaftesbury called moral conduct was governed by the desire for esteem. Berkeley and Butler thought that proper conduct could not be governed by social approval or censure. Butler pointed out: 'If shame, and delight in esteem, be spoken as real, as any settled ground of pain or pleasure, both these must be in proportion to the supposed wisdom and worth of him by whom we are contemned or esteemed.'[82]

The alternative between the judgment of society and the judgment of God, manifest in one's conscience, is presented by the Whig ideologist, Daniel Defoe. A gentleman who had been robbed by Moll Flanders after a liaison is confronted by a criminal friend of Moll's for purposes of blackmail. The gentleman says to Moll's friend: 'Madam, you are a stranger to me, but it is very unfortunate that you should be let into the secret of the worst action of my life and a thing I am justly ashamed of, in which the only satisfaction I had was that I thought it was known only to God and my own conscience.'[83] Contrary to Butler, Defoe thought that we shun the disesteem not only of worthy or wise individuals but also of individuals like Moll's friend. The eighteenth-century Enlightenment came to hold that social censure is a more effective guide to conduct than conscience. As Claude Adrien Helvétius was later to say: 'Experience tells us, that every action which does not expose us to legal punishment, or to dishonour, is an action performed in general without remorse.'[84]

Between Butler and Helvétius both in time and in doctrine, Laurence Sterne, in his sermon 'Advantages of Christianity to the World,' argued that we need vertical obligations (to God), not merely horizontal obligations (meeting the expectations of our fellows). One could claim that 'there is no need, that the everlasting laws of justice and mercy should be stretched down from above, – since they can be proved from more obvious mediums,' namely, social utility. 'That the necessities of society, and the impossibility of its subsisting otherwise, would point out the inconvenience, or if you will, – the duty of social virtues, is unquestionable: – but I firmly deny, that therefore religion and morality are independent of each other.'[85] Despite Sterne's firm denial, one can imagine a condescending smile lighting up the shade of Lord Shaftesbury and a man-devilish grin leavening the hellish toil of Bernard Mandeville's afterlife. The Enlightenment infiltrated the Church of England. Butler's attempt to balance secular philosophy and religion, prudence and conscience, reason and revelation, may not have accommodated the otherworldly destiny of Christians to the social world of the eighteenth century; but in the sermons of Sterne we can hear the accents of Mandevillean interest and the tones of Shaftesbury's social affections merging in the call of Protestant conscience.

Chapter 7

Professors and Nonprofessors of Presbyterian Conscience

Francis Hutcheson and the Politics of Scottish Universities

David Hume characterized the Presbyterian conscience as follows:

> The genius of that religion which prevailed in Scotland ... was far from inculcating deference and submission to the ecclesiastics, merely as such: or rather, by nourishing in every individual the highest raptures and ecstacies of devotion, it consecrated, in a manner, every individual, and in his own eyes bestowed a character on him much superior to what forms and ceremonious institutions could alone confer.[1]

Hume of course was no friend of what he took to be the dismal devotion, self-laceration, and egalitarianism of the Presbyterian conscience. Of the remarkable set of thinkers who comprised the Scottish Enlightenment, Hume stands out as a nonprofessor, a religious sceptic, and a person who failed to obtain a chair in a Scottish university.

After the Glorious Revolution of 1688, the supporters of the Stuart claim to the throne of England were driven from the Scottish universities, and Locke's *Essay concerning Human Understanding*, together with his *Second Treatise of Government*, became staples in the curricula of Scottish universities.[2] Gershom Carmichael came to prominence with the Lockean view that 'knowledge of natural law is not innate in men's minds' but is 'derived from the nature of things and their uninterrupted course, and a proper use of reason.'[3]

One of the leading members of the Scottish Enlightenment was Francis Hutcheson, the Ulster Presbyterian who taught philosophy at the University of Glasgow. Hutcheson's teachings about the natural goodness of humanity were far from orthodox from a Presbyterian standpoint, in that they countered prevailing views about the sinfulness of fallen man, with the result that Hutcheson was answerable to a Glasgow synod for his heterodoxy.[4] However, his optimism about human nature was not based on an acceptance of Lockean doctrine or a rejection of innate ideas. He championed Shaftesbury's moral sense and thus did not espouse Locke's rejection of conscience as an innate practical principle. When one disavowed innate ideas, Hutcheson thought, one was left with a morality based on self-interest. Hobbes, Pufendorf, and Locke banished 'old notions of natural affections, and kind instincts, the sensus communis, the decorum, and honestum.'[5]

Hutcheson's *An Inquiry into the Original of our Ideas of Beauty and Virtue* was a defence of the ideas of Lord Shaftesbury against those of Bernard Mandeville. Hutcheson insisted that the internal moral sense does not imply innate ideas any more than the external senses, but he also asserted that our moral sense is as natural as the principles of self-love and is antecedent to custom, education, and example.[6] Our moral sense is the natural conscience of a social being – our natural tendency to approve the virtues and censure the vices of others, regardless of their advantage or disadvantage to us. The love and esteem of our fellow humans is as essential to our being as the air we breathe. For Hutcheson, a humane and generous character was closely connected to a strong love of esteem,[7] although he did not agree with Mandeville that virtuous acts are motivated by a desire for social esteem.

The moral sense is intimately associated with human sociality. According to Hutcheson, the seventeenth-century predecessors of Mandeville dismissed humanity's moral sense because they did not recognize the social nature of human beings. The philosophers of the Scottish Enlightenment were unanimous in espousing the sociable views of the 'elegant Lord Shaftesbury' against Hobbesian and Mandevillean egoism, however much Mandeville's principle of self-interested exchanges informed the pages of Smith's *The Wealth of Nations*. As Donald Winch dryly put it, 'self-confessed Hobbists or Mandevillians are hard to find.'[8] For example, Hutcheson's contemporary and critic, Archibald Campbell, wrote: 'We must desire the *Love* and *Esteem* of other rational agents, *that is*, that they like and approve of our being in happiness.'[9] Adam Ferguson wrote: 'As man is formed for society, he is justly made to enjoy or to suffer under the approbation or disapprobation of other men, as well as his own.'[10] Egoism is an untenable position, Hutcheson thought, because of the 'natural contagiousness' of pleasures and pains; humans communicate their suffering and share their joy with others.[11]

The moral sense, for Hutcheson, is more the cause than the effect of social approbation or disapprobation, but the latter can reinforce or impair the former. Perhaps responding to Mandeville's critique of Shaftesbury's sense of honour, Hutcheson distinguished honour, which aims at distinction, from conscience or moral sense, which aims at the common good: 'We may sometimes find an high *Sense of Honour* and desire of *Applause*, where there is indeed a *moral Sense*, but a very weak one, very much perverted, so as to be influenced by *popular Opinion*, and made subservient to it.'[12] The moral sense may be impaired, just as the senses of sight and hearing may be impaired. Hutcheson admitted that it is difficult to understand how reason could correct an impairment of the moral sense, except by recalling the moral sense to its earlier judgments or by relating it to the 'general sense of Mankind.'[13] Judgments of spectators are generally reliable to confirm the judgments of one's moral sense.[14] Hutcheson did not clarify how public opinion corrects as well as impairs the moral sense.

The conscience of Shaftesbury and Hutcheson is different from the individual conscience of Luther and Milton in that it is not dependent on Revelation and, also, is the product of human society. Protestant conscience mainly involves judgments on oneself; in contrast, the moral sense mainly involves making spectatorial judgments of approbation or disapprobation on the actions of others, and then applying the spectator's point of view to one's own conduct. Like Butler and Shaftesbury, Hutcheson thought that one could not understand moral conduct from the premises of egoist psychology; we do not describe morally attractive actions as such because we have an interest or pleasure in them, although witnessing virtuous actions raises pleasure in us.[15] The moral sense is bound up with human sociality – with the natural contagiousness of pleasure, with repugnance at seeing fellow creatures suffer, and with the desire to live in the favourable estimation of one's peers. If we lacked a moral sense, Hutcheson asserted, we would not be delighted with honour; love of honour presupposes a sense of moral virtue, both in the individuals pursuing the honour and in those conferring it.[16] Hutcheson implied that honour recognizes a pre-existing moral sense; it does not construct that moral sense, although it may pervert or impair it in those overly in need of popular acclaim.

Hutcheson's moral sense is more social than the seventeenth-century conscience; it is also less rational judgment than natural instinct. Butler equated reason and conscience as the supreme human authority; Hutcheson called reason the 'permanent counsellor' to conscience or the moral sense.[17] While the position of counsellor sounds more exalted than Humean reason as slave, Hutcheson's morality, like Hume's, is one of feeling, unlike Butler's morality of conscience as rational judgment.

Hume on Conscience and Freedom of Conscience

David Hume is notable for eschewing the word *conscience* in his philosophy. Even more consistently than Voltaire and Diderot, Hume avoided a word with superstitious connotations of 'the God within,' and with a political legacy of rebellion and civil war, which Hume, like Hobbes, felt to be the *summum malum*. Hume allowed the word to appear in his *History of England*, but generally in the context of an account of freedom of conscience, which Hume favoured when understood as religious toleration under the aegis of an established latitudinarian church.

For the leading thinkers of the Enlightenment, freedom of conscience was Hobbesian Erastianism, not Miltonian or Lockean separation of church and state. Voltaire taught that the first law of nature was toleration, which is inherently tied to human frailty,[18] and also maintained that 'reason informs us that the prince must be absolute master of all ecclesiastical policy, with no restrictions whatsoever.'[19] Diderot also sounded a Hobbesian note when he asserted: 'I do not like to include in acts of sovereignty people who preach of a being superior to the sovereign, and who attribute to that being whatever pleases them ... I do not like to give weight and consideration to those who speak in the name of the Almighty. Religion is a buttress which almost always ends up collapsing the house.'[20]

Like Voltaire, Diderot was convinced that the state must control all aspects of religious doctrines and practices.[21] Hume, Voltaire, and Diderot are counterexamples to the common view that Enlightenment thinkers championed freedom of conscience, understood as the separation of church and state. For example, Charles Griswold Jr writes: 'The arguments against the legitimacy of a state-supported religion and, in the extreme case, of a religious monopoly are so integral a part of Enlightenment effort to put politics on a stable and just foundation as to constitute one of the controlling themes of the period.'[22]

Much like Voltaire and Diderot, Hume combined Hobbesian scepticism with Erastianism. As opponents of the anarchic Protestant conscience, enlightened sceptics supported religious toleration under the name of freedom of conscience but were disinclined to separate church and state. Hume favoured government monopoly rather than free competition in the religion business, on the basis that the separation of ecclesiastical and civil authority creates instability and civil war.[23] More realistically than Locke, who thought persecution ineffective, Hume saw that the heavy hand of the state could promote religious uniformity (at least before dissenting sects became solidly rooted): 'Persecution may, indeed, seem better calculated to make hypocrites than converts; but experience teaches us, that the habits of hypocrisy often turn into reality; and the children, at least, ignorant of the dissimulation of their parents, may happily be educated in more orthodox tenets.'[24]

Besides providing security for property and authority, an established church diminishes religious enthusiasm, zeal, and even piety. A ceremonial religion tends 'to mollify that fierce and gloomy spirit of devotion.' Hume compared the Presbyterian conscience to a dog with its master; a man with the sense that God is behind him becomes invincibly aggressive.[25] The Puritan conscience is inherently republican; Presbyterianism and monarchy are incompatible; while the surplice and crown, bishops and kings, are bound together.[26] By means of church establishment, Hume wrote, the government bribes the indolence of spiritual guides.[27] As John B. Stewart put Hume's point: 'Put the clergy on the government payroll, and their interest in popular religious fervor wanes.'[28]

Despite his affinity with Hobbes with respect to the anarchic character of Protestant conscience and the government's role in organized religion, Hume distanced himself from the most philosophic of British political theorists: 'Hobbes's politics are fitted only to promote tyranny, and his ethics to promote licentiousness.'[29]

Hume's objection to Hobbes was similar to his distaste for Puritans: he perceived their egalitarian rejection of authority, together with their repudiation of custom and sociality, as undermining the love of reputation, honour, and fame and as diminishing the fear of shame and dishonour. Indeed, Puritan republicanism veers toward Hobbesian egoism, licentiousness, and tyranny. In deprecating 'the sentiments of shame, duty, and honour,' the Puritans undermined the natural counters to selfishness and ambition: 'The saint, resigned over to superior guidance, was at full liberty to gratify all his appetites, disguised under the appearance of pious zeal.'[30] Despite his affinity with Hobbes on the relationship between religion and politics, Hume supported the comfortable sociability of the eighteenth century, as opposed to the uneasy individualism of the Puritan or Hobbesian: 'The steady attention alone to so important an interest as that of eternal salvation is apt to extinguish the benevolent affections, and beget a narrow, contracted selfishness.'[31]

Hobbes was critical of the claims of conscience; Hume in his philosophic work ignored the call of conscience – that is, the experience many have had in being bound by conscience. Whereas Bishop Butler, Rousseau, and Kant thought that conscience was an argument for God's existence from the design of the moral world, Hume did not discuss conscience in his *Dialogues concerning Natural Religion*. Indeed, in his *An Enquiry concerning the Principles of Morals*, Hume seemed to go out of his way to avoid using the word *conscience*: 'Inward peace of mind, consciousness of integrity, a satisfactory review of our conduct; these are circumstances very requisite to happiness, and will be cherished and cultivated by every honest man, who feels the importance of them.'[32]

Whereas his contemporaries would have said that a good conscience is essential to a happy life, Hume's philosophic precision mandated the longer version of the same message. Indeed, Hume asserted that there is 'no proper name in our language' for 'the *sentiment* of conscious worth, the self-satisfaction proceeding from a review of a man's own conduct and character.'[33] Perhaps we might understand Hume's repudiation of the language of conscience in terms of his systematic use of the psychology of social approbation and disapprobation; sympathy and social approbation replace the god within and individual judgment of good and evil. A central principle of Hume's *Treatise of Human Nature* asserts that '*no action can be virtuous, or morally good, unless there be in human nature some motive to produce it, distinct from the sense of its morality.*'[34] Conscience does not seem to be a motive for Hume, as is sympathy and the desire for esteem; virtue is not its own reward. Hume defined virtue as '*whatever mental action or quality gives to a spectator the pleasing sentiment of approbation;* and vice the contrary.'[35] Hutcheson, and later Smith, came close to identifying what conscience dictates with what spectators approve; but neither defined virtue as what is socially approved and vice as what is disapproved.

Hume was also bolder than his compatriots in following up the Hobbesian equation of love of virtue with love of praise. Robert Clayton criticized Hume: 'For though true it is, that all virtuous Actions merit, and generally do meet with, Approbation; yet it is not equally true that every Thing which meets with Approbation is *Virtue*.'[36] Hume's friend and kinsman, Henry Home, Lord Kames, also thought Hume wrong to reduce the rules of morality to norms of social acceptability.[37] However, for Hume the desire for social esteem is – and ought to be – the master passion of social beings; complementing the market where one is paid in money for putting some socially useful good or service on the market, one is paid in social esteem for forgoing profit for public service. Hume claimed to 'esteem the man, whose self-love, by whatever means, is so directed as to give him a concern for others, and render him serviceable to society' and to 'hate or despise him, who has no regard to any thing beyond his own gratifications and enjoyments.'[38]

The love of fame was the dominant passion in Hume's life; it was also, for him, the most solid basis of moral conduct – the ruling principle 'in all generous minds, and ... often the grand object of all their desires and undertakings':

> By our continual and earnest pursuit of a character, a name, a reputation in the world, we bring our own deportment and conduct frequently in review, and consider how they appear in the eyes of those, who approach and regard us. This constant habit of surveying ourselves, as it were, in reflection, keeps alive all the sentiments of right and wrong, and begets, in noble natures, a certain reverence for themselves as well as others; which is the surest guardian of every virtue.[39]

Whereas character is often opposed to reputation, *a* character is a reputation. We see ourselves as others see us, and keep in the path of rectitude in order to maintain a favourable reputation. Moral character is a product of our desire for a good reputation. One cannot rely on conscience as one can on the desire for social approval: 'And our regard to a character with others seems to arise only from a care of preserving a character with ourselves; and in order to attain this end, we find it necessary to prop our tottering judgment on the corresponding approbation of mankind.'[40] Here, Hume is not saying that our concern with reputation is derivative of our concern for character. Rather the reverse – and it is precisely in this reversal that Hume's boldness and originality consists. Hume's repudiation of the myth of individual inner-directedness was complete: 'Our opinions of all kinds are strongly affected by society and sympathy, and it is almost impossible for us to support any principle or sentiment, against the universal consent of every one, with whom we have any friendship or correspondence.'[41]

Hume thought that we cannot pride ourselves on anything unless the grounds of our self-satisfaction 'be also obvious to others, and engage the approbation of the spectators.'[42] The universal desire for fame and applause serves individuals 'to fix and confirm their favourable opinion of themselves.'[43]

Hume's repudiation of conscience was philosophically and theologically radical but socially and politically conservative. Harvey Chisick distinguished between Hume's enlightened conservatism and the traditional conservatism of Samuel Johnson, who recognized 'the religious obligation of charity and the secular obligation of paternalism.' Johnson is reported to have said that 'a decent provision for the poor is the true test of civilization.' In Chisick's view, Hume recognized no obligations to the poor: 'Hume, I think, would have regarded the terms in which Dr. Johnson expressed himself as outmoded, for he recognised no obligation on the part of society or of any individual to provide for another.'[44]

On the other hand, R.A. Houston writes that the Enlightenment language of sympathy and benevolence subjected the objects of sympathy to social control – to hierarchies of beneficent givers and recipients of benevolence.[45] Hume used the language of sympathy and benevolence, yet his writings on political economy emphasized market self-dependence, as his more egalitarian friend, Adam Smith, was to do in *The Wealth of Nations*. For Hume, moral virtues derived from historically changing assessments of utility rather than from divine strictures graven on the heart; in effect, this standpoint transformed traditional Christian vices such as greed, avarice, uncharitableness, and vanity into civilized virtues. Anticipating Smith's transmogrification of Mandeville's vices, which power a capitalist economy, into virtues, Hume wrote of Mandeville: 'And indeed it seems upon any system of morality, little less than a contradiction in terms, to talk of a vice, which is in general beneficial to society.'[46] Christian vices become capitalist virtues.

Whereas later eighteenth-century thinkers, including free thinkers like Thomas Paine and William Godwin, invoked conscience and the

Christian gospel against the capitalist ethos, Hume, although a Tory, was consistently enlightened to remain a firm adherent of Whig commercialism and a staunch opponent of Protestant conscience. Whereas later romantics and radicals espoused Rousseau's view that conscience, or the ability to make moral choices, is the definitive faculty of human beings and the basis of their claims to moral equality, Hume departed from rationalism along the path of habit, not conscience. Gilles Deleuze aptly captures the spirit of Hume's philosophical radicalism and political conservatism: 'We are habits, nothing but habits – the habit of saying "I." Perhaps, there is no more striking answer to the problem of the self.'[47]

Hume thought that human beings are moved by their passions and interests. Impulsiveness and self-centredness are controlled by the market (within which one can maximize one's own interest only by providing some useful good or service to others), by the social psychology of approval and censure (which rewards socially useful conduct with esteem and punishes socially harmful behaviour with scorn or hatred), and by habituation to the expectations of others. Hume repudiates the anarchic and egalitarian character of the Presbyterian conscience and thus typifies, according to J.G.A. Pocock, the conservative Enlightenment.[48] As Knud Haakonssen writes, the conservative Enlightenment 'constituted the mainstream of the Enlightenment.'[49] Nevertheless, none of Hume's compatriots in the Scottish Enlightenment repudiated the language of conscience to the extent he did, and none were as forthright in identifying moral conduct with what is socially approved or disapproved and in declaring the desire for reputation to be the most solid basis of virtue. In this respect, Hume was closer to Diderot, Helvétius, and Holbach than Hutcheson, Reid, Steuart, Smith, Millar, Stewart, and Ferguson.

Adam Smith: The Problem of Praise and Praiseworthiness

The so-called Adam Smith problem consists in unifying, or making a coherent whole of, his two most notable works – *The Wealth of Nations* and *The Theory of Moral Sentiments*. The former is a work of economic rationality, the latter of social sensibility. The former is predicated on a model of economic man as rational maximizer moved by self-interest; the latter presents human beings less abstractly, as moved not simply by money but by the desire for social approval and self-approbation, by esteem and conscience, by sympathy with and benevolence for one's fellow human beings. Thus *The Wealth of Nations* can be read as an abstraction of human experience, which is presented more fully and concretely in *The Theory of Moral Sentiments*. A cynic might suggest that the abstraction of economic man as acquisitive calculator has become our reality, and that Smith's theory of conscience as the impartial spectator, with its attendant social psychology of sympathy and benevolence, is the sentimental sententiousness of a Scottish professor detached from 'the real world.' An unfriendly death notice in *The Times* (16 August 1790) suggested that the professor of moral philosophy learned from 'the real world':

> The [Glasgow] College was torn by parties, and Dr. S[mith] embraced that side which was most popular among the people of condition; that is, the rich merchants of the town, among whom he was well received, and from whose conversation ... he learned many facts necessary for improving his Lectures; for living in a great commercial town, he had converted the chair of Moral Philosophy into a professorship of trade and finance.[50]

Donald Winch has argued that some of the disparity between *The Theory of Moral Sentiments* and *The Wealth of Nations* is a result of Smith's readers confusing sympathy with benevolence.[51] Since an analysis of *The Wealth of Nations* lies beyond my present purpose of clarifying the meaning of conscience, I will limit my comparison of Smith's two major works to those features which might illuminate his *Theory of Moral Sentiments*. Peter Minowitz asserts that '*The Wealth of Nations* is an atheistic and anti-Christian work ... *The Theory of Moral Sentiments*, on the other hand, is full of God, and features little of the blatant irreligiosity of *The Wealth of Nations*.'[52] Another apparent difference is voiced by Vivienne Brown, who holds that *The Wealth of Nations* has a monological character, with actors calculating their main chance, and with inferences being drawn from the assumption of prudent action; whereas *The Theory of Moral Sentiments* has a dialogical character, that is, it reads as a continuing dialogue between the moral agent or actor and the impartial spectator as judge.[53]

If *The Wealth of Nations* is prototypically individualist, *The Theory of Moral Sentiments* appears to be 'communitarian' or even 'collectivist.' V.P. Hope points out that Smith's conscience as impartial spectator 'is a collective person embodying a shared sense of what is decent and fair.'[54] A consensus of moral judgment arises from an actor's desire for social approval, the spectator's sympathy with the actor's situation and aims, the approbation or disapprobation of the spectators, and the internalization or modification of that judgment in the conscience of the actor. According to Knud Haakonssen, Smith thought that sympathetic identification of spectators with agents arises from a view of the situation and not, as with Hume, from witnessing the expression of another's passion and forming a similar passion or impression from ideas in one's own experience.[55] Moreover, Smith's conscience, as D.D. Raphael points out, is not a direct reflection of public opinion, of social esteem and censure, in that the actor is better informed or has inside knowledge of the facts of his situation and his motives.[56]

In Smith's moral theory, individual conscience wrestles with social approval. Smith evaded the boldness of Hume's social conformism in his refusal to reduce what is praiseworthy into what is praised, the 'demigod within the breast' into the judgments of external spectators. He declared: 'The man without aims at praise, the man within at praise-worthiness.'[57] He retained some traditional Protestant individualism against the enlightened conformism of Hume and contemporary French sceptics. If we accept Mark Hulliung's view that the core of the Enlightenment was the attempt to replace the idol of God with that of Society,[58] Smith tempered his commitment to Humean enlightenment with professorial prudence or moderation. Smith declared that 'this demigod within the breast appears ... partly of immortal, yet partly too of mortal extraction.'[59]

Smith's mortal extraction of conscience paralleled the account of his friend Hume:

> Nature, when she formed man for society, endowed him with an original desire to please, and an original aversion to offend his brethren. She taught him to feel pleasure in their favourable, and pain in their unfavourable regard. She rendered their approbation most flattering and most agreeable to him for its own sake; and their disapprobation, most mortifying and most offensive.[60]

The mortal seems to take on immortality in a different phrasing of the same idea:

> The all-wise Author of Nature has ... taught man to respect the sentiments and judgments of his brethren; to be more or less pleased when they approve of his conduct, and to be more or less hurt when they disapprove of it. He has made man, if I may say so, the immediate judge

of mankind; ... and appointed him his viceregent upon earth, to superintend the behaviour of his brethren.[61]

Smith went on to say that while people have an immediate judge in their fellow humans, they appeal 'to a much higher tribunal, to the tribunal of their own consciences, to that of the supposed impartial and well-informed spectator, to that of the man within the breast, the great judge and arbiter of their conduct.'[62]

Moral judgments are not innate but are the acquired products of our social environment; in Hobbes's state of nature or on Robinson Crusoe's deserted island, there would be no judgments of conscience. As Charles Griswold Jr points out, Smith's view of 'our natural dependence on others for our self-conception' means that our moral self-awareness is acquired through social interaction.[63] A lone individual 'is provided with no mirror which can present' his motives and sentiments to his self-inspection, but 'bring him into society, and he is immediately provided with the mirror which he wanted before.'[64] The mirror of self-approbation or disapprobation is the eyes of others; one sees oneself with the eyes of others. Moral conduct requires us to place ourselves in the situation of others, and view our own conduct through their eyes, and then approve or disapprove of our conduct as we see it from their perspective. Through this procedure of self-examination, which Smith says is as painful as a surgeon operating on himself, we 'pull off the mysterious veil of self-delusion, which covers from his view the deformities of his own conduct.'[65] Our self-assessment is thereby purged of the blind partiality or bias that is normal in cases where one is a judge in one's own cause. Samuel Fleischacker correctly observes that it was not so much the sympathy of spectators for actors and vice versa as the *impartiality* of the sympathy that distinguished Smith from his philosophic predecessors: 'Smith's insistence that sympathy be impartial would by itself be at least a shift of emphasis from Hutcheson's and Hume's theories of moral approbation.'[66] A conscientious individual divides herself into two persons: an *agent* who is plaintiff and defendant, and a *spectator* who makes an impartial judgment of the cause.

Like Hume, Smith thought that our uncertainty about our own merit and our strong need to think well of ourselves makes us desire the good opinion of others.[67] Indeed, no one is so inner-directed as to be unmoved by the adverse judgments of others, of friends and family.[68] Mathematicians and natural philosophers or scientists, who know the truth and importance of their discoveries, are most independent of public opinion, Smith thought, whereas poets and moral philosophers are vain, anxious for approval, and subject to public opinion.[69] Can we infer that Smith, like Diderot, D'Alembert, and Condorcet, thought men of science should lead public opinion, and the rest should follow it? Smith does not explain how science and conscience escape the web of social expectations and the reinforcement of subjective certainty.

All men desire praise, which is 'to appear fit for society,' whereas the man of conscience desires to be praiseworthy or 'to be really fit' for society.[70] 'The love of praiseworthiness is by no means derived altogether from the love of praise,' although 'they resemble one another, though they are connected, and often blended with one another.'[71] Smith deprecated the 'coarse and rustic eloquence' of Mandeville, who thought all virtue to be vanity, derived from a love of praise or commendation. Rather, Smith intoned, 'rendering ourselves the proper objects of esteem and approbation, cannot with any propriety be called vanity.'[72] The ghost of Mandeville haunted the pages of *The Theory of Moral Sentiments* as well as *The Wealth of Nations*. Smith emphasized the quality over the quantity of approbation; the considered approbation of one wise man is worth more 'than all the noisy applauses of ten thousand ignorant though enthusiastic admirers.'[73] Perhaps the difference between praise and praiseworthiness is the difference between temporary acclaim and enduring fame, or between uninformed and informed approval. In a friendly elbow to the ribs, Hume wrote to his friend on the popularity of *The Theory of Moral Sentiments* (for which Hume would have given his eye teeth): 'Nothing, indeed, can be a stronger presumption of falsehood than the approbation of the multitude.'[74] If Smith thought Hume a wise man, then he was not very inner-directed at the time of Hume's candidacy for the Chair of Logic at Glasgow in 1751. T.D. Campbell and Ian Ross write: 'Smith did not stand up for him, but was swayed by the consideration that public opinion would be unfavourable and that the "interest" of the University dictated acceding to that opinion.'[75] When Peter Minowitz states that Smith comes close to reducing morality to what 'the many' praise or blame,[76] he runs counter to numerous *professed* statements of Smith to the contrary.

Smith gave more weight to the quality than the quantity of the approbation, to praiseworthiness than the actual praise of uninformed persons; but he did not clearly distinguish admiration, approbation, and approval.[77] We may give our approbation to what is permissible;

prudent and lawful acquisition may earn our approbation without our admiration. We may admire a charming or cunning rogue without approving of him, and even admire the greatness of successful criminality without giving it our approbation. If we are apt to shade our assessments of the conduct of others, we are also prone to making nuanced judgments about ourselves, admiring where we cannot approve and approving where we cannot admire.

Moral sentiments, Smith thought, 'suppose the idea of some other being, who is the natural judge of the person that feels them; and it is only by sympathy with the decisions of the arbiter of his conduct, that he can conceive, either the triumph of self-applause, or the shame of self-condemnation.'[78] Individual self-assessment is closely tied to social approval. To be sure, the individual conscience perceives things that are hidden to society; and even if the agent is completely certain that no one will know of his misdeed, the impartial spectator within will unleash the 'natural pangs of an affrighted conscience.'[79] Conscience internalizes social standards and judges individuals with the eyes of society even when there are no witnesses to their actions. Conscience, rather than benevolence or humanity, prompts self-sacrifice to the interests of others; one not only wants social esteem but also wants to think well of oneself.[80]

Individual self-assessment is closely tied to social approval; and approval or disapproval of others is connected to self-assessment. Conscience, or the impartial spectator, constructs rules to bind itself from the things it abhors in others; the construction of general rules is an antidote to self-deceit.[81] Conscience may begin with real spectators (Jiminy Crickets, as it were, on the shoulder of Pinocchio before he matures and becomes a real boy), but those spectators are internalized as they are idealized. Smith referred to 'that great discipline which Nature has established for the acquisition of ... every ... virtue; a regard to the sentiments of the real or supposed spectator of our conduct.'[82] In the second to the fifth editions of *Moral Sentiments*, Smith referred to conscience as 'the representative of mankind, and substitute of the Deity.'[83] As distinct from ideal spectators, actual spectators may be biased or prejudiced. Smith seemed to contend with Hume's view that we naturally tend to favour our own immediate circle, and to have limited sympathy for those beyond it: 'The propriety of our moral sentiments is never so apt to be corrupted, as when the indulgent and partial spectator is at hand, while the indifferent and impartial one is at a great distance.'[84] We are corrupted as curly-headed boys by indulgent mothers when the lord and master is at work, by our class and nationality when we judge those of our own or a different class and nationality, and so forth. From the habit of consulting one's conscience, Smith wrote, 'he does not merely affect the sentiments of the impartial spectator. He really adopts them. He almost identifies himself with, he almost becomes himself that impartial spectator, and scarce even feels but as that great arbiter of his conduct directs him to feel.'[85]

We might note here that unlike Rousseau, Kant, Coleridge, and Kierkegaard, Smith did not identify the self with the conscience; the empirical self and its habits, memories, and feelings are not fused with conscience, or with the adopted sentiments of the ideal spectator. However, we might also note that Smith's impartial spectator echoes the certainty of Protestant conscience, of Luther, Knox, and Milton, rather than the scepticism of his enlightened contemporaries such as Hume, Voltaire, and Diderot. Smith enjoined us to attend to 'the man within the breast, the supposed impartial spectator, the great judge and arbiter of our conduct. If we place ourselves completely in his situation, if we really view ourselves with his eyes, and as he views us, and listen with diligent and reverential attention to what he suggests to us, his voice will never deceive us. We stand in need of no casuistic rules to direct our conduct.'[86]

Smith's reconstruction of Protestant conscience in the categories of Enlightenment social psychology is impressive, in that it merges the inner-directedness of the god within with the other-orientedness of social approval and censure. Knud Haakonssen asserts that the standpoint of an impartial spectator implies a general rule (like John Rawls's veil of ignorance) by means of which we gain independence from prevailing social mores.[87] However, it is questionable whether Smith thought we could ever achieve a condition of impartial judgment, in that we sympathize with others on the basis of our own sentiments. Smith advanced the following claim, which is not only questionable in itself but also fatal to the ideal of impartiality: 'The man who feels little for his own misfortunes must always feel less for those of other people, and be less disposed to relieve them. The man who feels little resentment for the injuries which are done to himself, must always have less for those which are done to other people, and be less disposed either to protect or avenge them.'[88]

Smith's claim is questionable, not only because there are occasional saints who feel their own afflictions and injuries less than they do those of others, but also because it undermines his objective of achieving a consensus among people of different class, gender, and nationality. Socially dominant groups, and those who think themselves oppressed by them, would have insufficient sympathy with the situation and perspective of others to search for a common standpoint, let alone arrive at one. As is well known, Smith thought beggars were worthy of contempt (not sympathy, compassion, humanity, or benevolence), because beggary 'can seldom happen without some misconduct, and some very considerable misconduct too.'[89] Not all beggars would see matters as clearly as Smith; nor would they necessarily accept his version of the facts (directed at 'whining and melancholy moralists,' such as Pascal, who think some are not entitled to happiness when others are in misery): 'Take the whole earth at an average, for one man who suffers pain and misery, you will find twenty in prosperity and joy, or at least in tolerable circumstances.'[90]

Despite the difficulties in establishing the standpoint of the impartial spectator, or even the grounds of a search for one, Smith's *Theory of Moral Sentiments* seems to me the supreme effort in the English-speaking world to articulate the dictates of the Protestant conscience in the language of the Enlightenment.[91] In asserting that Smith gave voice to Protestant conscience, I do not mean to side either with Minowitz's view that Smith was a secret atheist or with Campbell and Ross's view that Smith's 'express conviction is that the ordinary rules of morality are rightly regarded as the voice of God.'[92] That Smith expressed or professed that moral rules are to be regarded as the voice of God does not entail that he had an inner conviction that moral rules are to be so regarded. My method derives from the very English injunction of Hobbes that to conduct an inquisition upon a person's soul or secret intentions is contrary to the rights of conscience. Smith is to be understood as he professed himself to the company he kept and the people whose approval he sought. It is a cardinal position of the post-Lockean Enlightenment that a man's conscience is formed by his education, company, and social environment, and particularly by those whose approval he seeks. To the degree that Smith's conscience was governed by public opinion or the desire for social approbation, he was in accord with the central creed of the Enlightenment. Hume's philosophy accorded with the friendship he practised. If Donald Winch holds as a calumny Smith's death notice in *The Times* that 'he embraced that side which was most popular among the people of condition' and 'converted the chair of Moral Philosophy into a professorship of trade and finance,'[93] Winch must be sentimentally attached to Protestant inner-directedness rather than enlightened other-orientedness.

Chapter 8

Conscience as Tiger and Lamb

Rousseau, Radicalism, and Romanticism

In *A Vindication of the Rights of Woman*, Mary Wollstonecraft wrote: 'Our own conscience is the most enlightened philosopher.'[1] In this chapter I explore the place of conscience in radical thought from the time of the American and French revolutions. In doing so, I hope to clarify the relationship between enlightened reason and Protestant conscience in what could be called the Radical Enlightenment, or what I should prefer to call the radical opposition to the mainstream of Enlightenment thought.

To clarify the meaning of Wollstonecraft's thought, we must touch on the place of conscience in the ideas of Jean-Jacques Rousseau, whose relationship to Enlightenment thought was complex and ambivalent.[2] Wollstonecraft, like Paine, Godwin, and Blake, followed Rousseau's critique of civilized inequality – of the injustice of hereditary aristocracy and of the growing inequalities of commercial societies. English radicals sided with Rousseau rather than with Adam Smith, who thought the increasing inequality of commercial society was compensated for by the increased self-dependence of market relationships and by the (alleged) fact that even the poorest in contemporary capitalist societies fare better than the richest members of precapitalist societies. Although Paine used Smith's *laissez-faire* principles to attack aristocracy and militaristic government in *Common Sense* and *The Rights of Man*, he came to advocate a redistributive role for the state by means of inheritance taxes. In *Agrarian Justice*, Paine sounded a Rousseauan note that one also hears in the works of Wollstonecraft, Godwin, and Blake: 'The most affluent and the most miserable of the human race are to be found in the countries that are called civilized.' Paine's conclusion was that since poverty is caused by commercial civilization, civilization owes a comfortable subsistence to all individuals bound in commercial relationships.[3] English radicals also espoused Rousseau's use of conscience as the voice of the sturdy plebeian. In his *Discourse on the Arts and the Sciences*, Rousseau took aim at *les lumières*:

> What good is it to seek our happiness in the opinion of another if we can find it within ourselves. Let us leave to others the care of informing peoples of their duties, and limit ourselves to fulfilling well our own. We do not need to know more than this.
>
> O virtue! Sublime science of simple souls, are so many difficulties and preparations needed to know you? Are not your principles engraved in all hearts, and is it not enough in order to learn your laws to commune with oneself and listen to the voice of one's conscience in the silence of the passions? That is true philosophy.[4]

Rousseau contended that it was impertinent for literary educators and the leaders of public opinion to instruct other people on their duties even while undermining, in their attacks on the divine inner voice, people's right to judge for themselves what is appropriate to their innermost selves in their particular circumstances. Rousseau understood conscience as standing in opposition to the social self – to public opinion that threatens to swamp one's individuality. (Much later, but in the same vein, Heidegger in *Being and Time* would perceive conscience as a call to one's social self from one's authentic self.) Conscience is the voice of nonconformist and romantic reaction to the hierarchic sociability of the conservative Enlightenment.

Despite Blake's rejection of what he took to be anti-Christian deism in Rousseau – 'Mock on, mock on, Voltaire, Rousseau!'[5] – he echoed Rousseau in perceiving conscience as the divine and infallible voice of the common man, the certainty of the oppressed that oppression is wrong. In his magnificent defence of Paine as a better Christian than the Lockean Whig, Bishop Watson, who attacked Paine's deism as atheism and who defended God's providential division of humanity into rich and poor classes, Blake declared: 'Conscience in those that have it is unequivocal.'[6] Evidently, Blake thought Paine's defence of freedom of conscience and the disestablishment of religion more important than the anti-Christian tone of Paine's deism; state religion, the poet thought, is the source of all cruelty.[7] It was Watson, not Paine, who represented the dark satanic mills of Lockean rationalism; the 'state trickster,' as Blake called the bishop, used Locke's opposition to conscience as an innate idea to bolster his view that God made both rich and poor.[8] Conscience is not, as Locke and Watson had it, mere opinion, the contingent product of one's upbringing and company: 'If Conscience is not a Criterion of Moral Rectitude, What is it? He who thinks Honesty is changeable knows nothing about it. Contemptible Falsehood & Wickedness. Virtue & Honesty, or the dictates of Conscience, are of no doubtful Signification to anyone. Opinion is one Thing. Principle another. No Man can change his Principles. Every Man changes his Opinions.'[9] Blake's use of conscience combines moral individualism with class solidarity. As Christopher Hill wrote of the antinomians of the seventeenth century, 'the inner light was a bond of unity because God *did* in fact say similar things to the mechanics who formed his congregations.'[10]

Paine's *Agrarian Justice*, published in response to Watson, begins with this self-evident truth: 'It is wrong to say that God made *Rich* and *Poor*; he made only *Male* and *Female*; and he gave them the earth for their inheritance.'[11] Mary Wollstonecraft agreed with Rousseau and Paine that class differences are not divinely appointed, but she did not agree with them that gender differences are God's creation. Indeed, Rousseau thought that men by their nature are designed for the inner-directedness of Protestant conscience, while women by their nature are designed for the government of public opinion. Women's nature makes their reputation more important than their character, and as a result their conduct should be governed by public opinion. In short, Rousseau thought women should be raised in precisely the manner that his enlightened adversaries thought men are, and ought to be, habituated to moral conduct – namely, by a desire for social esteem and a fear of social censure. For Rousseau, 'opinion is the grave of virtue among men and its throne among women.'[12] Thus men are to follow their own inner compass but women must follow external maps, or what is laid out for them by public opinion. Rousseau seems to be saying that the philosophy of Hume, Diderot, and D'Holbach is fine for women but ruinous for men.

Wollstonecraft wanted to universalize Rousseau's moral individualism; women as well as men were to be subject to no other authority than their own conscience. However, for Wollstonecraft (as for Paine and Godwin) reason and conscience were 'synonymous terms.'[13] Rousseau and Blake differentiated reason and conscience. Rousseau asserted that 'by reason alone, independent of conscience, no natural law can be established.'[14] Blake declaimed: 'Conscience was sent, a Guard to Reason, Reason once fairer than the light, till foul'd in Knowledge's dark Prison house.'[15]

Another affinity between Rousseau and Blake is that both men thought conscience to be a friend of desire. This runs counter to the Freudian or Enlightenment idea that the superego and libido are opposed – that conscience restrains desire whereas reason serves it. Rousseau and Blake saw conscience and eroticism as partners, not enemies. The Savoyard vicar's paean to conscience in *Emile* is cribbed from Rousseau's soulful addresses to Sophie d'Houdetot, a married woman and lover of Rousseau's friend Saint-Lambert. In his letters to d'Houdetot, Rousseau appeals to conscience to loosen the hold of mere public opinion, which bars a fusion of Jean-Jacques and Sophie's souls.[16] Blake for his part did not distinguish between *eros* and *agape*, sexual love and Christian charity. Nor did he distinguish between conscience and imagination:[17] in his prophetic works, they are the constitutive features of individuality, as opposed to impersonal reason, or 'Urizen.' Urizen is 'your-reason' (i.e., not my conscience), or the horizon of Enlightenment reason, prudential self-interest, and publicly accepted norms repressing the individuality of each person.[18] According to E.P. Thompson, the appeal to antinomian conscience was 'a way of breaking out from received wisdom and moralizing and entering upon new possibilities.'[19] Conscience, for Blake, is opposed to the conformity and normality of enlightened reason.

Mary Wollstonecraft appeared to accept the romantic proverb of Blake's that 'the road of excess leads to the palace of wisdom.'[20] In *A Vindication of the Rights of Woman*, she wrote:

> One reason why men have superior judgment, and more fortitude than women, is undoubtedly this, that they give a freer scope to the grand passions, and by more frequently going astray enlarge their minds. If then by the exercise of their own reason they fix on some stable principle, they probably have to thank the force of their passions, nourished by *false* views of life, and permitted to overleap the boundary that secures content.[21]

Wollstonecraft suggested a reason why conscience enjoys a central place in romantic poetry, in the poems of Byron, Wordsworth, Coleridge, and Blake. Conscience, like imagination, has a transgressive quality; if romantic poetry broke through the boundaries of the Augustan age, guilt for doing so was also grist for poetic mills. Conscience is more attractive than prudence, who as Blake wrote, 'is a rich ugly old maid courted by incapacity.'[22]

Radical Conscience and the American War

At the outbreak of the American War of Independence, William Blake was in his late teens, the same age as William Wordsworth, Ludwig van Beethoven, and Georg Wilhelm Friedrich Hegel when the French Revolution dawned. In *The Prelude* (XI.108–9), Wordsworth wrote: 'Bliss was it in that dawn to be alive, / But to be young was very heaven!' At the end of his life, Hegel looked back on the French Revolution (unswayed, as the mere poets were, by the Terror and the Napoleonic period) as follows: 'This was accordingly a glorious mental dawn. All thinking beings shared in the jubilation of this epoch. Emotions of a lofty character stirred men's minds at that time; a spiritual enthusiasm thrilled through the world, as if the reconciliation between the Divine and the Secular was now first accomplished.'[23]

Thomas Paine was in his late thirties when he arrived in America in 1774, past the time of youthful enthusiasm. The following year, his *Common Sense* provided an ideological warrant for rebellion against the mother country. Paine's readers were the sons and daughters of those described, by Wordsworth, as *The Pilgrim Fathers*: 'Men they were who would not bend; / Blest Pilgrims, surely, as they took for guide / A will by sovereign Conscience sanctified ...'[24]

Although a latecomer to America, Paine shared the dissenting background that had driven the earlier Pilgrims to America. Paine was raised as a Quaker and wished to be buried as a Quaker. There is debate among Paine's biographers whether Quaker beliefs informed his political practice.[25] Edward H. Davidson and William J. Scheik write: 'The Quaker doctrine of the Inward Light, "the true Light, which lighteth every man" (John 1:9), may have imparted a special sense of the individual that, however unexamined, possibly continued to empower, even legitimize, Paine's later proto-Emersonian voice, particularly when speaking authoritatively against the authority of established religion.'[26]

Scholars have been more inclined to call Paine's thought deist or pantheist rather than atheist, whether or not they find residues of Quaker conscience within the enlightened freethinker. Thomas Jefferson drew our attention to national differences in the political theological creed of the Enlightenment: refugees from priestly religions called themselves deists in Protestant countries, whereas in Catholic countries they called themselves atheists.[27] His compatriot and fellow deist, Benjamin Franklin, professed his belief immediately after the American rebellion against the British empire had succeeded: 'If I had ever before been an Atheist, I should now have been convinced of the Being and Government of a Deity! It is he [sic] who abases the Proud and favours the Humble.'[28]

Deists might also point beyond the evidence that religion favours the righteous, to the utility of religion. Voltaire notoriously wrote: 'I want my attorney, my tailor, my servants, even my wife to believe in God, and I think that then I shall be robbed and cuckolded less often.'[29] Franklin advised Paine that his writings attacking organized religion might undermine morality, particularly among young people.[30] Whether Paine was a pantheist, an atheist, or a deist, there is a distinctly Protestant tone to *Common Sense*. Scripture, Paine told us, is unequivocally against monarchical government; that is why it is withheld from the public in Catholic countries: 'for monarchy, in every instance, is the popery of government.'[31] In *Common Sense*, Paine sets forth freedom of conscience as a fundamental principle: 'above all things the free exercise of religion, according to the dictates of conscience.'[32] Freedom of conscience, for Paine, is not mere religious toleration. In *The Rights of Man* he wrote: 'Toleration is not the *opposite* of Intolerance, but is the *counterfeit* of it. Both are despotisms. The one assumes to itself the right of with-holding Liberty of Conscience, and the other of granting it.'[33]

Paine's *Common Sense* is an odd mixture of enlightened reason and Protestant conscience. Paine stated that government would not be necessary 'were the impulses of conscience clear, uniform, and irresistibly obeyed' and then asserted that the first society's rules were 'enforced by no other penalty than public disesteem.'[34] Thomas Jefferson also confused the moral sense or conscience with public esteem or disesteem: 'Man was destined for society. His morality, therefore, was to be formed to this object. He was endowed with a sense of right and wrong, merely relative to this.'[35]

If Paine was unclear whether conscience is an internal directive or a reflex of public opinion, he was also unclear whether freedom of conscience, the upholding of which is the prime duty of governments, should be extended to conscientious objectors to the American cause.

Tories in America were, for him, traitors, and deserved the penalty befitting the most heinous of crimes.[36] The Quakers who professed conscientious objection to participating in the War of Independence were such traitors. Paine supported the Scotch-Irish settlers who wanted both a break with England and a more vigorous prosecution of war against the Indians; in this, he set himself against the pacifist Pennsylvanians, who favoured negotiation with the Native Americans and in fact took up arms on behalf of Indians who were being slaughtered by the white settlers.[37] Paine wrote that Quakers had no right to publish their pacifist position; they were mixing religion and politics and mistaking party for conscience. Paine, as John Keane notes, was 'cocksure' that the Quakers were violating their principles. Paine wrote that he reproached the Society of Friends not 'because you are *Quakers*, but because ye pretend to *be* and are *not* Quakers.'[38] Paine supported the Free Quakers, who thought pacifism less important than conscience, or the cause of the white Protestant Americans. If the mainstream Quakers were soft on Black slavery, on Catholic rights (at the time of both the Glorious Revolution and the Quebec Act of 1774), and on the suppression of Native Americans, Paine's *Common Sense* pointed out that the British had 'stirred up the Indians and the Negroes to destroy us.'[39] In an us-them situation, Native and Black Americans were not *us*.

For Paine, conscience unambiguously pointed to the American cause, rather than neutrality or support for the British. As William C. Kashatus III notes: 'However, to single out pacifism as the sole test of Quaker conviction is to denigrate the very basis of Quaker thought itself, the Inner Light, which guides the individual in his search for religious and moral truth. Paine then, like his associates of the "Free Quaker milieu," was following the leading of his Inner Light in his conviction as to the rightness of the Revolutionary cause.'[40]

Paine thought the Quakers were hypocrites who wished to maintain the British connection in America and so must clearly be scorning conscience for material advantage. Such a charge is unworthy, since the Quakers suffered enormous material losses during the war, and after the war would not buy land taken by force from the French or American Tories.[41] That Paine acquired land and 'my boy Joe' for his services to the American cause did not condition his principled convictions about the cause of liberty in the British Empire.[42]

How can we assess the rightness of the revolutionary cause? The Machiavellian would say by its success; the American rebellion succeeded and hence became the American Revolution or the War of Independence. On the other hand, Edmund Burke supported the American Revolution precisely because it was *not* a revolution – that is, it was not a disruption of property, of inherited economic and political practices, of a tradition of doing things; it was successful because it maintained a British way of life in America, and an existing social structure, while altering the form of government. But if, *contra* Burke, the Revolution changed life for the Americans, can we be sure that the lot of Blacks, Amerindians, and Catholics – the most likely beneficiaries of an English victory – would have improved if the British rather than the Americans had won the war? Perhaps the British lion would have become more arrogant and oppressive had it won the war, and would not have abolished slavery when it did, and would not have honoured its treaty obligations with the Indians better than the white settlers. Perhaps a British victory would not have prevented the bloody civil war of the next century, and perhaps America would not have evolved to political independence (as Canada did), without a military victory. We cannot really judge historical actors properly in consequentialist terms because we cannot accurately weigh counterfactuals (what would have happened if ...). At the same time, one may wish to avoid the covert consequentialism of Whiggish history that accepts the winning side as the deserving side – specifically, the conclusion of Paine scholars (and Paine himself) that his conscience directed him to the side of righteousness in the American rebellion against the British.

Conscience, Natural Rights, and the French Revolution

If Edmund Burke was a friend to the American Revolution, his opposition to the French Revolution was early and vigorous. He thought revolution disrupted traditions in which known and determinate rights existed; by exchanging concrete rights for metaphysical abstractions or natural rights, it undermined the civil rights that Frenchmen, and particularly Englishmen, had come to enjoy. He insisted: 'Men cannot enjoy the rights of an uncivil and of a civil state together.'[43] The first law of nature is that individuals renounce the right of private judgment and execution of the laws of nature when they enter civil society: 'One of the first motives to civil society, and which becomes one of its fundamental rules, is *that no man should be judge in his own cause*.'[44] Once one limits the natural right of self-government, politics becomes a matter of prudence, of skilful assessments of social utility, not matters of principle. Politics is a matter of practical know-how acquired through the experience of estate management; it is not theoretical knowledge acquired from reading some manuals on the rights of man.

If the conservative Whig statesman, Burke, was hostile to the idea of natural rights, and specifically to the rights of conscience or the rights of private judgment on which the other natural rights rest, the reforming lawyer, Jeremy Bentham, was apoplectic on the subject. The rhetoric of natural rights, Bentham opined, is 'cut-throat,' 'terrorist language,' 'dangerous nonsense,' 'nonsense upon stilts.'[45] He elaborated:

> The dictates of reason and utility are the result of circumstances which require genius to discover, strength of mind to weigh, and patience to investigate: the language of natural rights require [sic] nothing but a hard front, a hard heart and an unblushing countenance. It is from beginning to end so much flat assertion: it neither has any thing to do with reason nor will endure the mention of it. It lays down as a fundamental and inviolable principle whatever is in dispute: admit it, you are an honest fellow, a true patriot: question it, or so much as ask for a proof of it, you are whatever is most odious, sinning equally against truth and against conscience.[46]

Bentham opposed the long uphill road of reason to the slippery downhill slope of conscience. Reason is a matter for trained lawyers, immersed in a utilitarian tradition of thinking; conscience is the easy and unlearned path to the cut-throat assertion of natural rights.

To counter the popularity of Burke's *Reflections*, Mary Wollstonecraft rushed to print with *A Vindication of the Rights of Men*, but the popular best-seller was Paine's *Rights of Man*. The intuition of both proponents and opponents of natural rights is that natural rights rest on conscience, or the individual judgment of right and wrong. Burke opposed natural rights because of the priority they gave to the right of private judgment, a judgment exercised by those inexperienced in estate management or (see Bentham) unlearned in utilitarian doctrine. In response to Burke's contention that one cannot enjoy the rights of a civil and uncivil state together, Paine countered that the right of private judgment is an inalienable natural right, while the right to execute the laws of nature is a civil right – punishment is to be conducted by civil authorities.[47] Paine did not want to leave uncontested Burke's alternative – namely, that all rights are determined by civil authorities. His answer to Burke would not have satisfied Locke – for what point is there to a right of private judgment if the means of executing such judgments is left in the hands of the civil authorities – but it seemed satisfactory to Paine's many readers.

John Keane says that the sales of a half-million copies in a decade made *The Rights of Man* 'the most widely read book of all time, in any language.'[48] Perhaps Keane was taking into account the quality as well as the quantity of books sold, since Paine wrote of the Bible: 'I can write a better book myself.'[49] Keane asserts that when Paine was writing *The Age of Reason*, he 'was certainly conscious of standing humbly before his Maker.'[50] In *The Age of Reason*, Paine asserted: 'My own mind is my own church.'[51] While worshipful to his own church, Paine insisted that there is no sanctity or authority in the Bible or the Koran.[52] In assessing Keane's claim that Paine stood humbly before God, we might recall John Dryden's claim that celebration of conscience and Christian humility are incompatible. William Blake, as we will see, thought that Christianity is anything but a religion of humility because it insists, unlike other monotheistic religions, that the divine is present in human beings. Although he abhorred deism, Blake thought Paine's *Age of Reason* to be an honest criticism of orthodox Christianity.[53] In the course of his heart-warming defence of Paine against the Lockean Bishop Watson, Blake declared: 'The Bible or Peculiar Word of God, Exclusive of Conscience or the Word of God Universal, is that Abomination, which, like the Jewish ceremonies, is for ever removed & henceforth every man may converse with God & be a King & Priest in his own house.'[54]

Blake's words are not the hot air of Enlightenment rhetoric; they have the weight of conviction behind them. To be sure, Mary Wollstonecraft could have added some words of her own to Blake's celebration of conscience above the Bible.

We must now consider the relationship between conscience of freethinkers and Biblical teaching. Paine's advocacy, in *Agrarian Justice* and in the second part of *The Rights of Man* of an extensive welfare state to eliminate poverty, funded by a graduated estate tax, was based on the proposition that God did not make the rich and the poor and that 'land ... is the free gift of the Creator in common to the human race.'[55] Similarly, the anarchist freethinker William Godwin reaffirmed the traditional Christian teaching that property is a trust rather than a right, and cited the Bible to support his view of distributive justice.[56] Whether Godwin was a theist or an atheist at the time of writing *Political Justice* is a matter for scholarly debate.[57] Not unjustly, he has been described as 'a terrier at the throat of Christianity and, shaking it this way and that, nothing will persuade him to let go.'⁵⁸ Thus F.E.L. Priestley noted the irony in Godwin's affirming the Christian duty to assist the needy with one's property, and citing the Bible to justify his position:

> It is noteworthy that on the subject of property he is willing to appeal to the Bible. His references – Mark 10.21, and Acts 2.44–5 – are aptly chosen, although Godwin would disapprove of the heavenly reward offered in the first, and of the community of possession in the second. If he had added a further reference to 1 Corinthians 9.7,8, he could have presented his own attitude as complete Christian doctrine: the Pauline statement of the right to the produce of one's labour combined with the injunction to share with the needy gives precisely Godwin's point of view.⁵⁹

Perhaps Blake was right that Paine was a better Christian than his opponents thought, and perhaps people like Paine were better Christians than they thought themselves to be. Mark Philp argues that Godwin's thought, whether theist or atheist, was structured by the tradition of Protestant Dissent, in which conscience or the right and duty of private judgment enjoys pride of place.⁶⁰ Godwin declared: 'The universal exercise of private judgment is a doctrine so unspeakably beautiful, that the true politician will certainly feel infinite reluctance in admitting the idea of interfering with it.'⁶¹

Godwin's political thought is a more consistently libertarian form of Paine's egalitarian doctrine. Like Paine, Godwin thought that 'government is, abstractly taken, an evil, an usurpation upon the private judgment and individual conscience of mankind.'⁶² Although Godwin agreed with Paine in essential economic doctrine, he was reluctant to use the 'brute regulations' of law to regulate conduct and redistribute wealth without first transforming the understanding or conscience of those subject to laws and taxes.⁶³ 'There is but one power to which I can yield a heart-felt obedience, the decision of my own understanding, the dictate of my own conscience.'⁶⁴ In obeying law, Godwin said, we either obey others' decisions or our own; however we may attempt to adhere to heteronomous law, we are condemned to autonomy – 'will not conscience in spite of ourselves whisper us, "This decree is equitable, and this is founded in mistake"?'⁶⁵

Godwin insisted that conscience does not merely pertain to an inner realm of the mind, and that freedom of conscience is not merely a synonym for freedom of religion: 'It is commonly said, "that positive institutions ought to leave me free in matters of conscience, but may properly interfere in my conduct in civil concerns." But this distinction seems to have been very lightly taken up. What sort of moralist must he be, whose conscience is silent in what passes in his intercourse with other men?'[66]

Conscience has a proper role in civil and secular concerns, and is not to be limited to purely religious matters. Indeed, Godwin was offended 'that men should have affirmed religion to be the sacred province of conscience, while moral duty is left undefined to the decision of the magistrate.'[67] The anarchist anticipated John Stuart Mill's secular championship of conscience when he asserted that to disregard the dictates of conscience is to 'abdicate the most valuable part of the character of a man.'[68] He seemed to argue that the dictates of conscience are a more reliable guide than demonstrable knowledge:

> If there be any truth more unquestionable than the rest, it is, that every man is bound to the exercise of his faculties in the discovery of right, and to the carrying into effect all the right with which he is acquainted. It may be granted, that an infallible standard, if it could be discovered, would be considerably beneficial. But this infallible standard itself would be of little use in human affairs, unless it had the property of reasoning as well as deciding, of enlightening the mind as well as constraining the body.[69]

Godwin's thought seemed to exemplify W.H. Auden's dictum: 'Truth is Catholic, but the search for it is Protestant.'[70] Godwin's *Political Justice* combined belief in universal standards of truth and justice[71] with conscience or fallible judgment in the application of these rules.

Godwin diverged from the tradition of Rational Dissent in refusing to recognize that 'erroneous conscience' has any authority.'[72] This refusal suggests that the rights of subjectivity are trumped by objective reason, and that the right of individual judgment is subject to standards of rational utility.[73] Was Godwin (and later John Stuart Mill) more on the side of secular utility or (with Rational Dissent) on the side of rights of conscience? Certainly, Godwin thought freedom of association must be curtailed in terms of public utility.[74] Individualists such as Hobbes and Rousseau thought freedom of groups less precious than personal freedoms, and supported limits to the freedom to associate with others in sects and parties. But Godwin expected more from public discussion than Hobbes or Rousseau (who thought solitary meditation or listening to one's heart more fruitful paths to truth), and thus one is more surprised that he disassociates the rights of conscience from the right to meet and discuss public matters. Freedom of speech and of association would seem to be essential stepping stones to Godwin's anarchist utopia. Before everyone followed the dictates of conscience, conflicting views of what is right and wrong would have to be settled by public discussions. Godwin did not elaborate the later doctrine of John Stuart Mill that public utility and individual freedom could not conflict – that my right to speak is based on the public's need to hear me rather than on some natural right to free expression.

Godwin followed the Lockean Enlightenment in rejecting the idea of conscience as innate; one's conscience is formed by prenatal and postnatal impressions.[75] One's character is largely a product of one's education and social environment. But the mind is not just the passive product of circumstances. Godwin anticipated Mill in asserting that the moral and intellectual muscles are enlarged by exercise.[76] Conscience is moral muscle-building.

A.J. Ayer stated that Paine 'did not understand the nature of capitalism.'[77] He underemphasized the social divisions that resulted from competition and overrated the power and readiness of the exploited to defend themselves. What Ayer says about Paine is equally valid for Godwin. But would it be a fair comment on Blake? Is the Christian soul immune from the diseases of the capitalist body politic? Are secular thinkers like Paine and Godwin to be held to different standards than Christian poets? Whatever the answer to these questions, the use of conscience by Paine, Wollstonecraft, Godwin, and Blake is an egalitarian protest against capitalist enlightenment and the oppression and hierarchy inherent in capitalism that Locke, Hume, and Smith either accepted or ignored.

Philosophy and Poetry

Plato may have been unduly severe in declaring a permanent war between philosophy and poetry. Even so, the two have remained alternative paths, notwithstanding that at the turn of the nineteenth century there were philosophic poets such as Goethe, Hölderlin, and Schiller in Germany and Blake and Coleridge in England. However, while Germany produced Kant, Fichte, Schelling, Hegel, Herder, and

Schopenhauer, England in the same period produced Blake, Wordsworth, Byron, Coleridge, Shelley, and Keats. Blake helps explain why eighteenth-century England did not have an Enlightenment.

Complementing the views of contemporary historians who think England did not have an Enlightenment because the English did not need one – they had become enlightened in the seventeenth century – Blake viewed Bacon (*The Advancement of Learning*), Locke (*An Essay Concerning Human Understanding*), and Newton (*Principia* and *Opticks*) as the architects of the satanic mills that darkened England's green and pleasant land. Locke had praised the experimental philosophy of Bacon and Newton and had declared philosophy to be the underlabour to Newtonian physics[78] (besting the foreign thought of Descartes and Leibniz), and as a result, natural philosophy had become Newtonian physics. Locke's distinction between the primary qualities of substances ('solidity, extension, figure, motion or rest, and number' and secondary qualities 'colours, sounds, tastes, etc.') suggests that reality is primarily what is measurable.[79] The cold, gleaming eye of Blake's *Newton* bodies forth Blake's vision of satanic Urizen (a copy of which ironically now graces the courtyard of the British Library). If Locke reduced natural philosophy to Newtonian physics, he also prepared the way for the collapse of moral philosophy into economics – it was he, after all, who eliminated any natural law restrictions to the acquisition of property and who declared economic growth to be 'the great art of government.'[80] The marriage of natural philosophy (physics) and moral philosophy (economics) in technology was the specifically British gift to the world. But Blake could not accept the views of Locke and Smith that misery is an anomaly in commercial civilizations, and that the poorest in capitalist societies fare better than the richest in precapitalist societies. His *London* begins:

> I wander through each chartered street
> Near where the chartered Thames does flow,
> And mark in every face I meet
> Marks of weakness, marks of woe.

The repetition of 'chartered' and 'marks' indicates a view of property closer to Paine and Godwin than to Locke and Smith. As Northrop Frye indicated, Blake's age was structured by 'Lockian philosophy, Deist religion, social injustice and warfare.'[81] Blake was radically opposed to liberal doctrines of class harmony, and referred in this way to the class of producers and the class of devourers:

These two classes of men are always upon earth, and they should be enemies; whoever tries to reconcile them seeks to destroy existence. Religion is an endeavour to reconcile the two.

Note. Jesus Christ did not wish to unite but to separate them, as in the parable of sheep and goats. And he says, 'I came not to send peace, but a sword.'[82]

When Blake prayed, 'May God us keep: From single vision and Newton's sleep,' he had in mind, besides the conformism and class conciliationism of the Enlightenment, its complacent hostility to speculative philosophy. David Hume wrote: 'In Newton this island may boast of having produced the greatest and rarest genius that ever arose for the ornamentation and instruction of the species.'[83] Doubtless having in mind Locke's self-assessment as an underlabourer to Newtonian physics, Hume declared Locke 'a great Philosopher, and a just and modest Reasoner.'[84] Hume exhibited the dogmatic certainty that if a book did not contain abstract reasoning about number or experimental reasoning about fact, 'commit it then to the flames: For it can contain nothing but sophistry and illusion.'[85] Gibbon shared Hume's view that sensible men will put the boots to speculative philosophy (not of course history, which deals with fact). Gibbon advised Joseph Priestley to renounce philosophical theology and stick 'to those sciences in which real and useful improvements can be made.'[86] After Blake's death but on the same trajectory of sceptical enlightenment as Locke, Hume, and Gibbon, John Stuart Mill wrote: 'If it were possible to blot entirely out the whole of German metaphysics, the whole of Christian theology, and the whole of the Roman and English systems of technical jurisprudence, and were to direct all the minds that expand their faculties in these pursuits to useful speculations or practice, there would be talent enough set at liberty to change the face of the world.'[87]

If these activities are worse than wasteful, poetry is not serviceable to the religion of progress, however it may repair the emotional cripples sacrificed to that religion. Mill wrote: 'The regeneration of the world in its present stage is a matter for business, and it would be as rational to keep accounts or write invoices in verse as to attempt to do the work of human improvement in it.'[88]

Blake's fundamental impulse was the same as the great tradition of German idealism, namely, to reject a conception of mind as passive – a position that Blake thought arose from Urizen (Bacon, Locke, and Newton). Blake insisted that imagination and conscience construct aesthetic and moral worlds, whereas Enlightenment reason is bounded by the impressions of the five senses, and the reflections or memories of sensory experience. In 'objective' knowledge of the natural world, human understanding is passive; whereas in moral conduct, reason and conscience are active partners in constructing what we should do; and in imagination, an alternative to the natural order is revealed. In *Jerusalem* (plate 93), Blake declaimed:

> If Bacon, Newton, Locke
> Deny a conscience in man, & the communion of saints & angels,
> Contemning the Divine Vision & fruition, worshipping the *deus*
> Of the heathen, the god of this world, & the goddess Nature,[89]

From the standpoint of Enlightenment reason, Blake was mad: in the light of day, the midsummer night's dream of the lunatic, lover, and poet is the converse of reason. Blake's 'madness' must be understood in the context of the sleepy complacency of the English to speculative philosophy. Perhaps Blake's idiosyncrasy represents the mainstream of English spirituality driven from philosophy into the form of poetry that has come to be known as Romanticism.

Blake was not alone in his refusal to deconstruct conscience as conditioned opinion contingent upon our upbringing and social environment, and to replace the internal compass by public opinion. In *The Island*, Lord Byron wrote:

> Yet still there whispers the small voice within,
> Heard through Gain's silence, and o'er Glory's din:
> Whatever creed be taught or land be trod,
> Man's conscience is the oracle of God![90]

In *The Excursion* (IV.222–7), Wordsworth also praised the god within:

> But, above all, the victory is most sure
> For him, who, seeking faith by virtue, strives
> To yield entire submission to the law
> Of conscience – conscience reverenced and obeyed
> As God's most intimate presence in the soul
> And his most perfect image in the world.

Perhaps more interesting to the historian of ideas is that Wordsworth's affirmation of conscience is simultaneously a turning away from the social man of the eighteenth century. The Enlightenment seemed to end, for Wordsworth, in the Terror that followed the French Revolution. *The Excursion* (IV.260–5) continues:

> For that other loss,
> The loss of confidence in social man,
> By the unexpected transports of our age
> Carried so high, that every thought, which looked
> Beyond the temporal destiny of the kind,
> To many seemed superfluous.

Blake's views on conscience are less orthodox than those of Byron and Wordsworth as presented above. Blake thought Wordsworth the greatest poet of the age, but thought him a pagan for worshipping nature rather than spirit; moreover, Blake did not abandon the ideals of the French Revolution, as Wordsworth and Coleridge did.[91] What Blake admired in Byron was his transgressive quality, his supersession of conventional limits. Blake's *The Ghost of Abel* was dedicated to Lord Byron, whose romantic drama *Cain, a Mystery* was under threat of prosecution for immorality and blasphemy.[92] Blake scholars, who have uncritically accepted Enlightenment ideas through Freud, have equated Freud's superego with the repressive workmaster Urizen.[93] However, for Blake, conscience is on the side of freedom and desire, as opposed to the repressive conformism of Urizen (the rational norms of the Enlightenment's social man, Humean habits, prudential calculations of utility). For Blake, as Northrop Frye noted, 'the loins were the place of the Last Judgment.'[94] Conscience and love know no rules:

> Love to faults is always blind,
> Always is to joy inclined,
> Lawless, winged and unconfined,
> And breaks all chains from every mind.
>
> Deceit to secrecy confined,
> Lawful, cautious and refined,
> To every thing but interest blind –
> And forges fetters for the mind.[95]

Bacon, Newton, and Locke, Blake said, 'deny a conscience in men' when they worship 'the god of this world, & the goddess Nature.' What did Blake mean when he stated that Bacon and his followers replaced conscience by the god of this world? In a harsh response to Bacon's essay 'of Praise' – and specifically to Bacon's statement that 'praise is the reflection of virtue' – Blake roared, 'Villain! did Christ Seek the Praise of the Rulers?'[96] His seemingly unjust response illuminates precisely what the social men of the Enlightenment thought should replace individual conscience – namely, the approbation or disapprobation of others, and particularly, of the powerful.

Words bursting around Blake's engraving *The Laocoon* help to explain what Blake meant by 'the god of this world, & the goddess Nature'; they exclaim that 'Money ... is The Great Satan or Reason,' that the Bible is 'the Great Code of Art,' that 'Art is the Tree of Life,' that 'Science is the Tree of Death,' that Imagination 'The Eternal Body of Man' delivers us 'from Nature and Imitation.'[97] Mastery over nature through obedience to her laws, and rational calculation of interest and control of impulse, and these things harnessed to the maximization of money: this constitutes the reason of Bacon, Newton, and Locke, who do not recognize a transcendent realm, and who deprecate as unreal and 'subjective' the worlds of imagination and conscience. When Blake claimed that 'all deities exist in the human breast,'[98] he was not affirming an enlightened deism or atheism. Rather the reverse. Deism or natural religion is a refusal to believe in the identity of the divine and human. Locke's 'cloven fiction' is the philosopher's insistence on separating God and man, transforming God into a distant and abstract 'Nobodaddy.'[99] Locke's loveless doctrine comes under Blake's concentrated fire: 'Innate Ideas are in Every Man, Born with him; they are truly Himself. The Man who says that we have No innate Ideas must be a Fool & Knave, Having No Con-Science or Innate Science.'[100] Whereas Locke thought personal identity rested in consciousness or our memory of experiences and our reflections upon them, Blake thought we are truly our consciences or the ideas we bring to order our moral experience. Blake was not championing irrational conscience as opposed to Lockean conscienceless reason; rather, he wanted to harmonize reason and conscience. Reason, Blake thought, was 'once fairer than the light' until Bacon, Newton, and Locke 'fowl'd' it by separating reason from the divine, and then 'Conscience was sent, a Guard to Reason.'[101] In *King Edward the Third*, Blake writes that reason would not be 'forlorn if conscience is his friend.' Conscience is an attractive friend because her voice is 'sweeter than music in a summer's eve.'[102] Nor, when Blake emphasized that conscience is innate, was he denying that conscience is developed through its exercise, or may be nurtured or crippled in different environments.

Blake should not be taken as a complete enemy of Enlightenment, despite his writing around the engraving of Laocoon. He wished to harmonize art and science, imagination and reason. The conclusion of *Vala, or the Four Zoas* could be an Enlightenment dream; it envisages imagination 'to form the golden armour of science / For intellectual war. The war of swords departed now, / The dark religions are departed, & sweet science reigns.'[103] However, Enlightenment reason is hostile to revolutionary conscience – 'For Luvah is France, the victim of the spectres of Albion.'[104] These spectres are not Burke and Bentham, opponents of the right of individual judgment, but 'Bacon, Newton & Locke.' Bishop Watson cited Locke, not Burke or Bentham, in his opposition to the egalitarian conscience animating the French Revolution. Blake was an unrepentant friend of the French Revolution, although his poem of that name was never published and only the first of seven books survived. Although Blake was acquitted in his trial (where he was charged with seditiously favouring Bonaparte over George III and his troops), Blake's judges and jurors knew nothing of Blake's writings or his friendships with Paine, Wollstonecraft, and other radicals.[105] In *Vala, or the Four Zoas* Blake sang forth:

The thrones of kings are shaken; they have lost their robes and crowns.
The poor smite their oppressors, they awake up to the harvest;
The naked warriors rush together down to the sea-shore
Trembling before the multitudes of slaves now set at liberty;
They are become like wintry flocks, like forests stripped of leaves.
The oppressed pursue like the wind; there is no room for escape.[106]

Luvah/Orc, the revolutionary spirit (and his female emanation Vala), cut off from the imaginative Urthona/Los (and his female emanation Enitharmon, conscience, the offspring of Urthona and the female emanation [Enion] of the compassionate Tharmas) and the rational, controlling Urizen, is inadequate to the task of world transformation. Urizen (the enlightened reason of Bacon, Hobbes, and Locke, passed on to the deism of Voltaire and Rousseau) is the enemy of Luvah, or revolutionary Christian love. In *The French Revolution*, Blake celebrated the 'spectres of religious men weeping: In winds driven out of the abbeys, their naked souls shiver in keen open air,: Driven out by the fiery cloud of Voltaire, and the thunderous rocks of Rousseau.'[107] But looking back at the French Revolution in *Jerusalem*, Blake called deism an enemy to Christianity and to the human race. Deism is dogmatic and destructive to those who cannot espouse the 'impossible absurdity' of a natural religion: 'Voltaire, Rousseau, Gibbon, Hume charge the spiritually religious with hypocrisy. But how a monk, or a Methodist either, can be a hypocrite, I cannot conceive.' Was Blake tarring thinkers indiscriminately? And in particular, was he wrong to lump Rousseau with Voltaire, Hume, and Gibbon? If so, his assessment of Rousseau seems to have been based on reading, not hearsay: 'Rousseau thought men good by nature; he found them evil & found no friend. Friendship cannot exist without forgiveness of sins continually. The book written by Rousseau called his *Confessions* is an apology & cloak for his sins & not a confession.'[108]

Blake thought that Rousseau's total rejection of Christian teaching on original sin – Rousseau thought he was naturally good and only corrupted by an oppressive society – was only partially valid. Rousseau's position, in Blake's view, led him to ignore his sins and thus to be incapable of overcoming them through conscientious self-examination, of confessions to those against whom one sinned, and of mutual forgiveness. For Blake, Rousseau wrongly portrayed redemption in nature rather than in spirit. Deist naturalism, Blake thought, is destructive:

> When Satan first the black bow bent
> And the moral law from the Gospel rent,
> He forged the law into a sword
> And spilled the blood of mercy's Lord.[109]

In the introduction to the third chapter of *Jerusalem*, Blake assailed the deists for abandoning Christian love; yet in his introduction to the fourth chapter, he admonished Christians not to turn their backs on art and science.

Blake was of the tradition of Milton, of revolutionary Christian liberty, but he was not untouched by the spirit of Enlightenment: 'Remember how Calvin & Luther in fury premature / Sewed war & stern division between papist & protestants! / Let it not be so now. O go not forth in martyrdoms & wars.'[110]

In *Vala or the Four Zoas*, eternal man was redeemed when 'Urizen gave the horses of light into the hands of Luvah.'[111] In *Jerusalem*, we have the same theme: 'And where Luther ends Adam begins again in eternal circle / To awake the prisoners of death – to bring Albion again / With Luvah into light eternal, in his eternal day.'[112]

If Blake could not resurrect Albion's conscience from enlightened sleep, no one could. E.P. Thompson intelligently set forth the issue between Blake and the Enlightenment:

> Blake could see no way to derive such an affirmation of love from naturalistic psychology, which was, at its very root, derivative from self-interest. Hence he must, even when in his most 'Jacobin' and revolutionary temper, hold fast to the Everlasting Gospel of his older antinomian faith. To create the New Jerusalem something must be brought in from outside the rationalist system, and that something could only be found in the non-rational image of Jesus, in the affirmatives of Mercy, Pity, Peace and Love.[113]

England may not have had an Enlightenment but she had its greatest critic.

Conscience and Revolution

Was E.P. Thompson right to see in conscience an antihegemonic discourse countering the enlightened reason of the comfortably situated?[114] When Mary Wollstonecraft asserted that conscience is the most enlightened philosopher, she was countering not only Burke's and Bentham's reactive view of conscience as the basis of natural rights but also Rousseau's sexist view that only men can follow their inner compass (a view not disavowed by Paine, or Blake, and even Wollstonecraft's husband, Godwin.)[115] Like Wollstonecraft, Paine and Godwin identified conscience with reason. Paine and Godwin, despite their militant opposition to Christianity, used the authority of the Bible and traditional Christian conceptions of property (as a trust to be used for the common good) to support the egalitarianism they wished to add to liberalism. Godwin's libertarian or anarchist insistence that force must never be used to inaugurate a new egalitarian era led him to withdraw from revolution in favour of protracted mental reform. Paine, Wollstonecraft, and Blake rode the revolutionary tiger farther than Godwin. What separated Paine from Blake pertained to the identity of, or difference between, the tiger of democratic revolution and the lamb of Christian love.

Was Bishop Watson, who attacked Paine and defended social inequality, a friend or enemy of the Enlightenment? Paine and Blake supported freedom of conscience, which for them meant the disestablishment of religion and the complete separation of church and state. But Hobbes, Mandeville, Voltaire, Hume, and Diderot considered a state church the best means to achieve enlightened toleration. Hume thought that church establishment would kill off religious enthusiasm more effectively than the separation of church and state. The tolerant Whig bishop was closer in spirit to Hume than to enthusiasts such as Paine, Blake, and Richard Price. Paine's American deist friends advised him on the utility of religion in promoting enlightened ideas. Watson's defence of class inequalities accorded with the mainstreams of the Scottish and French Enlightenment, and his defence of hierarchy used Locke's opposition to innate ideas and conscience. Blake saw in Watson the image of Urizen, the serpentine wisdom of the Enlightenment. Paine saw Watson as the enemy of the age of reason.

Conscience was central to Blake because it presented the divine in man. For him, conscience was like Jesus, the God in human form. Paine professed to be a friend to God and an enemy to Christianity; Blake appeared more friendly to Jesus than God, old Nobodaddy: 'God is only an Allegory of Kings & nothing Else ... God is The Ghost of the Priest & King, who Exist, whereas God exists not except for their Effluvia.'[116]

Blake's conscience may appear narcissistic, blasphemous, and intolerant. He seemed to equate Jesus with himself and himself with Jesus:

> The vision of Christ that thou dost see
> Is my vision's greatest enemy:
> Thine has a great hook nose like thine,
> Mine has a snub nose like to mine;[117]

As the Enlightenment consistently maintained, the spirit of Christian love is narrow-minded and intolerant. As John Dryden observed, conscience and humility are incompatible. Blake proclaimed: 'If humility is Christianity, you, O Jews, are the true Christians.'[118] For non-Christians, God is remote. However, conscience for Blake is the pride and power that divinity is within, the confidence that a New Jerusalem can be built. Enlightened men know better.

Chapter 9

Individualist Conscience and Nationalist Prejudice

William Wordsworth tied together Protestant conscience and the English tongue: 'We must be free or die, who speak the tongue / That Shakespeare spake; the faith and morals hold / Which Milton held.'[1]

Although John Stuart Mill associated 'the noblest language' with the love of freedom,[2] he did not explicitly support Wordsworth's view that Protestantism informed the English character – that indeed it constituted, as much as the language, Englishness. (Perhaps if we excluded the Irish we could link Protestantism to the British character; but Mill, although of Scots background and with Scottish connections, considered himself English.) He did think the English were 'incomparably the most conscientious of all nations,' a nation whose moral superiority 'has consisted in greater tenderness of conscience' than other nations.[3] While Mill's liberalism was undoubtedly closer to the secular Protestantism of Paine and Godwin than to the overt anti-Catholicism of Milton and Locke, he thought there was a tension between Catholicism and liberalism: 'Timidity of conscience ... has so often driven highly gifted men into Romanism from the need of a firmer support than they can find in the independent conclusions of their own judgment.'[4]

Two years after John Stuart Mill died, Cardinal Newman found himself taunted by the Liberal prime minister William Gladstone with respect to the compatibility of liberal citizenship and the doctrine of papal infallibility, and declared: 'I can see no inconsistency in my being at once a good Catholic and a good Englishman.'[5] The claims of an internationalist church and a nation-state are compatible.

Newman proved that he spoke the tongue that Shakespeare spake when he described conscience as 'personal, peremptory, unargumentative, irresponsible, minatory, definitive.'[6] Newman's thoughtful defence of conscience or the right of private judgment might well be taken to be the faith and morals of Milton. However, he asserted that 'it is the Protestant doctrine that Private Judgment is our *ordinary* guide in religious matters, but I use it ... in very extraordinary and rare, nay, impossible emergencies.'[7] Newman certainly was not the first Catholic to celebrate conscience or the right of individual judgment, but as far as I am aware, he was the first Catholic to authorize conscience above church authority: 'Certainly, if I am obliged to bring religion into after-dinner toasts, (which indeed does not seem quite the thing) I shall drink, – to the Pope, if you please, – still, to Conscience first, and to the Pope afterwards.'[8]

In saying so, Newman established that he was both a Catholic and an Englishman. For the essence of Englishness, according to John Stuart Mill, is independent judgment, the ability to think for oneself. Mill wrote to Auguste Comte: 'I believe that there is less of a feeling of nationality among the English than among other civilized people. Today they have far fewer prejudices and national biases than the peoples of the continent.'[9]

Although less anti-Catholic than Locke and many other liberals, Mill would have been reluctant to join Newman in a toast to the pope. In his correspondence with Comte, Mill discovered that Catholic atheists were different from Protestant atheists: Comte lacked the respect for freedom of conscience that is customary in Protestant countries.[10] As a liberal, Mill would have felt it vulgar nationalism to toast the Queen. But would he have joined Newman in a toast to conscience?

If Mill had understood Newman's conscience as God's voice or as a divine gift within us, he would have rejected it, since Mill remained faithful to his father's and Bentham's unbelief. If conscience is understood as innate – or as Newman put it, within 'all classes and conditions of men, for high and low, young and old, men and women, independently of books, of educated reasoning, or of philosophy'[11] – Mill probably would have rejected the idea as unprogressive, as implying that 'moral judgments and feelings cannot be susceptible of any improvement.'[12] In Mill's view, conscience, like intellect, was something to be trained; along with the advancement of knowledge and the cultivation of aesthetic sensibilities, the training of the moral faculty was an integral part of a liberal education.[13] Conscience, for Mill, was acquired rather than innate, the product of one's early upbringing or education and the ongoing approbation or disapprobation of others.

Yet Mill's conscience emerged *despite* the Benthamite education administered by his father: 'I was so much accustomed to expect to be told what to do, either in the form of a direct command or of rebuke for not doing it, that I acquired a habit of leaving my moral agency to rest with my father, my conscience never speaking to me except by his voice.'[14]

Nevertheless, Mill claimed that his education was not indoctrination in Benthamite beliefs and conditioning in utilitarian norms; rather, he was educated to think for himself. An early draft of his *Autobiography* stated that his 'habit of thinking' for himself had been 'given' him by his father; this was amended in the published version: 'the habit of thinking for myself, which his mode of education had fostered ...'[15] Mill wrote to Carlyle on 22 October 1832: 'I was not *crammed*; my own thinking faculties were called into strong though partial play; & by their means I have been enabled to *remake* all my opinions.'[16] One might wonder here whether he was not just giving voice to empty liberal ideals; it would have been truly original had he said he was so conditioned in youth that he was incapable of thinking for himself. James Mill instructed his son 'to take the strongest interest in the Reformation, as the great and decisive contest against priestly tyranny for freedom of thought.'[17] James Mill, like Bentham and other enlightened liberals, favoured freedom of conscience but opposed conscience; conscientious intention leads people to do wrong, whereas utilitarian calculation avoids the pitfalls of conscience. Mill wrote of his father: 'Consistently carrying out the doctrine, that the object of praise and blame should be the discouragement of wrong conduct and the encouragement of right, he refused to let his praise or blame be influenced by the motive of the agent.'[18]

John Mill strongly deprecated Bentham for ignoring conscience as 'this great fact of human nature,' and as a motive distinct from public opinion or social approval and disapproval.[19] Indeed, Bentham's philosophy would lead to 'the despotism of Public Opinion.'[20] 'The doctrine of Locke, that we have no *innate* moral sense' should not be, Mill wrote, 'perverted into the doctrine that we have no moral sense at all.'[21] Liberal philosophers have debated, usually on the basis of *Utilitarianism*, whether Mill's internal sanction of conscience is or is not reducible to the external sanction of social approbation.[22] The only clear answer is that the question is not easily answered. When David Lyons says that 'I think we do no favor to Mill if we emphasize his assimilation of internal to external sanctions,'[23] he is implying that

Mill was unclear and that Enlightenment moral psychology is inadequate.

The question of whether Mill, whom Gladstone called 'the saint of rationalism,' would have joined Newman in a toast to conscience is not easily resolved. Would Mill have joined Hume, Voltaire, Diderot, Helvétius, d'Holbach, Bentham, James Mill, and Comte in abstaining from Newman's toast? Is adherence to conscience unenlightened prejudice, an illusion of those who think themselves independent-minded, even a nationalist self-deception? In this chapter I will attempt to address these questions in exploring the conflicting sources of Mill's thought, his ties to and break from paternal enlightenment doctrine, and the ultimately unsatisfactory relationship in *On Liberty* and *Utilitarianism* between self-culture and social conditioning, conscience and social censure, individual judgment and public opinion.

Coleridge on Conscience and Nationality

Samuel Taylor Coleridge was at one with Blake in thinking that Enlightenment philosophy deprecated imagination and conscience and, in doing so, degraded reason into the service of profit and creature comforts. Just as Blake scorned the 'naturalism' of Bacon, Newton, and Locke, Coleridge exclaimed: 'O what an awful Being is Conscience! and how infra-bestial the Locks, Priestleys, Humes, Condillacs and the dehumanizing race of fashionable Metaphysicians ... *Cata*physicians (i.e. *Contra*naturalists) when I spoke of them as *Agents*; but when I regard them merely in *themselves & passive*, I should call them *Hypo*physicians, i.e. *below Nature.*'[24]

Indeed, Coleridge's thought centred on a championship of Christian conscience above Enlightenment consciousness: 'Observe, This is the corner-stone of *my* system, ethical, metaphysical and theological – the priority, namely, both in dignity and order of generation of the Conscience to the Consciousness in Man.'[25]

Coleridge here did not mean so much the priority of faith over reason in humans, or of what is immortal over what is mortal; rather, he meant the priority of the active mind (what he found in German philosophy) over the passive mind, the *tabula rasa* of the British empirical tradition. Moral agency, Coleridge thought, arises prior to intellectual reflection as representations of past sense impressions. He stated that as 'the Heart is the Life of the Head,' so 'Consciousness ... is but the Reflex of Conscience.'[26]

Individualist Conscience and Nationalist Prejudice   157

For Coleridge and for Blake, the priority of conscience over consciousness did not mean that moral strictness had greater importance than imaginative spontaneity, as in Matthew Arnold's distinction between Hebraism and Hellenism: 'The governing idea of Hellenism is *spontaneity of consciousness;* that of Hebraism, *strictness of conscience.*'[27] For Blake and Coleridge, conscience was not opposed to nature; it was not a supernatural order imposed as a straight-jacket on natural spontaneity and its artistic expression. Conscience is as much spontaneity as strictness, as much freedom as obedience. Coleridge endorsed Rousseau's and Kant's philosophy of freedom: 'No Power on Earth can oblige me to act against my Conscience.'[28]

If Blake's libertarian conscience veered toward a patriotic love of one's own, Coleridge's conscience attached him to the language and customs of his country: 'A most important truth [is] that the Law of Justice, that is, of unconditional Obedience to the Conscience knits us to earth, to the flesh and blood of our human nature with all its food and fuel of Affections, predilections of Language & Country.' In contrast, 'the doctrine of Expedience inevitably unloosens the soul from its centripetal Instincts, makes man a thing of generalities and ideal abstractions, Shadows.'[29] Enlightenment rationalism, like Catholicism, is rootless cosmopolitanism; Protestant conscience attaches us to our own. The abstract man of the Enlightenment, governed by rational utility, is like a balloon 'with props unpropped, floating between earth & heaven without belonging to either.'[30] Coleridge insisted that conscience attaches us to our own, but he also had a more inclusive notion of what constituted his own culture than was usual among his contemporaries. As Richard Holmes writes, 'Coleridge always argued for the integral role of the Jewish intellectual in the national culture.'[31] His melodrama *Osario* or *Remorse* championed a Moorish insurrection against Spanish persecution; it exhibited sensitivity to nationalistic feelings and antipathy to the Church that oppressed them.

Coleridge was inspired to write *On the Constitution of the Church and State* (1829) (for which Mill had the highest admiration) out of apprehension for the Bill for Relief of Roman Catholics. Mill admired Coleridge's openness and toleration, and offered no criticism of Coleridge's insistence that a church must be a national church, that is, a state-established church. Mill cited admiringly Coleridge's image that Christianity (the invisible catholic church) is like an olive tree in relation to the vines, bearing the fruit fermented in national communions: 'As the olive tree is said in its growth to fertilize the surrounding soil, to invigorate the roots of the vines in its immediate neighbourhood, and to improve the strength and flavour of the wines; such is the relation of the Christian and the national church.'[32] The universal church exists *in* England, Coleridge declared, but 'the true Church *of* England is the National Church, or clerisy.'[33] Coleridge's clerisy are spiritual civil servants charged with maintaining national universities and providing a 'pastor, presbyter, or *parson*' in every parish, a schoolmaster in every parish, and poor relief for the aged and infirm. Just as Hegel's middle-class civil servants in *The Philosophy of Right* were the universal class mediating between the conservative particularism of the agricultural classes and the egoistic progressivism of the business classes, Coleridge's clerisy represents nationality in relationship to the principle of permanence of the landed classes and the principle of progress of the commercial classes.[34]

Countering both Tory and Whig doctrine, Coleridge maintained that an absolute right of property is appropriate only for commercial (as distinct from landed) property: 'a property, not connected with especial duties, a property not fiduciary or official, but arbitrary and unconditional, was in the light of our forefathers the brand of a Jew and an alien; not the distinction, not the right, or honour, of an English baron or gentleman.'[35] All property titles are subject to state service, but the state serves to protect property. The church is the custodian of nationality, as distinct from landed and personal property; it feeds the propertied classes by drawing up the worthiest of the lower classes. Thus, Henry VIII should have renationalized the land, wrongly taken from the nation by the Catholic Church, instead of selling church lands to private landowners; Coleridge asserted that 'every free subject in the nation has a living interest, a permanent, and likewise a possible personal and reversionary interest.'[36] Mill enjoyed the irony of a Tory sounding like a revolutionary socialist.

Coleridge's clerisy, as custodians of national property, recognize the Crown as the head of the church and function to promote national civilization, learning, spiritual solace, and material welfare. The élite of the clerisy cultivate the human spirit and enlarge knowledge, while the greater part function 'to preserve the stores, to guard the treasures, of past civilization, and thus to bind the present with the past; to perfect and add to the same and thus to connect the present with the future.'[37] Mill did not dismiss as Tory propaganda Coleridge's argument that a landed aristocracy and an established church were necessary to offset ubiquitous commercialism. He seemed to find some weight in Hume's argument that an established church was 'a "bulwark against fanaticism," a sedative to the religious spirit, to prevent it from disturbing the harmony of society or the tranquillity of states.'[38] Mill wrote favourably about Coleridge's view that the clerisy advances nationality or a national civilization.[39] Although, like his father, no friend of the established church and landed aristocracy, Mill accepted the clerisy and a leisured class as barriers against what Alexis de Tocqueville called 'the tyranny of the majority,' or the moral weight of conformist, monolithically middle-class public opinion.[40]

James Mill and Alexis de Tocqueville on Public Opinion

Forty years after its first edition in 1829, John Stuart Mill republished James Mill's *Analysis of the Phenomena of the Human Mind*. James Mill followed Adam Smith in distinguishing love of praise, as the primary feeling, from love of praiseworthiness, as the secondary feeling; but he also turned Smith's *Theory of Moral Sentiments* into practical prescriptions for educating children and improving the world. Praise and blame are decisive in raising children. James Mill wrote:

> It is this sensibility to praise and blame, in other words, the associations we have with them, which gives its effect to what is called POPULAR OPINION, or the POPULAR SANCTION, and, when the acts of Justice, Beneficence, Fortitude, and Prudence of other men are the objects of it, the MORAL SANCTION; *Popular Opinion*, being a phrase which expresses the Praise or Blame which the people bestow; and the *Sanction* being the good or evil consequences which men are accustomed to associate with that praise or blame.[41]

Just as Pavlov was to administer shocks and food to dogs for the progressive purpose of modifying 'instincts' and ultimately creating a more desirable human type, James Mill administered praise and blame to educate youth to the permanent interests of man as a progressive being:

> When Education is good, no part of morality will be reckoned of more importance than the distribution of Praise and Blame; no act will be considered more immoral than the misapplication of them. They are the great instruments we possess for ensuring moral acts on the part of our Fellow-creature; and when we squander away, or prostitute those great

causes of virtue, and thereby deprive them of a great part of their useful tendency, we do what in us lies to lessen the quantity of Virtue, and thence of Felicity, in the world.[42]

Whereas prostitution is usually seen as misuse of the capacity for love, James Mill was concerned about the misuse of the power of praise and blame. John Mill deprecated the lovelessness of his youthful education; in an early draft of his *Autobiography* he wrote: 'I thus grew up in the absence of love and in the presence of fear: and many and indelible are the effects of this bringing-up, in the stunting of my moral growth.'[43] But John Mill was not man enough, or was all too manlike, to blame his father for his loveless upbringing: 'That rarity in England, a really warm hearted mother, would in the first place have made my father a totally different being, and in the second would have made the children grow up loving and being loved.'[44] She drudged for her nine children but failed to provide her husband and children with the love and intellectual stimulation by which they could flourish. Mill's sister, Harriet Isabella, thought her brother's expectation that the mother be an intellectual companion to her husband, while working hard to support a growing family on slender means, was unreasonable and ungenerous.[45] Harriet Burrow Mill, a woman of 'startling beauty,' bore her husband nine children while bearing his contempt for her person and his contempt for the sexual act.[46] John Mill lived in fear of his father's censure 'but for her remonstrances I never had the slightest regard.'[47] In the published version of his *Autobiography*, John Stuart's mother disappeared.

Visible in the rejected versions of the *Autobiography* are useful addenda to James Mill's theory and practice of forming conscience through the instrument of praise and the weapon of blame. The recipient of praise and blame must consider the donor worthy of bestowing either one. John Mill so uncritically accepted his father's contempt, and that of his friends, for his mother that he held her estimation of him contemptible. Smith's distinction between praise and praiseworthiness (or blame and blameworthiness) may be reducible to imbalances of power, or in the case of Mill to the gendered imbalance of parental power in the loveless family.

The theoretical question is whether or not John Stuart Mill distinguished conscience (or the love of what is praiseworthy) from public opinion or social approval (or the love of praise and the fear of blame).

Although he deprecated Bentham for not distinguishing conscience from the desire for social approval, and although in *Utilitarianism* he distinguished 'the opinion of his fellow creatures' from 'the reproaches of his own conscience,'[48] he so qualified the distinction that he may have obliterated it. Conscience, he asserted, is a complex phenomenon arising from a complexity of circumstances and collateral associations such that self-esteem and the esteem of others, self-censure and social disapprobation, are impossible to disentangle. Conscience is acquired rather than innate, but it rests on the basis of 'powerful natural sentiment,' namely, 'the social feelings of mankind; the desire to be at unity with our fellow creatures, which is already a powerful principle in human nature, and happily one of those which tend to become stronger, even without express inculcation, from the influences of advancing civilization.'[49] Against the moral intuitionism of William Hamilton, Mill favoured the moral police of social censure; 'whoever cultivates a disposition to wrong, places his mind out of sympathy with the rest of his fellow creatures, and if they are aware of his disposition, becomes a natural object of their active dislike.'[50] Hume, Diderot, D'Holbach, Helvétius, Bentham, and James Mill adhered to this enlightened creed, but they did not talk, as John Mill did, about conscience.

In a letter to William George Ward dated 28 November 1859, Mill wrote that his father's *Analysis of the Phenomena of the Human Mind* was generally satisfactory, but he also acknowledged:

> The pains of conscience are certainly very different from those of dread of disapprobation; yet it might well be, that the innumerable associations of pain undergone, or pains feared and imagined as the consequence of wrong things done, or of wrong things which we have been tempted to do (especially in early life), may produce a general & intense feeling of recoil from wrongdoing in which no conscious influence of other people's disapprobation may be perceptible.[51]

Mill here advanced the essential Freudian teaching on the formation of the (unconscious) superego – as distinct from the conscious ego – but Freud, unlike Mill, did not present himself as a friend of conscience. Mill, like Freud, was an heir to the Enlightenment's opposition between conscience and consciousness; but he did not conclude, as Freud did, that conscience is other than the self or ego. To be sure,

Mill did not accept Coleridge's view (or that of his contemporaries, Emerson, Kierkegaard, and Proudhon)[52] that conscience is definitive of the self.

Mill's letter to Ward leaves the matter unclear whether he disagreed with his father's view that conscience is reducible to social approbation. Mill's letter continued with the assertion that conscience is 'a natural outgrowth from the social nature of man' and is derivative of social sympathy:

> I sympathize in their desire that I shd be punished: & (even apart from benevolence) the painfulness of not being in union with them makes me shrink from pursuing a line of conduct which would make my ends, wishes & purposes habitually conflict with theirs. To this fellow feeling with man may of course be added ... fellow feeling with God, & recoil from the idea of not being at union with Him. May I add, that even to an unbeliever there may be a feeling similar in nature towards an *ideal* God? as there may be towards an ideally perfect man, or towards our friends who are no more, even if we do not feel assured of their immortality.[53]

Whether to a real God or to an ideal and dead goddess, conscience betokens a longing for at-onement; pangs of conscience atone but, like the pangs of adolescence, express a longing for oneness. However much Mill intended to disarm opponents of his father's contention that virtue was reducible to the desire for social approbation, we may still wonder how the 'socialist' Mill, who desired to be at one with his fellows, is the same as the 'individualist' Mill, who braved the tyranny of public opinion to remain true to himself (and of course to his ideally perfect woman, whose voice replaced his father's as Mill's conscience).

Stefan Collini writes:

> As prompter of the national conscience, Mill derived certain advantages from his deliberately nurtured position as an outsider among the English governing classes. When the aim is to make one's readers morally uncomfortable, too great an intimacy can be an obstacle; Mill seems to have felt that his avoidance of 'society' helped to provide the requisite distance as well as to preserve a kind of uncorrupted purity of feeling.[54]

In this passage Collini points out what I think is a contradiction at the heart of Mill's account of conscience. Mill took the position of a

Individualist Conscience and Nationalist Prejudice 163

loner outside society, a gadfly pricking the national conscience, and from this stance as an outsider tried to make his fellow men and women both less complacent and less morally comfortable; yet in his theory of conscience (in *Utilitarianism* and his letter to Ward) he claimed that the basis of conscience is the natural desire to be at one with one's fellow human beings. While it is possible to reconcile these contradictory positions – dissent from actual social norms, consensus with ideal future norms – Mill never made the attempt, and thus his account of conscience is unsatisfactory.

The tension in Mill's account of conscience could perhaps be situated between his allegiance to his father's view that moral conduct is policed by public opinion, and his espousal of Alexis de Tocqueville's fear of the tyranny of middle-class opinion. Mill's enthusiasm for the idea of the tyranny of majoritarian opinion was somewhat muted by his recognition that Tocqueville's idea had become a Tory slogan used to block democratization of Britain.[55] He emphasized that the tyrannous majority in America did not wage war on property – Americans upheld all boundary stones as sacred – but he also acknowledged that in Europe, where there was less land and more people, the democratic principle of majority rule might render property titles insecure. Also, America was different from Europe in that it lacked 'a leisure class' and a 'highly instructed class.' To be sure Washington, Jefferson, Madison, and Monroe had all 'belonged to a class of proprietors maintained by the labour of slaves,' but a leisured ruling class was on the wane in Jacksonian America.[56] The power of the masses was increasing and the power of individuals diminishing; thus, 'the individual becomes so lost in the crowd, that though he depends more and more upon opinion, he is apt to depend less and less upon well-grounded opinion; upon the opinion of those who know him.'[57] Mill made it clear that the American emphasis on conscience and freedom of conscience produces the most thoughtless conformity; 'the right of private judgment, by being extended to the incompetent, ceases to be exercised even by the competent.' As a result, despite their assertion of the right to private judgment, the Americans are the least independent-minded of peoples.[58] Instead of appealing to religion or conscience, as Tocqueville did, as a means of endowing individuals with a sense of their own importance, Mill relied on enlightened public opinion to offset unenlightened public opinion. For 'the formation of the best public opinion, there should exist somewhere a great social support for opinions and sentiments different from those of the mass,' namely, 'an agricultural class, a leisured class, and a learned class.'[59] Coleridge's clerisy seemed to be the antidote to James Mill's majoritarianism, as de Tocqueville described the symptoms.

In his essay 'Utility of Religion,' Mill said that education, not religion, is the great moral authority; 'the commands of God are to young children' nothing 'more than the commands of their parents,' while 'the power of education is almost boundless.'[60] Embracing Enlightenment doctrine with both arms, Mill declared that 'the power of public opinion; of the praise and blame, the favour and disfavour, of their fellow creatures ... is a source of strength inherent in any system of moral belief which is generally adopted, whether connected with religion or not.'[61] People follow public opinion or social mores but 'flatter themselves that they are acting from the motive of conscience when they are doing in obedience to the inferior motive, things which their conscience approves.' Mill said that people often act contrary to their consciences in conformity to public opinion, but when conscience and public opinion pull in the same direction, their force is overpowering.[62]

To repeat, Mill never considered that religion might be useful as a means for reinforcing conscience as a bulwark against tyrannical public opinion; while conscience is juxtaposed to opinion, Mill favoured enlightened opinion as a counter to despotic opinion. However, while he held obedience to conscience to be superior to following public opinion, he never provided a philosophic account of why the latter is an inferior path to take. Was he such a captive to Victorian public opinion that he could not robustly put the boots to conscience, as Bentham and his father did? Mill asserted: 'There is no philosophy possible where fear of consequences is a stronger principle than love of truth.'[63] But he also maintained that a profession of irreligion would jeopardize any chance that he would be read in England.[64] Conversely, could he not have provided a philosophic account of the secular libertarianism of Godwin and Proudhon, based on conscience, the ability to make moral choices, as the definitive characteristic of humanity? Perhaps the closest Mill came to a philosophical account of conscience was in his celebrated work *On Liberty*.

On Liberty and Conscience

On Liberty celebrates 'freedom of conscience, in the most comprehensive sense; liberty of thought and feeling; absolute freedom of opinion and sentiment on all subjects, practical or speculative, scientific, moral, or theological.' In its most comprehensive sense, it is confined to 'the inward domain of consciousness.' Although in this book Mill defends liberty of tastes and pursuits (that do not harm others) and freedom of association, he does not contend that freedom of conscience licenses freedom of action. Freedom of speech, Mill states, inheres in freedom of thought or of conscience, but freedom of action apparently falls outside the scope of conscience.[65] Conscientious dissent, conscientious objection, free votes in Parliament, jury verdicts according to conscience, and the like, are not subjects of Mill's libertarian defence. With respect to conscience, one may wonder whether Mill was expanding Bentham's motto of a good citizen: 'To obey punctually; to censure freely.'[66]

Let us compare Hobbes and Mill. The Hobbesian social contract is based on the inalienable right of self-preservation, including the right to evade 'any dangerous or dishonourable office.' To avoid violating the natural right of cowardice, Hobbes recommended, in Chapter 21 of *Leviathan*, a professional army rather than a conscripted army. Mill asserted that 'though no good purpose is answered by inventing a contract in order to deduce social obligations,' each person is bound to bear 'his share (to be fixed on some equitable principle) of the labours and sacrifices incurred for defending the society or its members from injury and molestation.'[67] But Mill did not indicate whether he adhered to the republican principle of conscripted armies or the liberal principle of volunteer armies. Would he have supported the Hobbesian right of cowardice for those 'of feminine courage'? Could he have advanced beyond the unwillingness to die to conscientious objection or an unwillingness to kill for one's country? Would he have suggested some dangerous alternatives to warfare for those with a reluctance to kill, since his principle is that labours and sacrifices are to be shared equitably? We get no answers to these questions, because the rights of conscience in *On Liberty* are restricted to freedom of thought.

Rather than maintain respect for deference to conscience in the field of action, Mill argued for a right to do as one pleased insofar as one does not harm others. Conscience, Mill thought, tends toward intolerance; sincere bigots impose their ideas of a good life on others. Although a few great thinkers 'asserted freedom of conscience as an indefeasible right,' the case for tolerance was won by historical experience of utility, not by abstract assertions of natural right, or by religious indifference following the Puritan and Glorious Revolutions.[68] Freedom of conscience, for Mill, did not entail the doctrinaire separation of church and state. Like Hume, Mill thought an established church tended to diminish religious enthusiasm. Indeed, Mill recommended state provision for Catholic clergy in Ireland because priests would be more disliked if they were supported by taxes rather than by voluntary subscription, and less zealous if their living did not depend on the numbers of their flock. Supporting Catholic rather than dissenting clergymen would 'diminish the interest they now have in proselytism. Believing, as we do, the Catholic religion to be a bad one, we of course think it undesirable that proselytes should be made to it.'[69]

Mill's freedom of conscience meant sceptical toleration rather than the separation of church and state. But he recognized that enlightened tolerance came at a price: the English ceased to think. Mill explained why the English did not have a philosophic Enlightenment, as did the Scots, Americans, French, and Germans:

> The repose which followed the great struggles of the Reformation and the Commonwealth; the final victory over Popery and Puritanism, Jacobitism and Republicanism, and the lulling of the controversies which kept speculation and spiritual consciousness alive; the lethargy which came upon all governors and teachers, after their position in society became fixed; and the growing absorption of all classes in material interests – caused a character of mind to diffuse itself, with less of deep inward workings, and less capable of interpreting those it had, than had existed for centuries.[70]

Although *On Liberty* suggests that thought and freedom of thought are intimately associated – even that the latter is a necessary and sufficient condition of the former – it is clear that Mill was not celebrating the thoughtlessness of late eighteenth-century and nineteenth-century England. Sceptical toleration is not necessarily the same as freedom of conscience. If freedom of conscience combines sceptical toleration and burning zeal, then *On Liberty* seems to be championing conscience, not merely toleration. As Alan Ryan says, Mill's works 'are hymns to individuality, to intellectual boldness and fearlessness, to an intellectual life in which we care intensely that our thoughts and feelings should be ours.'[71] If science cares that our thoughts be true and our feelings healthy, conscience cares that our thoughts be truly our own (not aped, or custom-built, or fashionable).

Mill's doctrine seems to be secular Protestantism. As a youth, Mill used the pseudonym 'Wickliffe' in writing five letters defending the atheist Richard Carlisle and his right to free speech.[72] In *On Liberty*, Mill stated that the theory of Protestantism is that 'the intellect and judgment of mankind ought to be cultivated' and that 'the responsibility for the choice of a religion must be borne by each for himself, and cannot be thrown off upon teachers.'[73] However, the practice is different. Mill asserted, with the confidence of a Puritan preacher, that not one person in a thousand regulates his life by the Bible; the standard of the average man is 'the custom of his nation, his class, or his religious profession.'[74] In a letter to Arthur W. Greene (27 December 1861), Mill asserted that intolerance inheres in all religions, especially Catholicism and Islam:

> But the Protestant forms of Xtianity, not claiming for themselves any divinely confirmed infallibility, hold as a principle that the mode in which truth ought to be arrived at & the only legitimate mode of obtaining full assurance of it, is by the operation of the individual reason & conscience which makes the permission & even encouragement of free inquiry indispensable, in theory at least, however much the contrary may often be the case in practice.[75]

In his correspondence with Auguste Comte, Mill came to see that a Catholic atheist is different from a Protestant atheist, and that their different traditions divided them more than their commitment to militant secularism united them. Mill agreed with Comte that the ascendancy once enjoyed by priests should pass to philosophers, but he did not think the laity should defer to them as experts on moral and political matters.[76] Comte followed *les lumières* in wanting philosophers to organize as a hierarchical corporation, like the Catholic church, in a religion of reason. But the rationalist counter-hegemony of the French Enlightenment shared the authoritarian structure of the Catholic church it challenged, and thus is quite a different thing from Protestant conscience. From the Protestant and liberal point of view, Comte's religion of humanity would be 'the completest system of spiritual and temporal despotism.'[77] Comte denounced as outdated Protestant metaphysics 'the first of all the articles of the liberal creed, "the absolute right of free examination, or the dogma of unlimited liberty of conscience."'[78] Comte thought reason and conscience to be mutually inconsistent: conscience has no authority in the sciences. In the Comtean scheme, philosophers were to exercise 'a moral and intellectual authority, charged with the duty of guiding men's opinions and enlightening and warning their consciences.'[79]

Besides having an authoritarian political theory, Comte showed, Mill thought, 'a very insufficient understanding of the peculiar phenomenon of English development' in his historical writing: 'His failure consists chiefly in want of appreciation of Protestantism; ... like almost all thinkers, even unbelievers, who have lived and thought exclusively in a Catholic atmosphere, he sees ... the Reformation as a merely destructive movement.'[80] Protestantism cultivated 'the intelligence and conscience of the individual believer' and promoted literacy among the poor to enable them to have direct access to the Bible.[81] In Mill's view, Comte's Catholic neglect of conscience led him to oppose freedom of divorce and also to commit the error – often imputed to utilitarian moralists – of confusing the standard of policy (the general welfare) with the motive to virtuous conduct. In sum, Mill thought that 'M. Comte is accustomed to draw most of his ideas of moral cultivation from the discipline of the Catholic Church.'[82]

Could it be that Mill's libertarian principles are closer to Protestant conscience than to Enlightenment reason? Is the *form* of the pursuit of truth – that it be one's own – more important than its catholicity or universality? Mill was aware that the advancement of knowledge, or more generally, cultural flourishing, was possible without individual liberty, and that progress is possible without individuality.[83] Individual culture and moral choices, not just the progress of civilization and the greatest happiness, are at the core of *On Liberty*. Although stopping short of Kierkegaard, who thought that making moral choices is what makes us human, Mill asserted: 'The human faculties of perception, judgment, discriminative feeling, mental activity, and even moral preference, are exercised only in making a choice.'[84]

Mill's nonconformist conscience dictates that the choice be one's own, not that the choice be rational: 'The mental and moral powers, like the muscular powers, are improved only by being used.'[85] To exercise moral choice is to develop as a human being.

Mill seemed to side with Blake in viewing conscience and individuality as essentially compatible. As distinct from Freud, who opposed conscience and desire, Mill sided with Blake in seeing conscience as friendly to desire: 'It is not because men's desires are strong that they act ill; it is because their consciences are weak. There is no natural connection between strong impulses and a weak conscience. The natural connection is the other way.'[86] Like Blake, and like the freethinkers Paine and Godwin, Mill's social conscience was tied to the teaching of 'the greatest moral reformer,' Jesus of Nazareth. Mill wrote that Jesus was 'a standard of excellence and a model for imitation,' 'the pattern of perfection for humanity,' and that his precepts were 'permanent and ... universal.'[87] In Blakean manner, Mill declared: 'It is the God incarnate, more than the God of the Jews or of Nature, who being idealized has taken so great and salutary a hold on the modern mind. And whatever else may be taken away from us by rational criticism, Christ is still left.'[88]

A.O.J. Cockshutt wrote of Mill: 'One conviction, shared by so many of his contemporaries of all schools of thought, remained unchallenged in Mill's mind. It was the idea that we know for certain without argument what is good. But this belief in instinct or conscience or inspiration was precisely the one that Bentham set out to destroy.'[89]

Cockshutt may have underemphasized the element of defensive rhetoric in Mill's 'Theism' and in his assessment of Bentham. On the other hand, David Copp may have underemphasized the distance between Bentham and Mill when he asserted that no utilitarian theory can accept the precept of following the dictates of conscience. Copp wrote that for Mill, 'one is morally required to do only what it would be expedient for one's conscience to dictate.'[90] Mill's doctrine with respect to following the dictates of one's conscience seems to shunt back and forth between the poles of Protestant individualism and utilitarian collectivism; Cockshutt and Copp highlight the antitheses that Mill attempted to synthesize. Mill held a view of conscience as acquired not innate, as socially constructed not God-given, as the product of nurture or education not nature or instinct. Perhaps to distance Mill from Protestant thinkers, contemporary Mill scholars refer to the Millian value of autonomy – a word Mill did not use (perhaps because it was tied up with the Kantianism he disdained) – rather than the dictates of conscience.[91] Although the Millian conscience seems heteronomous (the product of education, environment, and social approbation or public opinion), Mill was committed to 'self-culture,' continual reappraisal of the norms to which one has become habituated, self-respect and inner-directedness – precisely the aspects of human nature Mill found lacking in Bentham's utilitarianism.[92] According to Bernard Semmel, 'Mill understood that a good society could not long survive the eclipse of a freely chosen virtue.'[93] That virtue be freely chosen, not rationally calculated, is the essence of conscience.

Self, Consciousness, and Conscience

In the preceding section, I tried to demonstrate the implicitly Protestant character of Mill's doctrine of conscience and its rights to freedom. In this section, I wish to establish some of the barriers to a coherent account of conscience in Mill's writing. These barriers are psychological, ontological, ethical, and political: ambivalence about his father's moral education, a naturalism that understands human beings as part of the causal order of nature, a utilitarian conception of the good as a calculation of consequences, and a liberal apprehension that intuitive moralities tend to be either conservative justifications of prevailing mores or anarchist irrationalism.

Reflections about Mill's ambivalence about his father's mode of educating him might seem impertinent, if the construction of Mill's conscience were not, together with the propriety of his love affair with Harriet Taylor, the main theme of his *Autobiography*. According to the Freudian mythology, young men have to 'kill' their fathers in order to become independent, but in doing so they divinize their fathers and introject their idealized father as their superego. Mill, as is well known, fell into a nervous collapse during his crisis of faith in his father's religion of progress; he felt that if all the reforms for which he and his father had striven were to be actualized, he would not be happy. He attempted to heal himself by reading Coleridge and romantic poets, but his depression did not lift until he read Jean Francois Marmontel's *Memoirs* 'which relates his father's death' and how the son 'would supply the place' of the dead father: 'From this moment my burthen grew lighter. The oppression of the thought that all feeling was dead within me, was gone. I was no longer hopeless: I was not a stock or a stone.'[94]

However, Mill could not kill off his father's Enlightenment doctrine:

> In psychology, his fundamental doctrine was the formation of all human character by circumstances, through the universal Principle of Association, and the consequent unlimited possibility of improving the moral and intellectual condition of mankind by education. Of all his doctrines none was more important than this, or needs more to be insisted upon: unfortunately there is none which is more contradictory to the prevailing tendencies of speculation, both in his time and since.[95]

Mill knew that his father's doctrine (i.e., that conscience is not an innate practical principle) was hardly idiosyncratic; indeed, it was common to Hume, Hartley, Diderot, D'Holbach, Helvétius, and Bentham.

Individualist Conscience and Nationalist Prejudice   171

If his father's doctrine is an important truth that must be declared repeatedly in the face of hostile opinion, one may wonder why Mill berated Bentham for ignoring conscience in his moral doctrine.

Mill retained the prejudice that only empiricist epistemology and associationist psychology inhibit 'deep seated prejudices' and 'bad institutions.'[96] Alan Ryan points out that Mill was being unfair in linking the conservative Henry Mansell to Sir William Hamilton, who was as liberal in matters of politics and education as his mentor, Immanuel Kant; implausibly, Mill wanted to line up progressives under the banner of association and reactionaries under the banner of intuition.[97] The doctrine that conscience is innate runs counter to Mill's progressivist intuitions.[98]

The least formidable barrier to embracing a notion of conscience, in my opinion, is the utilitarian doctrine that goodness is determined by a calculation of consequences rather than by a purity of intentions. Mill's notion of utility is so elastic that we can comprehend conflicting tendencies within it – indeed, it is difficult to see what could be excluded from Mill's felicific calculus. In his *System of Logic*, Mill says happiness means 'both in the comparatively humble sense, of pleasure and freedom from pain, and in the higher meaning, of rendering life, not what it now is almost universally, puerile and insignificant – but such as human beings with highly developed faculties can care to have.'[99] His father's complete disdain for pleasure, Mill thought, was not inconsistent with utilitarianism; rather, it was a lofty form of it.[100] We are familiar with Mill's argument in *Utilitarianism* that it is better to be a dissatisfied Socrates than a pig satisfied, because the former has the ability to choose and the latter does not; and with his appeal in *On Liberty* to 'utility in the largest sense, grounded in the permanent interests of man as a progressive being.'[101] The elasticity of Mill's utilitarianism holds in flabby muscles, and smooths over unsightly lumps, and thus could stretch to the usefulness of good intentions and inner motivations, if notions of conscience were consistent with Mill's educational psychology, his liberal progressivism, and his naturalist ontology and empiricist epistemology.

The most formidable barrier to the espousal of conscience in Millian doctrine is his naturalism, that is, his view that human beings are predictable elements in a world of natural causes and effects.[102] If conscience resides in the irreducibility of moral prescription to causal prediction, of 'the ought' to 'the is,' of what is worthy of desire to what is in fact desired, then Mill rejected an irreducible conscience. Mill's *Examination of Hamilton* was a sustained rejection of Kantian freedom in favour of a naturalist determinism: 'The whole philosophy of Sir W. Hamilton seems to have its character determined by the requirements of the doctrine of Free-will.'[103] Mill's opposition to this doctrine has raised some questions among his admirers.

Alan Ryan points out that Mill's account dissolves the self into motives and lacks an account of moral agency.[104] In Benthamite fashion, Mill asserted that responsibility means punishment (although he added self-reproach to the sanctions of law and public opinion). Our sense of responsibility, Mill stated, was taught to us by our parents and tutors, and reinforced by the prevailing climate of opinion, and confirmed by personal reflection on our life experience. Human actions are predictable and thus are not *free* in the sense of Kant's and Hamilton's free will.[105] The ascription of free agency is not essential for legal and moral responsibility; belief in the amiability of benevolent conduct and the odiousness of malevolent conduct is 'sufficient for the ends of society and for the individual conscience.'[106] If a criminal is capable of being moved by the threat of punishment, then the punishment is just; and capital punishment provides an additional reason for would-be criminals to avoid invading the rights of others. Alan Ryan offers to defend criminals condemned to death insofar as the prosecution consistently maintains Mill's determinist line; Ryan thinks some members of a jury of common men and women would absolve a bad character, if they recognized such character as the product of poor upbringing and unfavourable social circumstances.[107] Curiously, Mill found it morally intolerable that God could consign to Hell those He knew could not help being sinners.

Mill's naturalism is consistent with the view that 'we are under a moral obligation to seek the improvement of our character.'[108] In his *Examination of Hamilton*, Mill does not explain the basis of this obligation, but presumably it is based, as in *Utilitarianism*, on the natural desire of humans to be at one with their fellows. To be sure, Mill's naturalism is consistent with the propositions that 'Art is as much Nature as anything else' and that 'every respectable attribute of humanity is the result not of instinct, but of victory over instinct.'[109] One might then wonder if the instinct to be at one with our fellow human beings – the basis of our moral obligation – is to be obeyed or overcome.

In Coleridge's epistemology, conscience has primacy; in contrast, Mill's naturalistic epistemology and psychology postulates the primacy of consciousness.[110] Mill elaborated: 'Consciousness tells me what

I do or feel. What I am *able* to do, is not a subject of consciousness. Consciousness is not prophetic; we are conscious of what is, not of what will or can be. We can never know that we are able to do a thing, except from having done it, or something equal and similar to it.'[111] Whereas conscience is prophetic, oriented to the future and to decisions of what we should do and who we should be, consciousness seems to be backward looking, tied to memory and habit, the product of past experiences rather than the agent of new experiences. Consciousness can determine what is prudent from past experiences; it can calculate what most effectively promotes the general welfare; and it can predict what policies will and will not work; but it cannot prescribe for us the right course of conduct.

Nor can consciousness determine personal identity. Consciousness links us to our past by memory and to the future by expectation, but ultimately the self or mind is a 'succession of manifold feelings' or psychic states. Mill, to be sure, found this conception of the self unsatisfactory; mind as 'a permanent possibility of feeling' and the self as a series of feelings aware of itself as a past and a future is finally inexplicable. The problem is how 'a series of feelings, the infinitely greater part of which is past or future, can be gathered up, as it were, into a single present conception, accompanied by a belief of reality.'[112] That is, Mill's problem is that most people are unsatisfied with the view of the self as a possibility rather than a reality, and with a reduction of self to present consciousness of past memories and future expectations. Mill candidly confessed: 'I do not profess to have adequately accounted for the belief in Mind.' He attributed 'a reality to the Ego – to my own mind – different from that real existence as a Permanent Possibility, which is the only reality I acknowledge in Matter.'[113] The question is whether Mill's attribution of a reality to the self is philosophically justified.

Jonathan Loesburg claims that 'Mill needs a concept of an active self-consciousness to put into motion the act of self-reform or education that is the model for him of a freely willed moment.'[114] Loesburg, however, finds it highly questionable whether that needed concept is available within Mill's philosophy. Alan Ryan claims that Mill's naturalistic or mechanistic conception of mind 'destroys our concept of personal identity; the agent disappears, to be replaced by a spectator of events occurring at a location which we somehow continue to call "him" ... This picture makes us unable to use any longer our former ideas about guilt and responsibility.'[115]

Mill's reduction of self to consciousness rather than conscience transforms agency into spectatorship, decision into *theoria*, openness of choice into the closedness of causal necessity. The dissolution of the empirical self in consciousness was not a theoretical problem for the post-Kantian tradition that portrayed the self as constituted by its moral choices and practical decisions. As Soren Kierkegaard wrote: 'He is a definite individual, in the choice he makes himself a definite individual, for he chooses himself.'[116] Outside the choice, humans are nothing, for moral choices constitute humanity: 'The choice itself is decisive for the content of the personality, through the choice the personality immerses itself in the thing chosen, and when it does not choose it withers away in consumption.'[117] Whereas Mill associated the idea of an innate conscience with a fixed or static view of human nature, Kierkegaard associated it with becoming rather than being, history rather than nature: 'the aesthetical in a man is that by which he is immediately what he is; the ethical is that whereby he becomes what he becomes.'[118]

Mill's fidelity to Enlightenment rationalism seems to have precluded a full commitment to, or a philosophical account of, Protestant conscience (in the manner of Kant, Fichte, Hegel, and Kierkegaard). He did not understand the self as constituted or defined by conscience. Nor did he understand the equality of human beings in terms of their moral choices; for Mill, the equality of humans was merely asserted – not, as for Hobbes, rationally justified – and was something to be gauged in terms of individual claims to welfare rather than capacity for moral choice. Freedom of conscience, for Mill, is detached from Milton's understanding of conscience. It hovers between Miltonian zeal and Humean scepticism, avoiding the anarchism of the former and the conservatism of the latter; but lacking a substantive account of conscience and personal identity, freedom of conscience gravitates toward sceptical tolerance. Lacking a philosophic account of conscience, Mill tended to identify conscience with opinion; thus, *On Liberty* tends toward a celebration of British opinionatedness.

Perhaps Mill was wise not to provide a philosophic foundation for his political doctrine. However, such an avoidance would have been alien to Mill, for two reasons. First, he rejected Carlyle's view that the worth of English political practice is inversely proportional to the worth of English philosophy. Theoretical weakness, Mill stated, was practical weakness: 'To act well without being able to say why one so acts is to act well only accidentally.'[119] Second, to base liberal theory on conscience rather than utility is antifoundationalist. To base liberalism on conscience is to base it on nothing – nothing other than moral choices.

Mill's theory emphasized that conscience is socially constructed but also is developed or modified by the individual exercise of moral choice. However, we might ask whether Mill was wedded to the view that the capacity for moral choice is not an innate human capacity, like speech. Perhaps specific moral content is socially constructed and historically variable (just as different languages are), but the capacity for moral choice (like that for speech) is innate. If Mill granted an innate poetic sense, why would he oppose an innate moral sense? Certainly, Mill thought it 'undeniable in point of fact, and consistent with the principles of a sound metaphysics, that there are poetic *natures*. There is a mental and physical constitution or temperament, particularly fitted for poetry.'[120]

Poetry is a national as well as an individual gift, and like conscience has the character of a soliloquy or individual meditation: 'Poetry ... is the natural fruit of solitude and meditation; eloquence, of intercourse with the world ... The French, who are the least poetical of all great and intellectual nations, are among the most eloquent: the French, also, being the most sociable, the vainest, and the least self-dependent.'[121]

The nation that is best able to think for itself is, of course, the most poetic. Mill asserted: 'It would be difficult for anyone to imagine that "Rule Britannia," for example, or "Scots wha hae," had no permanent influence on the higher regions of human character.'[122] Some of us might like a tighter definition of 'the higher regions of human character' before giving our assent to that proposition. According to Mill, Protestant interiority seemed to facilitate art; for him, Mozart and Beethoven were meditative, while Rossini and the Italian school were garrulous.[123]

As we have seen, Mill rejected Comte's positivism as a continuation of Catholicism and its universalist morality. Comte, in turn, rejected Mill's respect for the rights of conscience as obsolete Protestant metaphysics. Mill's view that the English were better able to think for themselves than continental Europeans because they had 'fewer prejudices and national biases' was, for Comte, an 'involuntary confirmation' that the English were profoundly nationalistic. Mill's response was that foreigners misjudge the English because Englishmen are not extroverted.[124] Foreigners think the English are moved by interest and national prejudice, when in fact they are moved by principle and moral duty: 'Englishmen, beyond all the rest of the human race, are so shy of professing virtues that they will even profess vices instead.'[125]

In reviewing William Gladstone's *The State in its Relations with the Church* (1839), Lord Macaulay wrote:

> There are two intelligible and consistent courses which may be followed with respect to the exercise of private judgment; the course of the Romanist, who interdicts private judgment because of its inevitable inconveniences; and the course of the Protestant, who permits private judgment in spite of its inevitable inconveniences. Both are more reasonable than Mr. Gladstone, who would have private judgment without its inevitable inconveniences.[126]

Whether Mill was closer to Macaulay's Protestant or the man who later became the Liberal prime minister is a matter for individual judgment.

Mill remained explicitly faithful to the tradition of British empiricism and implicitly faithful to the tradition of Protestant interiority. John Stuart Mill has become, as Stefan Collini has said, 'a national possession.'[127] But a philosopher, one who brings to full explicitness what is contained within a historical tradition, is not merely a national possession.

Conclusion

In this book I have contended that the liberal tradition of the English-speaking world has simultaneously attempted to deconstruct conscience and to champion its rights. British philosophers have tended to explain away conscience, presenting it as a contingent acquisition, the product of childrearing, education, and social environment, rather than attempting to understand the call of conscience as an interesting phenomenon, in the manner of Montaigne, Bayle, Rousseau, Kant, Fichte, Hegel, Kierkegaard, Nietzsche, Heidegger, Sartre, and Foucault. Richard Rorty has tried to open the horizons of Anglo-American liberalism to continental philosophy, but he has done so by separating philosophy from politics. In separating politics from a philosophical basis, Rorty has declared Mill's *On Liberty* to be the unsurpassed statement of liberal principles.[1] Liberal doctrine does not need philosophical foundations.

If the rights of conscience are not justified philosophically, then they may be said to rest on, or be suspended in, a liberal tradition. Rorty's liberalism rests on Humean and Burkean scepticism about human rights; rights are seen as rites, habitual practices handed on from generation to generation. When detached from universal principles, liberalism takes on a conservative character, namely, traditionalism combined (as we saw with John Stuart Mill) with a little Anglo-American smugness. Bertrand Russell, in his noble defence for violating the Defence of the Realm Act in World War One, followed Mill in asserting that Britain leads all other countries in cultivating a tradition of liberty: 'We have preserved, more than any other Power, respect for the individual conscience. It is for that that I stand.'[2] Russell seemed more self-conscious than Mill that his individualist creed depended on like-minded individualists; he also extended Mill's defence of the rights of conscience to an important area of moral choice. Russell's individual courage demonstrated that he knew he stood within a tradition, rather than alone against the despotism of custom and the tyranny of public opinion.

One can inhabit a tradition thoughtfully or thoughtlessly. Many liberals employ the vocabulary of conscience rhetorically, without having thoughtfully analysed conscience and its claims. For example, Michael Ignatieff uses the language of conscience without any purpose beyond indicating the depth of his care for others, and even though he makes it clear that conscience is a socially constructed myth.[3] Many of Ignatieff's spiritual ancestors in the Enlightenment had the intellectual cleanliness to eschew talk of conscience. The tradition of the Enlightenment, when inhabited thoughtlessly, may convert the language of conscience into empty rhetorical gestures.

In examining the heritage of the idea of conscience, I intended not only to chart out traditions of thought but also to reawaken philosophic questioning of the idea. During the Protestant Reformation, conscience signified an egalitarian protest against the privilege of learning, and specifically against the clerical monopoly over scriptural interpretation or judgment of what was necessary to salvation. In *Conscience and Its Critics* I have argued that the Protestant conscience initially may have fostered the growth of capitalism by emancipating property rights and commercial contracts from Christian natural law, but by the late eighteenth century it had become an egalitarian protest against capitalist inequality and a moral protest against enlightened reason as bourgeois calculation. Although St Paul's letter to the Romans (13:1–7) links conscience to conformity or obedience to authority – a theme taken up by both Luther and Calvin – the claims of conscience were often voices, not of conformity but of dissent. In Milton, in the Locke of *The Two Treatises of Government* and *Letters concerning Toleration*, and later in Price, Priestley, Paine, Godwin, Wollstonecraft, and Blake, the voice of dissent became revolutionary.

Conscience – the subjective conviction of right, and the mark of our innermost or ownmost individuality – is inherently lawless and anarchic; it prescribes for oneself rather than for others, and adopts a flexible measure, adjusted to the particularities of one's situation and character. The anarchic and potentially revolutionary character of conscience troubled Thomas Hobbes, who attempted to house anarchic conscience within the law (as rights of defendants and jurors) and thus provided a philosophic account of modern subjectivity in conjunction with a political solution. If the English-speaking world rightly prides itself on its poets, such as Shakespeare, Milton, Wordsworth, Blake, and Coleridge, *Conscience and Its Critics* pays homage to the English political philosopher and advocates building on Hobbesian foundations, that is, constructing an institutional setting for the homeless consciences of the world.

However, it was not Hobbes but Locke who set liberal doctrine on the track it has followed from the eighteenth century to the present day. The European and Scottish Enlightenment built on Locke's deconstruction of conscience as an innate practical principle, as God within the mind. Moral conduct was to be regulated by the radar of public opinion, by one's desire for social approval and fear of social censure. The mind is a *tabula rasa* on which the educators of public tastes can write their progressive opinions and have them reinforced or amended by other enlightened writers. Enlightenment intellectuals were as hierarchical as the Catholic church they opposed; they were sceptical, but not of their own authority as educators and taste-makers. Individuals are *equal* with respect to conscience, or the capacity for moral choice, as Rousseau or Blake thought; but they are also *unequal* with respect to reason, or the calculation of consequences, as Locke, Voltaire, Hume, and Diderot thought. Enlightenment thinkers did not want freedom *for* conscience; that is, they did not favour the emancipation of intolerant certitude, religious zeal, and revolutionary intransigence. For them, freedom of conscience tended to mean sceptical tolerance, not an immunity or sanctity for conscience. Enlightenment thinkers were divided on the question of the separation of church and state: Paine, Jefferson, and Kant followed Milton and Locke; and Mandeville, Voltaire, Hume, and Diderot followed Hobbes; while Smith and John Stuart Mill found merit in arguments both for establishing religion to diminish zeal, and for multiplying disestablished churches as a means for moderating pretensions to exclusive salvation.

In presenting Protestant conscience, and Enlightenment reason as antitheses, I am presenting an alternative narrative to that provided by J.B. Schneewind in *The Invention of Autonomy: A History of Modern Philosophy* and Charles Griswold Jr in *Adam Smith and the Virtues of Enlightenment*. Both Schneewind and Griswold see a harmonious conjunction of Protestantism and Enlightenment, and place thinkers such as Locke, Bayle, Hutcheson, Rousseau, and Kant within the Enlightenment; whereas I have presented each of these men with at least one foot in the opposite camp, that of Protestant conscience. Griswold writes: 'True religion is the privatized religion of morality and conscience beloved of Enlightenment figures.'[4] Schneewind asserts: 'The ethics of self-governance was created by both religious and antireligious philosophers ... [However,] the Enlightenment project [was] the effort to limit God's control over earthly life while keeping him essential to morality.'[5] From these views, at least the following questions arise: (1) Is 'the privatized religion of morality and conscience beloved of Enlightenment figures' equally espoused by religious and antireligious philosophers? (2) If the Enlightenment religion is one of conscience, why did most Enlightenment figures embrace Locke's rejection of conscience as an innate practical principle? (3) If enlightened conduct is to be regulated by individual conscience, why did Enlightenment thinkers almost universally espouse a social psychology and an ethics based on the desire for esteem and the fear of social censure?

The narratives of Schneewind and Griswold do not take into account a countermovement to conscience – namely, the rise of society and the regulation of conduct by social expectations. In this book I am suggesting that in the eighteenth century, as society replaced the god within as the guide to conduct, public opinion rather than individual judgment became the force directing individuals to their appointed end. Against this hierarchical conformity of enlightened reason, the romantic and radical voices of Rousseau and Blake sought to reintroduce individual conscience as the fulcrum of moral thought. Niklas Luhmann has charted the course of our narrative from the seventeenth to the eighteenth centuries:

> If we drop this religious or ontological warrant of individuality, we arrive at the *homme aimable*, the sociable person of the eighteenth century ... The results were disappointing, particularly for the self-conscious individual: somehow, the individual withdrew from interaction. By the end of the eighteenth century, the *homme du monde*, the *home de bonne compagnie*, was no longer an individual.[6]

The challenge for post-Enlightenment individuals, such as William Godwin and John Stuart Mill, was to reconceive the absolute importance of individual judgment once individuals are detached from the eternal destiny of Christian theology. I am by no means suggesting that John Stuart Mill's effort was ignoble or doomed from the outset, but I do believe that he was fettered by the Enlightenment social psychology he imbibed from his father. Subsequent liberals such as T.H. Green, John Rawls, and J.B. Schneewind have looked to Immanuel Kant rather than Mill to find an ontological basis for individual liberty. However, Rawls and his followers have attempted to eliminate the transcendental origins of Kantian autonomy. Charles Griswold, Jr, champions Adam Smith as an exemplar of enlightened modernity, and rightly so, but his Humean reconstruction of Smith's conscience makes individual judgment of what is praiseworthy dependent on social approval or public opinion. As an alternative to highlighting eighteenth-century thinkers such as Smith and Kant, my account features the thought of Thomas Hobbes. John Aubrey's *Lives* presents Hobbes as the most notable of that remarkable range of robust individuals who were so prominent before eighteenth-century conformism pinched the souls of the English. Hobbesian thought not only expresses an age of robust individuality but also includes conscience within its political philosophy. John Locke excommunicated conscience from the realm of philosophy, leaving it bedraggled and homeless in Whig doctrine.

For example, the abortion issue is intractable on Lockean premises. The 'right to choice' side espouses Lockean privacy rights, a woman's proprietorship over her person, while the 'right to life' side emphasizes the Lockean duty to protect life. (To be sure, both of these Lockean antitheses abstract from the circumstances in which women make hard moral choices, and thus transform socio-economic problems into individual moral questions, and so do not exhaust all the available options on reproductive rights and on the provision of health and welfare services.) Locke justifies a role for conscience outside the law, in the individual's judgment when positive law does not accord with higher law or when the government has abused its trust. Both abortionists and the killers of abortionists could find support in Locke's justification of private judgment in executing the laws of nature. For the Hobbesian, the killer of an abortionist could only make the plea of conscience if he presented himself, after the deed, to a court to face a trial of his peers, whom he himself selects. The killer of an abortionist could not plead conscience if he kept his deed hidden in criminal darkness. If the killers of abortionists are consistently acquitted by juries of their peers, then legislators must change the law until it can be upheld by the jury system. Jury verdicts according to conscience may be inconsistent – it is the function of legislators, not jurors, to follow the canons of rational consistency – but for Hobbes, jurors decide not only fact but also right.

Does John Rawls's defence of conscientious objection to warfare represent an advance on the Hobbesian right of cowardice – that is, on the right of self-preserving individuals to evade 'dangerous office'? Rawls maintains that the rights of conscience are integral to a liberal tradition; like Bertrand Russell, he supports civil disobedience and conscientious objection to warfare when it is reasonable. He recognizes that liberal and republican principles do not necessarily coincide: the latter dictate a conscript army, which Rawls not unreasonably believes is 'less likely to be an instrument of unjustified foreign adventures' than a professional army.[7] Following the path of Mill and Russell, but inverting the practice in some liberal democracies, Rawls maintains that conscientious objection must be based on political rather than religious principles.[8] Our horizontal obligations to our fellow citizens have political primacy over our vertical obligations to God. Individuals have no right to conscientious objection in just wars or when the defence of liberty is at stake. Those who refuse to be conscripted into military service must demonstrate that the aims of the war are unjust. However, Rawls recommends that liberal states accept limited conscientious refusal and civil disobedience as a means of encouraging opponents to express their opposition publicly and to appeal to publicly accepted principles. Rawls would replace the silent call of conscience with public debate that eschews religious principles in favour of the overlapping consensus of liberal democracies.

In effect, Rawls has replaced 'dumb' conscience with Kantian practical reason. The reasons of conscience are not communicable; publicly avowed conscience is mere self-advertising. Thus the difficulty with Rawls's proposal is that some individuals cannot put into words why they refuse to participate in the military, even if they have mastered the difference between just and unjust wars. For some individuals, life would not be worth living if they had to kill others in a cause they found questionable. An alternative to Rawls's proposal would be for liberal democracies to provide some dangerous alternatives to military service (in hospitals, jails, mines, fire departments, rescue services) to differentiate those unwilling to kill from those unwilling to die, and to distinguish genuine conscientious objection from Hobbesian rights of cowardice. Hobbes advocated a professional rather than a conscript army. But Rawls thought that with a professional army, the rights and duties of citizenship would be unequally borne by all classes of citizens. For Hobbesians who are unwilling to die for their country, the loss of citizenship might be the appropriate penalty; however, as Hobbes himself said, banishment is not punishment but merely a change of air. In other words, the institutionalized encouragement of dumb conscience, the silent call from what is most one's own to one's self, is an alternative goal to fostering communicative competence or enlightened intersubjectivity; both goals might be worthy objectives of liberal democracies.

Death and taxes are famously inevitable; yet it is by no means certain that liberal states, which legitimately hold the monopoly on violence in a given territory, are morally entitled to take life by capital punishment or by conscripting the unwilling into military service. The compulsory payment of taxes is not normally seen as an issue of conscience, presumably because it is considered natural to pursue tax avoidance (with the assistance of accountants and lawyers) or tax evasion (if one cannot or will not pay for legal tax avoidance). One can choose one's tax-creditable charitable donations, but one cannot earmark what percentage of one's taxes will go to public broadcasting, health services, the armed forces, transportation, education, and so on. If individuals could choose what government services to support with their tax money – perhaps paying a fee to cover the minor administrative difficulty (in the computer age) of co-ordinating planning and expenditures – they might be less unhappy about paying taxes and less inclined to see politicians and civil servants (who are indeed the only bulwark against the total sway of global capital) as the enemy. By opening up social spending to decisions of conscience we might attenuate the current trend in liberal democracies toward portraying citizens as consumers, and as passive and apathetic in their commitments.

Is maximizing the sphere of moral choice as integral to liberal principle as maximizing the range of consumer choice? Or is it anarchism to hope that citizens could contribute to the formation of government policies as taxpayers by designating a percentage of their tax payments to go to one or another area of government expenditure? Would it be unworkable for hospital administrators not to be able to conscript nurses and orderlies into abortion services? And would liberal democracies collapse without caucus discipline? That is, what would happen if free votes in Parliament, which do not constitute a vote of confidence in the government, were the rule rather than the exception?

And what would happen if jurors judged law as well as fact? Our Hobbesian project of institutionalizing anarchic conscience, even if politically feasible, might not serve to humanize our bureaucratic institutions serving corporate profit; indeed, it might serve to domesticate a naturally wild animal. However, the basic objection to enlarging the sphere of conscience is that productivity and technological efficiency dictate that we confine our range of choice to consumer choices. Nevertheless, as John Stuart Mill pointed out, commercial progress and moral atrophy can coexist; a commercial civilization can do without independent judgment, but the moral and intellectual muscles can only be developed through exercise.

The two contemporary political theorists who have thought most deeply about issues of conscience are Michael Walzer and George Kateb. Walzer, a social democratic or communitarian critic of liberal individualism, repeatedly draws our attention to the *con* in conscience. Thus 'conscience is a shared knowledge, an internalized acceptance of communal standards.'[9] This conception of 'an internalized acceptance of communal standards' drifts away from conscience in the direction of a Freudian superego cut off from the ego. For example, incest is not normally a matter for conscience insofar as there is universal acceptance of the communal norm that it is wrong. Matters for conscience usually arise when individuals experience conflicting demands from communal standards, or when ready-to-wear habits and customs do not fit the individual in her choice of activities and professions.

Walzer recognizes more candidly than Mill the problems associated with secularizing conscience: 'Conscience means shared (moral) knowledge, and if we share this knowledge with other people rather than with God, we will also share divergent accounts and interpretations of its meaning. So Conscience is itself divided. My home-base umpire calls a strike but is overruled by my third-base umpire.'[10]

Walzer wishes to liberate us from the great Umpire in the sky, internalized in the self as a supposedly omniscient and severe, but actually hypocritical and hypercritical, judge of all things fair and foul, strike or ball, safe or out. Since, as the Americans say, the umpire is always right, we would do better to have a number of umpires; the self should have a variety of consciences, just as presidents have advisers, and should be portrayed as 'a thickly populated circle, with me at the center surrounded by my self-critics who stand at different temporal and spatial removes.'[11] Walzer recognizes that '"consciences" is an odd plural when applied to a single self,' but he does not fully examine the relationship between the singular self and plural consciences. With respect to Walzer's analogies, there is a recognized order of precedence with respect to the authority of the home and third base umpires on particular decisions, and in the same vein, presidents can overrule advisers; but there is no clear relationship between me and my self-critics in Walzer's pluralist and republican model of the self (replacing the Platonic monarchical self, with reason ruling the conflicting claims of the desires for honour and sensual satisfaction, and the Christian version, with conscience replacing reason as monarch of the class-divided soul). Is there still a me, independent of my self-critics, who can attend to or dismiss criticism? Or is the me as divided as the critics who mill around the self? What is the relationship between the *me* being judged and the *I* that judges which critics are competent to make a worthy judgment?

Walzer's social democratic account of the relationship between consciences and the self is in some ways quite similar to the account of the arch-individualist, George Kateb. Kateb argues that personal integrity does not mean complacent at-oneness with the self, but rather a duality of a watcher and a watched. In the case of Socrates, his *daimonion* or inner voice joined with his reflective intelligence to watch over the integrity of his self: 'The watcher is not always morally suspicious; it is not the Christian conscience. Although it is distinct from the inner voice, the watcher does reinforce the work of the inner voice, but this voice prohibits Socrates from doing anything that may be *personally* bad – injurious – for himself to do. Neither the inside watcher nor the inner voice is *directly* moral.'[12]

Socratic rationalism, like Kateb's post-Enlightenment variant of it, is distinct from Protestant conscience. The nay-saying *daimonion* is self-protective rather than moral (or directly moral); and Kateb's practical judgment, following rational self-scrutiny, is more Hobbesian prudence than Kantian conscience, albeit with a little honour thrown in. That is, the self is distinct from its agents (reason and conscience), which serve to protect not only its physical or embodied existence but also its reputation or good name. Kateb shares with Walzer the view that the self should be conceived as dialogical rather than monological in character, with the self dividing itself into an auditor and inner voice, a spectator and an agent, and with reflective intelligence making decisions on the data brought to it by the inner eye and inner voice. *Logos* gathers and persuades the irrational elements of the soul in council; in this it is distinct from a monarchical conscience, which dictates to subaltern aspects of the self. However, Kateb's and Walzer's divided selves maintain an integrated core of self, surrounded by and distinct from its agents; they reproduce the Enlightenment's deconstruction of conscience (as consciences or watchers) as distinct from the conscious self, and the Freudian superego (pluralized) divided from the ego.

Walzer's and Kateb's analyses of conscience do us the service of throwing the identity of the self into question. Liberalism tends to employ a vocabulary of the self (self-interest, self-preservation, self-determination, self-governance, etc.), yet it rarely subjects the idea of the self to question. Walzer and Kateb seem to offer a new, more pluralist conception of a divided self, but their divisions reproduce Enlightenment or Freudian divisions, albeit with pluralist agents serving an integrated self. We might ask this question: if the conscience is to be pluralized into consciences, why is the self served by consciences or watchers not to be pluralized into selves?

Richard Rorty argues that liberalism should disassociate itself from any determinate conception of the self. He considers metaphysical any conception of human nature that attempts to bridge our *private* interest in creating a robust self, with our *public* commitments to minimize unnecessary suffering. Walzer's account of the relationship between plural consciences and a unitary self would be subject to Rorty's critique that there is no self to be discovered by reflective examination.[13] I have argued elsewhere that for Hobbes there is no self, or stable self-interest, prior to conscientiously giving one's word in the social contract.[14] Thus, it cannot be against self-interest to dishonour one's word, because one's self is constituted by promising. From Kierkegaard to Foucault, the self is created by one's moral choices. Conscience is founded on nothing; it is constitutive of the self. Conscience is thus 'postmodern' in the sense that it is not founded on anything and has no basis in reason.

For Kierkegaard, our tastes and consumer choices reveal who we are; our moral choices make us become what we choose to be. Conscience is central to human existence, in that a decision to terminate or not terminate a pregnancy or to fight or not to fight in a war is more definitive of who we are than our choice of hairstyles or our taste in contemporary painting. The entrenched liberal maxim that our fundamental freedom is freedom of conscience would not make sense unless conscience were definitive of who we are. If we violated our consciences, we would cease to be who we are. Freedom of conscience is fundamental because we *are* our moral choices.

My typology in *Conscience and Its Critics* has placed equality on the side of conscience and inequality on the side of reason: we are equal in our moral choices and unequal in our capacity to calculate consequences. It places certitude and intolerant zeal on the side of conscience and tolerant scepticism or religious indifference on the side of reason. Conscience has tended to be the voice of plebeian intransigence, not the voice of patrician pragmatism. Conscience mandates the separation of church and state; reason suggests sceptical toleration under a latitudinarian but established church. Individuality and conscience are at one pole, sociality and reason at the other. Conscience is the exercise of our own judgment, reason is the conformity of our judgment to nonsubjective standards of truth and justice. Conscience prescribes for oneself, reason prescribes for others. Conscience is silent, reason is vocal. Lawlessness and dissent are characteristics of conscience, while lawfulness and conformity are definitive of reason. Reason conforms to the rules, conscience does not. Conscience dissents from the laws of market distribution, enlightened reason defers to them. Enlightenment thinkers had good reason to replace the dictates of conscience with the rule of public opinion. But Rousseau and Blake were not irrational in portraying Enlightenment reason as conscienceless.

We might ask whether the Enlightenment prejudice against the innateness and divinity of conscience is warranted. If conscience is nothing more than socially constructed habits, there seems little reason to endow it with respect or to encourage its exercise. If conscience is mere opinion, then support for conscience encourages wilfulness rather than reasonableness. Blake may have been wrong that there is a divine spark in us all, something irreducible to nature and habit, something distinct from empirical consciousness – that which we receive passively through the senses and reflect on in memory. But he may have been right to think that something like a Golden Rule informs our experience and actively shapes the moral experience that defines who we are. The Coleridgean priority of conscience over consciousness presents us with an activist conception of mind and a conception of self constituted by one's moral choices, rather than – as Mill had it – a self that is prior to and the cause of one's moral choices.

The fact that Mill acknowledged that his account of selfhood or personal identity was unsatisfactory permits us to question whether the phenomenon of conscience can be subject to naturalistic explanation, and is explicable – or explained away – in terms of upbringing, associational habituation, social approbation and disapprobation, and the like. Mill associated the idea of an innate and supernatural conscience with political and religious conservatism. If this association is unwarranted, as Chapters 1, 3, 8, and 9 have attempted to demonstrate, we have yet to demonstrate the opposite – namely, that the idea of an acquired conscience is politically and religiously conservative.

In *Conscience and Its Critics* I have suggested that the replacement of conscience by reason signified the rule of public opinion, not the authority of individual judgment. I have intimated that the idea of the mind as a *tabula rasa* necessarily entails a social division between an élite (enlightened educators, leaders of public opinion, taste makers) and those who follow its lead. Perhaps, however, there is room for untutored conscience (or the judgments of common men and women) within Enlightenment horizons, as there was in Hobbes' account of trial by jury. The ultimate question is whether the idea of an acquired conscience is compatible with self-transformation and self-definition. Perhaps the philosophic alternative to understanding the self as conscience is to understand the self as habit. Humean conservatism is a consistent rejection of conscience as an innate practical principle.

One might ask whether it really matters whether the capacity for moral choice is innate or acquired. The capacity for language is both innate and acquired; it develops in almost all humans but is acquired in a social setting. Linguistic capacity is not acquired the same way a taste for oysters or the ability to ride a bicycle is acquired. Such tastes and abilities presuppose training and the proximity of oysters and bicycles, and thus are not universal. If linguistic skill can be acquired, then there can be no objection to the notion of conscience being similarly acquired. Extraordinary proficiency can be learned, but ordinary proficiency does not have to be deliberately inculcated or artificially cultivated.

Perhaps the question whether conscience is God-given or socially constructed, innate or acquired, is less important than whether it is essential or accidental, definitive of our humanity or a contingent product of our social circumstances. Besides our capacity for reasoned speech, is there some other characteristic – our aesthetic taste, our susceptibility to pain and pleasure, our dreams and imagination – that more adequately defines who we are? If so, the dialectic of reason and conscience should be superseded, as Hume, Diderot, and Bentham devoutly wished, with a vocabulary of habit, taste, and benevolence. But if we insist on the sanctity and inviolability of our own moral choices, and sometimes assent to the constraint that our own judgments about what is right for ourselves be subject to universally binding rules, then the Universal Declaration of Human Rights is warranted in emphasizing the human endowments of reason and conscience as most definitive of our common humanity.

Paul Ricoeur indicates why the dialectic between reason and conscience must be ongoing. While he does not want to reduce conscience to public opinion, Ricoeur contends that 'the decision taken at the end of a debate with oneself, at the heart of what we may call our innermost forum, our heart of hearts, will be considered all the more worthy of being called *wise* if it issues from a council ... Wisdom in judging and the pronouncement of wise judgment must always involve more than one person.'[15] However, wise council is not groupie conformity; rather, it is the result of inner debate and then public discussion.

I have tried to show that referring to 'reason and conscience' is not a redundancy. Conscience and reason are not identical to each other. Indeed, Protestant conscience and Enlightenment reason may have different class backgrounds. If the snobbish contempt of enlightened reason for individual conscience is unwarranted, the resentment of untutored conscience for the privilege of learning is a barrier to an amicable relationship with reason. The ongoing tension between reason and conscience has been productive – of what human beings are.

Notes

Introduction

1 *Universal Declaration of Human Rights*, in Jack Donnelly and Rhoda E. Howard, eds., *International Handbook of Human Rights* (Westport: Greenwood, 1987), pp. 459–61.
2 C.S. Lewis, *Studies in Words* (Cambridge: Cambridge University Press, 1991), p. 191.
3 John Stuart Mill, *Collected Works*, ed. John Robson (Toronto: University of Toronto Press, 1969–1990), vol. 10, p. 231; cf. vol. 15, pp. 649–50.
4 J.B. Schneewind, *Moral Philosophy from Montaigne to Kant* (Cambridge: Cambridge University Press, 1990); J. B. Schneewind, *The Invention of Autonomy: A History of Modern Moral Philosophy* (Cambridge: Cambridge University Press, 1998); Thomas Hill, Jr, 'Four Conceptions of Conscience,' in Ian Shapiro and Robert Adams, eds., *Integrity and Conscience*, Nomos Series, XL (New York: New York University Press, 1998), pp. 13–52.
5 Philosophic accounts of Kantian autonomy are much more common than philosophic accounts of conscience. However, accounts such as Schneewind's *The Invention of Autonomy* and Thomas E. Hill, Jr's *Autonomy and Self-Respect* (Cambridge: Cambridge University Press, 1991) have tended to distance themselves from the transcendental basis of the Kantian moral law. Contemporary Mill scholars assert that Mill, despite his distaste for Kantian philosophy, espoused the Kantian value of autonomy but 'detranscendentalized' it – that is, espoused Kant without God, freedom, and immortality.
6 Gilbert Ryle, *Collected Papers* (Bristol: Thoemmes, 1990), vol. 2, p. 185.
7 Schneewind, *The Invention of Autonomy*, p. 8.

8 David Hume, *An Enquiry Concerning the Principles of Morals*, ed. Tom L. Beauchamp (Oxford: Clarendon, 1998), IX.i.3, p. 73.
9 Denis Diderot, *Le fils naturel*, in *Oeuvres Complètes* (Paris: Société encyclopédique français et le Club français du livre, 1969–73), t. 3, p. 89.

1: Christian Conscience and the Protestant Reformation

1 Herman Rauschning, *Hitler Speaks* (London: Thornton Butterworth, 1939), p. 220.
2 R.J. Zwi Werblowsky, 'The Concept of Conscience in Jewish Perspective,' trans. R.F.C. Hull, in Curatorium of the C.G. Jung Institute, *Conscience* (Evanston: Northwestern University Press, 1970), pp. 81–7.
3 Martin Heidegger, *Being and Time*, trans. J. Macquarrie and E. Robinson (New York: Harper and Row, 1962), p. 343.
4 Jean Calvin, *Seneca's de Clementia*, cited in David Lee Foxgrover, 'John Calvin's Understanding of Conscience' (PhD dissertation, Claremont Graduate School, 1978), pp. 244–5.
5 Jean-Jacques Rousseau, *Julie or the New Heloise*, trans. Philip Stewart and Jean Vaché, vol. 6 of *The Collected Writings of Rousseau*, ed. Roger Masters and Christopher Kelly (Hanover: University Press of New England, 1997), p. 215.
6 C.A. Pierce, *Conscience in the New Testament* (London: SCM Press, 1955), p. 107.
7 Ibid., pp. 118, 129.
8 Ibid., pp. 118–19.
9 Friedrich Nietzsche, *The Will to Power*, trans. Walter Kaufmann (New York: Viking, 1968), p. 185.
10 Martin Luther, *Works*, ed. Jaroslav Pelikan (St Louis: Concordia Publishing House, 1958), vol. 32, pp. 130, 112.
11 Jaroslav Pelikan, *Obedient Rebels: Catholic Substance and Protestant Principle in Luther's Reformation* (London: SCM Press, 1964), pp. 21, 33, 101.
12 Ibid., vol. 4, p. 50.
13 Luther, cited in David Lee Foxgrover, 'John Calvin's Understanding of Conscience' (PhD dissertation, Claremont Graduate School, 1978), p. 40; Luther, *Works*, vol. 9, p. 123; also vol. 16, p. 107; vol. 18, p. 374.
14 Luther, *Works*, vol. 26, p. 10; vol. 46, p. 17; vol. 30, p. 125.
15 Ibid., vol. 27, p. 345.
16 Timothy C. Potts, *Conscience in Medieval Philosophy* (Cambridge: Cambridge University Press, 1980), p. 61.

17 St Thomas More, *The Complete Works*, ed. John Headley, trans. Sister Scholastica Mandeville (New Haven: Yale University Press, 1969), vol. 5, p. 305.
18 Luther, *Works*, vol. 21, pp. 236–7.
19 Cited in Jaroslav Pelikan, *Spirit versus Structure: Luther and the Institutions of the Church* (London: Collins, 1968), p. 73.
20 Luther, *Works*, vol. 2, p. 222.
21 Josef Pieper, *The Four Cardinal Virtues* (Notre Dame: Notre Dame University Press, 1966), p. 12. See also Albert R. Jonsen and Stephen Toulmin, *The Abuse of Casuistry: A History of Moral Reasoning* (Berkeley: University of California Press, 1988), p. 130.
22 St Thomas Aquinas, *The Summa Theologica*, trans. Fathers of the English Dominican Province (New York: Benzinger Bros., 1938), vol. 10, 2a2ae.2.
23 Pieper, *Four Cardinal Virtues*, p. 40.
24 Aquinas, *Summa Theologica*, vol. 4, 1.79.13; 1.79.12; Jonsen and Toulmin, *The Abuse of Casuistry*, p. 129.
25 Michael G. Baylor, *Action and Person: Conscience in Late Scholasticism and the Young Luther* (Leiden: E. J. Brill, 1977), p. 54; Jonsen and Toulmin, *The Abuse of Casuistry*, pp. 128–9.
26 Baylor, *Action and Person*, p. 190. Guenter Virt writes that St Thomas misconstrued *syneidesis* as *synderesis* from copying a mistake in Hieronymus's *Commentary on Ezekiel*; see 'Conscience in Conflict?' in *Conscience: An Interdisciplinary View* (Dordrecht: D. Reidel, 1987), p. 170. However, *synderesis* might simply have been a transcription of the Greek *synteresis*.
27 Harold J. Berman, *Law and Revolution: The Formation of the Western Legal Tradition* (Cambridge: Harvard University Press, 1983), p. 30.
28 Gordon J. Schochet, 'Why Should History Matter? Political Theory and the History of Discourse,' in J.G.A. Pocock, G.J. Schochet, and L.G. Schwoerer, eds., *The Varieties of British Political Thought, 1500–1800* (Cambridge: Cambridge University Press, 1993), p. 340.
29 Luther, *Works*, vol. 44, pp. 245–310.
30 Martin Luther, *Lectures on Romans*, trans. and ed. Wilhelm Pauck (London: SCM Press, 1961), p. 394.
31 Luther, *Works*, vol. 31, p. 372; vol. 3, p. 326; vol. 4, p. 323; vol. 22, p. 441; vol. 27, p. 13; vol. 44, pp. 235–42. vol. 44, p. 242.
32 Ibid., vol. 17, p. 189.
33 Ibid., p. 207; vol. 24, pp. 101–2.
34 Ibid., vol. 34, p. 323; vol. 22, pp. 225–6; vol. 21, p. 150.

35 Ibid., vol. 33, pp. 52–6.
36 Gerald Strauss, '"Barrabas": Luther as Barrabas,' in Peter Newman Brooks, ed., *Seven-Headed Luther: Essays in Commemoration of a Quincentenary 1483–1983* (Oxford: Clarendon, 1983), p.172.
37 Ibid., vol. 30, p. 80.
38 Ibid., vol. 29, p. 73.
39 Ibid., vol. 21, p. 47.
40 Ibid., vol. 45, p. 84.
41 Ibid., vol. 10, p. 32.
42 Ibid., vol. 46, p. 318.
43 Ibid., vol. 6, pp. 298–300; vol. 54, pp. 24–5.
44 Strauss, '"Barrabas,"' p. 175.
45 Lynda Roper, *Oedipus and the Devil: Witchcraft, Sexuality and Religion in Early Modern Europe* (London: Routledge, 1995), chap. 4; Christian Pearson, SSF, 'Line upon Line: Here a Little, There a Little: Some Letters of Martin Luther,' in Brooks, *Seven-Headed Luther*, pp. 297–301.
46 Luther, *Works*, vol. 35, p. 72.
47 Erik Erikson, *Young Man Luther* (London: Faber and Faber, 1958), p. 225.
48 David Warren Sabean, *Power in the Blood: Popular Culture and Village Discourse in Early Modern Germany* (Cambridge: Cambridge University Press, 1984), pp. 35, 173.
49 Georgia B. Christopher, *Milton and the Science of the Saints* (Princeton: Princeton University Press, 1982), p. 44.
50 Luther, *Works*, vol. 21, p. 349.
51 Christopher Hill, *The English Bible and the Seventeenth-Century Revolution* (London: Allen Lane, 1993), p. 416.
52 John Calvin, *Institutes of the Christian Religion*, trans. John Allen (London: James Clark & Co., 1935). vol. 2, p. 635; IV.xx.1–2.
53 *Calvini Opera*, vol. 49, p. 433; cited in Foxgrover, 'John Calvin's Understanding of Conscience,' p. 41.
54 Calvin, *Institutes*, vol. 2, p. 63; III.xix.2.
55 Ibid., p. 75; III.xix.16.
56 Ibid., p. 73; III.xix.14.
57 Christopher Morris, *Political Thought in England: Tyndale to Hooker* (London: Oxford University Press, 1965), p. 155.
58 Calvin, *Institutes*, vol. 2, p. 661; IV.xx.31.
59 Ibid., p. 75; III.xix.15; also, p. 368; IV.x.3.
60 Ibid., p. 75; III.xix. 15.
61 Calvin on 1 Corinthians, cited in Foxgrover, 'John Calvin's Understanding of Conscience,' p. 349.

Notes to pages 25–8   195

62 Calvin, *Institutes*, vol. 2, p. 367; IV.x.3.
63 Ibid., p. 649; IV.xx.16.
64 Ibid., p. 650; IV.xx.16.
65 William Tyndale, *The Obedience of a Christian Man* (Menston: Scolar Press, 1970), p. 153. The spelling has been modernized.
66 William Tyndale, *The Works*, ed. S.L. Greenslade (Glasgow: Blackie, 1938), p. 212.
67 Cited in Hill, *The English Bible*, p. 51.
68 More, *The Complete Works*, vol. 6, pp. 288–92.
69 Stephen Greenblatt, *Renaissance Self-Fashioning: From More to Shakespeare* (Chicago: University of Chicago Press, 1980), p. 80.
70 More, *Complete Works*, vol. 6, p. 405.
71 Christopher Hill, *Liberty against the Law: Some Seventeenth-Century Controversies* (London: Allen Lane, 1996), p. 181.
72 John Milton, *The Poems*, ed. H. Darbeshire (Oxford: Oxford University Press, 1961), p. 71.
73 Mou, *Complete Works*, vol. 4, pp. 221, 231.
74 Rudolf B. Gottfried, *A Conscience Undeflowered: A Lecture on Thomas More* (Lunenburg: Stinehour Press, 1957), p. 23.
75 John Fox, *The Book of the Martyrs* (London: The Book Society, 1931), p. 247.
76 William Baldwin, *A Treatise of Morall Philosophie* (1547), enlarged by Thomas Palfreyman 1640, reproduced (Gainesville: Scholars' Facsimiles & Reprints, 1967), p. 140; ix.2.
77 Elliot Rose, *Cases of Conscience* (Cambridge: Cambridge University Press, 1975), pp. 11–13.
78 John Knox, *The First Blast of the Trumpet against the Monstrous Regiment of Women* (1558), 1608, 8b, 56b.
79 *The Political Works of James I*, reprinted from 1616 edition, ed. Charles H. McIlwain (Cambridge: Harvard University Press, 1918), xi.
80 Cited in Christopher Morris, *Political Thought in England: Tyndale to Hooker* (London: Oxford University Press, 1965), p. 118.
81 Peter Lake, *Anglicans and Puritans? Presbyterianism and English Conformist Thought from Whitgift to Hooker* (London: Unwin Hyman, 1988), p. 154.
82 Robert R. Orr, *Reason and Authority: The Thought of William Chillingworth* (Oxford: Clarendon, 1967), p. 70.
83 William Perkins, *The Whole Treatise of the Cases of Conscience, Distinguished Into Three Books* (Cambridge: John Legat, 1606), I.iii.1.
84 Ibid., epistle dedicatory.
85 Ibid., II.xiv.5.

86 William Perkins, *The Work*, ed. Ian Breward (Abington: Appleford, 1970), p. 504.
87 Perkins, *Whole Treatise*, I.v.4.
88 William Ames, *Conscience with the Power and Cases Thereof* (n.p., 1639), I.i.1.
89 Ibid., I.iv.6; I.xiii.6.
90 Ibid., IV.iv.15.
91 Ibid., V.xxxiii.17.
92 Ibid., V.li–liv.
93 Robert Sanderson, *The Works in Six Volumes*, ed. W. Jacobson (Oxford: Oxford University Press, 1854), vol. 2, p. 127.
94 *Bishop Sanderson's Lectures on Conscience and Human Law* (1647), ed. and trans. C. Wordsworth (Lincoln: James Williamson, 1877), p. 23.
95 Ibid., p. 30.
96 Ibid., p. 26.
97 Jeremy Taylor, *Ductor Dubitantium, or The Rule of Conscience in all her General Measures: Serving as a great Instrument for the determination of Cases of Conscience* (London: Norton, 1676), I.i.3.5.
98 Ibid., I.ii.9.11–13.
99 Ibid., I.i.26.
100 Ames, *Conscience*, I.ix.3.
101 Pierre Bayle, *A Philosophic Commentary on These Words of the Gospel, Luke XIV, 23, Compel them to come in, that my House may be full* (1686), trans. John Fox (London: J. Darby, 1708), p. 272.
102 Jordan, *Development of Religious Toleration*, vol. 1, pp. 104, 169, 239.
103 Rose, *Cases of Conscience*, chap. 8.
104 Edmund Leites, 'Casuistry and Character,' in E. Leites ed., *Conscience and Casuistry in Early Modern Europe* (Cambridge: Cambridge University Press, 1988), p. 129.
105 Cited in Christopher Hill, *The World Turned Upside Down* (Harmondsworth: Penguin, 1984), p. 257.
106 Mary Carey, *A Word in Season to the Kingdom of England* (London: Giles Calvert, 1647), Thomason Tract E393, p. 5, 9; *New Jerusalem's Glory* (London 1651), Thomason Tract E1274, p. 238.
107 Cited in Perez Zagorin, *A History of Political Thought in the English Revolution* (London: Routledge and Kegan Paul, 1954), p. 37.
108 Cited in Hill, *Liberty against the Law*, p. 219.
109 Laurence Clarkson, *A Single Eye* (London, 1650), Thomason Tract E614, pp. A2, 9, 12.
110 Cited in Christopher Hill, *Milton and the English Revolution* (London: Faber & Faber, 1979), p. 476.

111 Pierre Bayle, *A General Dictionary* (London: James Bettenham, 1734–41), vol. 6, pp. 554–5.

2: Conscience Makes Cowards of Us All

1 Horace Howard Furness, *The Varorium Shakespeare* (Philadelphia: Lippincott, 1908), vol. 16, pp. 132–4.
2 Ibid., p. 415.
3 Johann Wolfgang von Goethe, *Maxims and Reflections*, trans. Thomas Bailey Saunders (London: Macmillan, 1908), p. 87.
4 See Michel de Montaigne, *The Essays*, trans. and ed. Jacob Zeitlin (New York: Alfred Knopf, 1934), vol. 1, chap. 14, 'That the taste of good and evil depends in a great measure upon the opinions we have of them.' The connection between Hamlet's subjectivism and Montaigne's is discussed in Robert F. Fleissner, *The Prince and the Professor: The Wittenberg Connection in Marlowe, Shakespeare, Goethe, and Frost* (Heidelberg: Carl Winter, 1986), p. 17; also pp. 20, 109–11. Scholars have not ascertained whether Shakespeare had read Montaigne's *Essays* in French or in Florio's translation, but similarities in outlook and expression are notable. Hiram Haydn, in *The Counter-Renaissance* (New York: Charles Scribner's Sons, 1950, p. 667), referred to the resemblance between Montaigne and Shakespeare, rather than to the influence of the former on the latter, in their 'essential philosophic conservatism, and perhaps in temper and outlook.' Serena Jourdan, in *The Sparrow and the Flea: The Sense of Providence in Shakespeare and Montaigne* (Salzburg: Institut für Anglistik und Amerikanistik, 1983), also emphasizes similarity in themes – nature, death, and conscience – rather than influence. Warren Boutcher, in Florio's Montaigne: Translation and Pragmatic Humanism in the Sixteenth Century' (PhD thesis, University of Cambridge, 1991), p. 248, questions the view that Montaigne 'challenged all orthodoxies and opened up a post-humanist, sceptical crisis in the mind' of Shakespeare.
5 Zeitlin, introduction to Montaigne, *Essays*, xc.
6 Pierre Bayle, *The Dictionary Historical and Critical of Mr. Peter Bayle*, 2nd edition, trans. Pierre des Maizeaux (London: Bettenham, 1734), vol. 4, p. 188.
7 Terry Eagleton, *William Shakespeare* (Oxford: Basil Blackwell, 1986), p. 72.
8 Hidekatsu Nojima, 'The Mirror of Hamlet,' in Yoshiko Ueno, *Hamlet in Japan* (New York: AMS Press, 1995), p. 29.
9 Stephen Greenblatt, *Shakespearean Negotiations: The Circulation of Social Energy in Renaissance England* (Berkeley: University of California Press, 1988), p. 54.

10 Voltaire, *Lettres philosophiques*, ed. Gustave Lanson (Paris: Edouard Cornély, 1909), vol. 2, p. 82.
11 Sigmund Freud, *New Introductory Lectures on Psychoanalysis and Other Works*, trans. James Strachey (London: Hogarth Press, 1964), p. 61.
12 Sigmund Freud, *The Origins of Psycho-Analysis: Letters to Wilhelm Fleiss, Drafts and Notes: 1887–1902*, ed. Marie Bonaparte, Anna Freud, and Ernst Kris, trans. Eric Mosbacher and James Strachey (London: Imago, 1954), p. 224; also *The Interpretation of Dreams* (London: George Allen and Unwin, 1982), pp. 264–5.
13 C.S. Lewis, *Studies in Words* (Cambridge: Cambridge University Press, 1991), p. 207.
14 Martin Luther, *Works*, ed. Jaroslav Pelikan (St Louis: Concordia Publishing House, 1958), vol. 32, p. 112.
15 William Perkins, *The Whole Treatise of the Cases of Conscience* (Cambridge: John Legat, 1606), 1.3.1.
16 J. Dover Wilson, *What Happens in Hamlet* (Cambridge: Cambridge University Press, 1951), p. 164.
17 Eleanor Prosser, *Hamlet and Revenge* (Stanford: Stanford University Press, 1971), p.102; Peter Mercer, *Hamlet and the Acting of Revenge* (London: Macmillan, 1967), p. 136; Fleissner, *The Prince and the Professor*, pp. 21–2.
18 Roland Mushat Frye, *Shakespeare and Christian Doctrine* (Princeton: University Press, 1963), p. 161; Mark Matheson, 'Hamlet and "A Matter Tender and Dangerous,"' *Shakespeare Quarterly* 46 (1995): 391.
19 Luther, *Works*, vol. 9, p. 129.
20 Andrew Cecil Bradley, *Shakespearean Tragedy* (London: Macmillan, 1904), p. 98.
21 Catherine Belsey, 'The Case of Hamlet's Conscience,' *Studies in Philology* 76 (1979): 127.
22 Eleanor Prosser, *Hamlet and Revenge* (Stanford: Stanford University Press, 1971), p. 169.
23 Haydn, *Counter-Renaissance*, p. 622.
24 John Valdesso, *Divine Considerations* (Cambridge: Roger Daniel, 1646), pp. 190–1. (First English translation was 1638.)
25 Michel de Montaigne, *The Essays*, trans. and ed. Jacob Zeitlin (New York: Alfred Knopf, 1934), vol. 3, chap. 12, pp. 260–1.
26 Ibid., vol. 2, chap. 16, p. 295.
27 Ibid., vol.3, chap. 2, p. 19.
28 Ibid., vol. 1, chap. 24, p. 112.
29 Josef Pieper, *The Four Cardinal Virtues* (Notre Dame: University of Notre Dame Press, 1966), pp. 10–11.

30 Ibid., p. 40.
31 See Israel Gollanz, *The Sources of Hamlet* (London: Oxford University Press, 1926). Shakespeare's *Hamlet* follows the plot of Saxo Grammaticus (and Francois de Belleforest's *History of Hamblet*, which also closely follows Saxo Grammaticus) until the time of the sea voyage to England.
32 Wilson, *What Happens in Hamlet*, pp. 39–44; Roland Mushat Frye, *The Renaissance Hamlet: Issues and Response in 1600* (Princeton: University Press, 1984), pp. 77–81.
33 Naoya Shiga's *The Diary of Claudius* suggests that Claudius is Hamlet's father. See Hiroshi Izubuchi, 'A Hamlet of Our Own: Some Japanese Adaptations,' in Uéno, *Hamlet in Japan*, p. 189.
34 Prosser, *Hamlet and Revenge*, p. 126; the most sustained reflection on Hamlet's age is in V. Oesterberg, *Prince Hamlet's Age* (Koebenhavn: A.F. Fhoest, 1924), who concludes (pp. 48–51) that Hamlet was a boy.
35 Howard Horace Furness, ed., *The Varorium Shakespeare*, William Shakespeare, *Hamlet* (Philadelphia: Lippincott, 1918), vol. 2, p. 80.
36 Bradley, *Shakespearean Tragedy*, p. 118.
37 Albert R. Jonsen and Stephen Toulmin, *The Abuse of Casuistry: A History of Moral Reasoning* (Berkeley: University of California Press, 1988), p. 165.
38 Frye, *The Renaissance Hamlet*, p. 47.
39 Yasumari Takahashi, 'Hamlet and the Anxiety of Modern Japan,' *Shakespeare Survey* 48 (1995): 101–2.
40 Francis Bacon, *Essays*, ed. J.M. Mitchell (London: Macmillan, 1959), p. 11.
41 Mercer, *Hamlet and the Acting of Revenge*, p. 137.
42 Julia Reinhard Lupton and Kenneth Reinhard, in *After Oedipus: Shakespeare in Psychoanalysis* (Ithaca: Cornell University Press, 1993), pp. 75–6, refer to a ghostly '"phallophany", the nauseating emergence of the nonsymbolized phallus from behind the veils of signification in the field of the (m)Other's demand.'
43 Gollanz, *Sources of Hamlet*, pp. 141, 263–83.
44 Ibid., pp. 68, 169, 195–7.
45 Montaigne, *Essays*, vol. 2, chap. 36, p. 407.
46 Jourdan, *The Sparrow and the Flea*, p. 141.

3: Conscience Makes Heroes of Us All

1 John Dryden, *The Poems*, ed. John Sargeaunt (London: Oxford University Press, 1910), preface to *The Hind and the Panther*, p. 117.
2 Ibid., p. 123; I.470–80.
3 Samuel Butler, *Hudibras* (London: J. Walker, 1817), p. 140; II.ii.299–302.

4 A.L. Rowse, *Milton the Puritan* (London: Macmillan, 1977), p. 101.
5 Gordon Rupp, 'Luther against "The Turk, The Pope And The Devil,"' in Peter Newman Brooks, ed., *Seven-Headed Luther: Essays in Commemoration of a Quincentenary 1483–1983* (Oxford: Clarendon, 1983), p. 273.
6 John Knox, *The First Blast of the Trumpet against the Monstrous Regiment of Women* (1558), 1608, p. 8b.
7 Thomas Dekker, *The Dramatic Works*, ed. Fredson Bowers (Cambridge: Cambridge University Press, 1958), vol. 3, p. 179.
8 Cited in Roy Porter, 'The Enlightenment in England,' in R. Porter and M. Teich, eds., *The Enlightenment in National Context* (Cambridge: Cambridge University Press, 1981), p. 15.
9 Northrop Frye, *Five Essays on Milton's Epic* (London: Routledge and Kegan Paul, 1966), p. 90.
10 John Milton, *Complete Prose Works* (New Haven: Yale University Press, 1953–82), vol. 6, p. 537.
11 Ibid., vol. 3, pp. 343, 321.
12 Ibid., vol. 7, p. 243.
13 Frye, *Five Essays*, p. 91.
14 Milton, *Complete Prose Works*, vol. 7, pp. 247–8.
15 Ibid., vol. 3, p. 297.
16 Ibid., vol. 7, p. 267.
17 Ibid., vol. 3, p. 297.
18 John Milton, *The Poems*, ed. H. Darbishire (Oxford: Oxford University Press, 1961), p. 171.
19 Immanuel Kant, *Foundation of the Metaphysics of Morals and What Is Enlightenment?*, trans. Lewis White Beck (Chicago: University of Chicago Press, 1950), pp. 287, 291; Jeremy Bentham, *A Fragment on Government*, ed. J.H. Burns and H.L.A. Hart (Cambridge: Cambridge University Press, 1988), p. 10.
20 Denis Diderot, *Political Writings*, trans. John Hope Mason and Robert Wokler (Cambridge: Cambridge University Press, 1992), p. 74.
21 John Milton, *Areopagitica* in *The Prose of John Milton*, ed. J. Max Patrick (New York: New York University Press, 1968), p. 329.
22 Karl Marx and Friedrich Engels, *Manifesto of the Communist Party*, in *Selected Works* (Moscow: Progress Publishers, 1968), p. 51.
23 Milton, *Complete Prose Works*, vol. 2, p. 535.
24 Ibid., pp. 563, 493, 565.
25 Ibid., vol. 3, p. 369.
26 Ibid., vol. 7, p. 249.
27 Ibid., vol. 6, p. 587.

28 Ibid., p. 583.
29 Samuel Rutherford, *A Free Disputation against pretended Liberty of Conscience* (London: Andrew Crook, 1649), ii.
30 Ibid., pp. 132, 323–27.
31 Jackie Disalvo, *War of Titans: Blake's Critique of Milton and the Politics of Religion* (Pittsburgh: University of Pittsburgh Press, 1983), p. 287.
32 Milton, *Complete Prose Works*, vol. 4, p. 636.
33 Christopher Hill, *Milton and the English Revolution* (London: Faber and Faber, 1979), p. 249.
34 Milton, *Complete Prose Works*, vol. 7, pp. 260–1.
35 Ibid., vol. 4, p. 382.
36 Ibid., vol. 3, pp. 320, 322, 343.
37 John Locke, *Two Treatises of Government*, ed. Peter Laslett (Cambridge: Cambridge University Press, 1988), II.78–81.
38 Milton, *Complete Prose Works*, vol. 2, pp. 306–7, 337; vol. 6, p. 366.
39 Ibid., vol. 2, pp. 246–7, 269, 273, 306–7, 673; vol. 6, p. 381.
40 Ibid., vol. 6, p. 373.
41 Rowse, *Milton the Puritan*, p. 20; C.S. Lewis' judgment, and argument to support it, may be found in Edward LeComte, *Milton and Sex* (London: Macmillan, 1978).
42 Ibid., vol. 2, pp. 247, 258.
43 Ibid., vol. 6, pp. 356–70.
44 Charles R. Geisst, *The Political Thought of Milton* (London: Macmillan, 1984), pp. 35–6.
45 Milton, *Complete Prose Works*, vol. 3, pp. 259–334; vol. 7, pp. 248–9, 253; vol. 8, pp. 429–30.
46 Christopher Hill, *Milton and the English Revolution* (London: Faber and Faber, 1979), p. 153.
47 Ibid., pp. 306–7.
48 Milton, *Complete Prose Works*, vol. 3, pp. 479, 497, 597.
49 Ibid., vol. 7, p. 253.
50 Ibid., p. 292.
51 Ibid., vol. 8, p. 432.
52 Ibid., vol. 7, pp. 420–1.
53 Perez Zagorin, *Milton: Aristocrat and Rebel; The Poet and His Politics* (Woodbridge: D.S. Brewer, 1992), p. 106.
54 Hill, *Milton and the English Revolution*, p. 156.
55 Michael Walzer, *The Revolution of the Saints: A Study in the Origins of Radical Politics* (London: Weidenfeld and Nicolson, 1966), pp. 12, 21.
56 Milton, *Complete Prose Works*, vol. 3, p. 198.

202   Notes to pages 61-6

57 Ibid., vol. 4, p. 338.
58 Thomas Hobbes, *The English Works*, ed. W. Molesworth (London: J. Bohn, 1840), vol. 6, p. 368.
59 Milton, *The Poems*, vol. 1, p. 65.
60 Michel de Montaigne, *The Essays*, trans. and ed. Jacob Zeitlin (New York: Alfred Knopf, 1934), vol. 1, chap. 27, p. 161.

4: Hobbes on Conscience outside and inside the Law

1 W.K. Jordan, *The Development of Religious Toleration in England* (Gloucester: Peter Smith, 1965), vol. 1, pp. 17–18; Gordon J. Schochet, 'John Locke and Religious Toleration,' in Lois G. Schwoerer, ed., *The Revolution of 1688–1689: Changing Perspectives* (Cambridge: Cambridge University Press, 1992), p. 150.
2 Immanuel Kant, *Foundation of the Metaphysics of Morals and What Is Enlightenment?*, trans. Lewis White Beck (Chicago: University of Chicago Press, 1950), p. 291.
3 Ibid., p. 257.
4 Jean Bodin, *The Six Bookes of a Commonweale*, facsimile reprint of 1606 translation by Richard Knolles, ed. Kenneth D. McCrae (Cambridge: Harvard University Press, 1962), III.iii, pp. 299–300.
5 Ibid., I.viii, pp. 90–106.
6 Ibid., IV.vii, pp. 535–9.
7 Michel de Montaigne, *The Essays*, trans. and ed. Jacob Zeitlin (New York: Alfred Knopf, 1934), vol. 1, chap. 56, pp. 277–81.
8 Peter Burke, *Montaigne* (Oxford: Oxford University Press, 1981), p. 22.
9 Voltaire, *Oeuvres Complètes* (Paris: Garnier, 1879), vol. 20, p. 518.
10 See Isaac Kramnick, *The Portable Enlightenment Reader* (Harmondsworth: Penguin, 1995), and Stuart Brown, *British Philosophy and the Age of Enlightenment* (London: Routledge, 1996).
11 Norman Hampson, *The Enlightenment* (Harmondsworth: Penguin, 1968), p. 29.
12 Voltaire, *La Voix du sage et du peuple* (Amsterdam, 1750), p. 8.
13 R.E. Ewin, *Virtues and Rights: The Moral Philosophy of Thomas Hobbes* (Boulder: Westview, 1991), pp. 5, 46–8, 201–4.
14 J.W. Allen, *English Political Thought 1603–1644* (London: Methuen, 1938), p. 367.
15 Benjamin Whichcote, *Moral and Religious Aphorisms*, no. 60, cited in Jordan, *Development of Religious Toleration*, vol. 4, p. 102.

16 William Godwin, *History of the Commonwealth of England from Its Commencement, to the Restoration of Charles the Second* (London: Henry Colburn, 1824), vol. 1, p. 91.
17 Mark Whitaker, 'Hobbes's View of the Reformation,' *History of Political Thought* 9 (1988), 51.
18 Margaret Samson, '"Will You Hear What a Casuist He Is?": Thomas Hobbes as Director of Conscience,' *History of Political Thought* 11 (1990), 727–9.
19 Joseph Cropsey, introduction to Thomas Hobbes, *A Dialogue between a Philosopher and a Student of the Common Laws of England* (Chicago: University of Chicago Press, 1971), pp. 25–6.
20 Hobbes, *The English Works*, ed. W. Molesworth (London: J. Bohn, 1840), vol. 6, p. 190.
21 Ibid., vol. 7, pp. 225–6.
22 John Dunn, 'The Claim to Freedom of Conscience: Freedom of Speech, Freedom of Thought, Freedom of Worship?' in O.P. Grell, J.I. Israel, and N. Tyacke, eds., *From Persecution to Toleration: The Glorious Revolution and Reason in England* (Oxford: Clarendon Press, 1991), p. 176.
23 Richard Tuck, *Hobbes* (Oxford: University Press, 1989), p. 49.
24 See James R. Stoner, Jr, *Common Law and Liberal Theory: Coke, Hobbes and the Origins of American Constitutionalism* (Lawrence: University of Kansas Press, 1992), p. 48; Cropsey, ed., *A Dialogue between a Philosopher and a Student*, pp. 25–6, 72.
25 Thomas Hobbes, *Leviathan*, ed. M. Oakeshott (New York: Collier, 1968), chap. 7, p. 41.
26 Ibid.
27 Jordan, *Development of Religious Toleration*, vol. 4, p. 307.
28 Benedict de Spinoza, *Tractatus Theologico-Politicus*, chap. 14, in A.G. Wernham, trans. and ed., *The Political Works* (Oxford: Clarendon, 1958), p. 111.
29 Hobbes, *English Works*, vol. 4, p. 188.
30 Jordan, *Development of Religious Toleration*, vol. 4, p. 307.
31 Hobbes, *English Works*, vol. 4, p. 30.
32 Hobbes, *Leviathan*, chap 29, pp. 211–12.
33 Ibid., chap. 30, p. 224.
34 Ibid., chap. 46, p. 448.
35 Montaigne, *Essays*, vol. 1, chap. 5, p. 31.
36 Hobbes, *Leviathan*, chap. 14, p. 92.
37 Ibid.

38 Ibid., chap. 28, p. 206.
39 John Langbein, *Torture and the Law of Proof* (Chicago: University of Chicago Press, 1977), pp. 3–4, 73.
40 David P. Bien, *The Calas Affair: Persecution, Toleration, and Heresy in Eighteenth Century Toulouse* (Princeton: Princeton University Press, 1960), p. 82.
41 Hobbes, *Leviathan*, chap. 28, p. 203.
42 Ibid., p. 204.
43 Ibid., chap. 21, p. 144.
44 Ibid.
45 Ibid., chap. 23, p. 158.
46 Ibid.
47 Ibid., p. 159.
48 Hobbes, *English Works*, vol. 6, p. 65; Hobbes, *Leviathan*, chap. 23, p. 159.
49 Hobbes, *English Works*, vol. 6, p. 61.
50 Ibid., p. 77.
51 Ibid., p. 118.
52 Ibid., p. 95.
53 Ibid., chap. 26, p. 184.
54 Ibid.
55 James C. Cockburn, *A History of English Assizes 1558–1714* (Cambridge: University Press, 1972), p. 123.
56 Thomas A. Green, *Verdict According to Conscience* (Chicago, University of Chicago Press, 1985), pp. 153–75.
57 Thomas A. Green, 'The English Criminal Trial Jury and the Law-Finding Traditions,' in J.S. Cockburn and T.A. Green, eds., *Twelve Good Men and True: The Criminal Trial Jury in England* (Princeton: Princeton University Press, 1988), pp. 48–9.
58 Cockburn, *English Assizes*, p. 127.
59 Hobbes, Dialogue, in *English Works*, vol. 6, pp. 138–40.
60 Hobbes, *Leviathan*, chap. 30, p. 220.
61 Stephen Holmes, 'Political Psychology in Hobbes's *Behemoth*,' in M.G. Dietz, ed., *Thomas Hobbes and Political Theory* (Lawrence: University of Kansas, 1990), p. 140.
62 Hobbes, *Leviathan*, chap. 30, p. 227.
63 Hobbes, *English Works*, vol. 6, p. 227.
64 John Locke, *The Works* (London: Thomas Tegg, 1823), vol. 6, pp. 358, 362, 532.
65 R.E. Ewin, in *Virtues and Rights: The Moral Philosophy of Thomas Hobbes* (Boulder: Westview Press, 1991), distinguishes Hobbesian toleration from liberty of conscience, defends Hobbes's view that conscience should not

be understood as opposed to law, and supports 'a proper distinction' between conscience and private conscience. Ewen does not, however, relate Hobbesian conscience to the rights of defendants and jurors. James R. Stoner, Jr, in *Common Law and Liberal Theory*, pp. 109–22, discusses Hobbes's support for trial by jury but does not relate jury verdicts to the question of conscience. Thomas Green, in *Verdict According to Conscience*, relates conscience to jury verdicts but does not discuss Hobbes.

66 William Walwin, *Juries Justified: or A WORD of CORRECTION to Mr. Henry Robinson; for His seven Objections against Trial of Causes, by Juries of twelve men* (London: Robert Wood, 1651), pp. 4, 8.

5: Enlightened Reason versus Protestant Conscience in John Locke

1 Hans Arsleff, 'Locke's Influence,' in Vere Chappell, ed., *The Cambridge Companion to Locke* (Cambridge: Cambridge University Press, 1994), p. 252.
2 Benjamin Franklin, *The Writings*, ed. Albert Henry Smyth (New York: Macmillan, 1907), vol. 10, p. 148.
3 Nathan Tarkov, *Locke's Education for Liberty* (Chicago: University of Chicago Press, 1984), p. 1; David Wootton, ed., *John Locke: Political Writings* (London: Penguin, 1993), p. 9.
4 Wootton, *John Locke: Political Writings*, pp. 110–19.
5 Ibid., pp. 111–12.
6 Cited in Stephen Darwall, *The British Moralist and the Internal 'Ought': 1640–1740* (Cambridge: Cambridge University Press, 1995), p. 177.
7 John Locke, *An Essay concerning Human Understanding* (London: Thomas Bassett, 1690), II.xxvii.7, p. 158.
8 Ibid., II.xxvii.10, p. 158.
9 Ibid., II.xxvii.12, p. 159.
10 Wootton, ed., *John Locke: Political Writings*, p. 232.
11 Peter Gay, ed., *John Locke on Education* (New York: Columbia University Press, 1964), p. 36.
12 Locke, *Essay*, II.xxvii.12, pp. 159–60.
13 John Locke, *The Educational Writings*, ed. J.L. Axtell (Cambridge: Cambridge University Press, 1968), p. 325.
14 J.G.A. Pocock, 'Post-Puritan England and the Problem of the Enlightenment,' in Perez Zagorin, ed., *Culture and Politics from Puritanism to the Enlightenment* (Berkeley: University of California Press, 1980), p. 106; Roy Porter, 'The Enlightenment in England,' in R. Porter and M. Teich, eds., *The Enlightenment in National Context* (Cambridge: Cambridge University Press, 1981), p. 5.

15 Knud Haakonssen, 'Enlightened Dissent,' in K. Haakonssen ed., *Rational Dissent in Eighteenth-Century Britain* (Cambridge: Cambridge University Press, 1996), p. 3.
16 Gilbert Ryle, *Collected Papers* (Bristol: Thoemmes, 1990), vol. 1, p. 147.
17 Neal Wood, *The Politics of Locke's Philosophy: A Social Study of 'An Essay concerning Human Understanding'* (Berkeley: University of California Press, 1983), p. 140.
18 James Tully, *An Approach to Political Philosophy: Locke in Contexts* (Cambridge: Cambridge University Press, 1993), p. 53.
19 Ralph Cudworth, *The True Intellectual System of the Universe* (London: Richard Royston, 1678). Cudworth's influence on Locke is discussed in Stephen Darwall, *The British Moralists and the Internal 'Ought': 1640–1740* (Cambridge: Cambridge University Press, 1995), chaps. 5–6, although Darwall does not discuss Cudworth's invention of the word 'consciousness,' hitherto contained within the word 'conscience,' and the influence of the differentiation of consciousness and conscience on Locke.
20 Catherine Glyn Davies, *Conscience as Consciousness: The Idea of Self-Awareness in French Philosophic Writing from Descartes to Diderot* (Oxford: The Voltaire Society, 1990), chap. 2.
21 Ibid., p. 29.
22 Ibid., pp. 44, 50.
23 Denis Diderot et Jean D'Alembert, *L'Encyclopédie ou Dictionaire raisonné des sciences, des arts et des métiers (1751)* (New York: Readex Microprint Corporation, 1969), t. 3, p. 902.
24 Wayne Glausser, 'Three Approaches to Locke and the Slave Trade,' *Journal of the History of Ideas* 21 (1990): 212.
25 Cited in John Marshall, *John Locke: Resistance, Religion and Responsibility* (Cambridge: Cambridge University Press, 1994), p. 443.
26 John Locke, *The Reasonableness of Christianity* (London: George Virtue, 1836), sect. 174, p. 197; sect. 175, p. 201; sect. 174, p. 199.
27 John Locke, *The Works* (London: Thomas Tegg, 1823), vol. 6, pp. 358, 362, 532.
28 Ibid., p. 257.
29 Ibid., p. 44.
30 Michael S. Rabieh, 'The Reasonableness of Locke, or the Questionableness of Christianity,' *The Journal of Politics* 53 (1991): 955.
31 Marshall, *John Locke*, p. 197.
32 Wootton, *John Locke: Political Writings*, p. 145.
33 Ibid., pp. 153, 165, 174.
34 Ibid., p. 186.

35 Ibid., p. 199.
36 Ibid., pp. 197, 201.
37 Ibid., p. 202.
38 Ibid., pp. 204, 232, 198.
39 Ibid., p. 203.
40 Ibid., pp. 203–4.
41 Locke, *Works*, vol. 6, p. 472.
42 Wootton, *John Locke: Political Writings*, p. 434.
43 Ibid., p. 427.
44 Ibid., p. 410.
45 *A Letter to a Member of Parliament for Liberty of Conscience, By a Person of Honour* (London: Richard Baldwin, 1689), p. 4.
46 Cited in James E. Ernst, *The Political Thought of Roger Williams* (Seattle: University of Washington Press, 1979), p. 188.
47 Richard Hubberthorn, Samuel Fisher, and Francis Howgill, *Persecution Inconsistent with Christianity, Humane Society, and the Honour of Princes* (London, 1670), p. 22.
48 Jeremy Waldron, *Liberal Rights: Collected Papers 1981–1991* (Cambridge: Cambridge University Press, 1993), p. 163.
49 Locke, *Works*, vol. 6, p. 27.
50 Wootton, *John Locke: Political Writings*, p. 104.
51 Marshall, *John Locke*, p. 359.
52 John Dunn, 'The Claim to Freedom of Conscience: Freedom of Speech, Freedom of Thought, Freedom of Worship?' in O.P. Grell, J.I. Israel, and N. Tyacke, eds., *From Persecution to Toleration: The Glorious Revolution and Reason in England* (Oxford: Clarendon Press, 1991), p. 178.
53 John Locke, *A New Method of making Common-Place-Books* (London: J. Greenwood, 1706), p. 21.
54 Thomas Jefferson, *The Complete Jefferson*, ed. Saul K. Padover (New York: Duell, Sloan and Pearce, 1943), p. 945.
55 Waldron, *Liberal Rights*, p. 165; James Tully ed., *John Locke, A Letter concerning Toleration* (Indianapolis: Hackett, 1983), p. 8.
56 A. John Simmons, *On the Edge of Anarchy: Locke, Consent and the Limits of Society* (Princeton: Princeton University Press, 1993), p. 126; Wootton, *John Locke: Political Writings*, p. 96.
57 Tully, *John Locke: A Letter*, p. 8.
58 Mark Goldie, 'John Locke's Circle and James II,' *The Historical Journal* 35 (1992): 586.
59 Richard S. Dunn, 'William Penn's Odyssey: From Child of Light to Absentee Landlord,' in J. Morrell, P. Slack, and D. Woolf, eds., *Public Duty*

and *Private Conscience in Seventeenth-Century England* (Oxford: Clarendon, 1993), p. 318.
60 J.R. Jones, 'The Revolution in Context,' in J.R. Jones, ed., *Liberty Secured? Britain before and after 1688* (Stanford: Stanford University Press, 1992), p. 17.
61 Daniel Defoe, *A Letter to a Dissenter from his Friend at the Hague, Concerning the Penal Laws and the Test; shewing that the Popular Plea for Liberty of Conscience is not concerned in that Question* (London, 1688), pp. 2–4.
62 Daniel Defoe, *A New Test of the Church of England's Loyalty: Or, Whiggish Loyalty and Church Liberty Compared* (London, 1702), p. 13; also Daniel Defoe, *Persecution Anatomized* (London, 1705), p. 2.
63 Pierre Bayle, *A Philosophic Commentary on These Words of the Gospel, Luke XIV, 23, Compel them to come in, that my House may be full* (1686), trans. John Fox (London: J. Darby, 1708), pp. 92, 361.
64 Ibid., p. 230.
65 Wootton, *John Locke: Political Writings*, p. 105.
66 R.J. Howells, *Pierre Jurieu: Antinomian Radical* (Durham: University of Durham, 1983), p. 54.
67 Cited in Guy Howard Dodge, *The Political Thought of the Huguenots of the Dispersion: With Special Reference to the Thought and Influence of Pierre Jurieu* (New York: Columbia University Press, 1947), p. 29.
68 Tully, *An Approach to Political Philosophy*, p. 60.
69 Locke, *Works*, vol. 6, p. 47.
70 Ibid., p. 143.
71 John W. Yolton, *A Locke Dictionary* (Oxford: Blackwell, 1993), p. 49.
72 Ibid., p. 50.
73 Peter Laslett, ed., introduction to John Locke, *Two Treatises of Government* (Cambridge: Cambridge University Press, 1988), p. 217.
74 Ibid., p. 40.
75 C.B. Macpherson, *The Political Theory of Possessive Individualism* (Oxford: Oxford University Press, 1962), pp. 194–7; Ruth Grant, *John Locke's Liberalism* (Chicago: University of Chicago Press, 1987), pp. 131–5; Simmons, *On the Edge of Anarchy*, pp. 65–7.
76 Tully, *An Approach to Political Philosophy*, pp. 317, 40.
77 Gordon J. Schochet, 'Why Should History Matter? Political Theory and the History of Discourse,' in J.G.A. Pocock, G.J. Schochet, and L.G. Schwoerer, eds., *The Varieties of British Political Thought* (Cambridge: Cambridge University Press, 1993), p. 327.
78 Tully, An Approach to Political Philosophy, p. 22.

79 Richard Ashcraft, *Revolutionary Politics and Locke's 'Two Treatises of Government'* (Princeton: Princeton University Press, 1986); Martin Hughes, 'Locke on Taxation and Suffrage,' *History of Political Thought* 11 (1990): 423–42.
80 Goldie, 'John Locke's Circle,' 578.
81 John Dunn, *The Political Thought of John Locke* (Cambridge: Cambridge University Press, 1969), pp. 50–1.
82 Locke, *Works*, vol. 6, p. 135.
83 John M. Beattie, 'London Juries in the 1690s,' in J.S. Cockburn and T.A. Green, eds., *Twelve Good Men and True: The Criminal Trial Jury in England, 1200–1800* (Princeton: Princeton University Press, 1988), p. 214.
84 Marshall, *John Locke*, pp. 229–33, 251.
85 Wootton, *John Locke: Political Writings*, p. 154.
86 Ibid., p. 236.
87 Thomas Pangle provided this suggestion.
88 Wootton, *John Locke: Political Writings*, p. 224.
89 Ibid., pp. 43–4.
90 Ibid., p. 224.
91 Adam Smith, *Lectures on Justice, Police, Revenue and Arms* (1763), ed. E. Cannan (New York: Augustus Kelley, 1964), p. 52.

6: Aristocratic Honour, Bourgeois Interest, and Anglican Conscience

1 Mary Maples Dunn, *William Penn: Politics and Conscience* (Princeton: Princeton University Press, 1967), pp. 134–5; J.A.W. Gunn, *Politics and the Public Interest in the Seventeenth Century* (Toronto: University of Toronto Press, 1969), chap. 4.
2 Jonathan Swift, *The Prose Works*, ed. H. Davis, (Oxford: Blackwell, 1948), vol. 9, p. 150.
3 Ibid., p. 153.
4 Ibid., pp. 155–6.
5 Anthony Ashley Cooper, 3rd Earl of Shaftesbury, *Characteristics of Men, Manners, Opinions, Times, etc.* (London: Grant Richards, 1900), vol. 1, p. 262.
6 Ibid., pp. 305–6.
7 Ibid., p. 122; vol. 1, no. 3, p. 96; vol. 2, no. 2, p. 220.
8 Anthony Ashley Cooper, 3rd Earl of Shaftesbury, *Complete Works*, ed. G. Hemmerlich and W. Benda (Stuttgart: Frommann-Holzboog, 1981), vol. 1, no. 3, p. 72.

9 Ibid., p. 24.
10 Ibid., vol. 2, no. 2, p. 148.
11 Ibid., p. 194.
12 Ibid., p. 122.
13 Ibid., pp. 88, 112–14.
14 Ibid., p. 88.
15 Ibid., vol. 1, no. 3, p. 96.
16 Paul Henri Thiry, baron d'Holbach, 'Common Sense, or Natural Ideas Opposed to Supernatural,' in Isaac Kramnick, *The Portable Enlightenment Reader* (Harmondsworth: Penguin, 1995), pp. 148–9.
17 Shaftesbury, *Complete Works*, vol. 2, no. 1, pp. 340, 346.
18 Ibid., vol. 2, no. 2, p. 90.
19 Claude Adrien Helvétius, *De l'esprit* (New York: Burt Franklin, 1810), reprinted 1970, p. 408.
20 Edward Andrew, *The Genealogy of Values: The Aesthetic Economy of Nietzsche and Proust* (Lantham: Rowman and Littlefield, 1995), chap. 3.
21 Shaftesbury, *Complete Works*, vol. 1, no. 2, p. 354.
22 Shaftesbury, *Characteristics*, vol. 1, pp. 216, 218.
23 Ibid., vol. 2, p. 255.
24 Shaftesbury, *Complete Works*, vol. 1, no. 1, pp. 274, 286, 270; vol. 1, no. 2, p. 224.
25 William Blake, *Complete Writings*, ed. Geoffrey Keynes (London: Oxford University Press, 1972), p. 548.
26 Bernard Mandeville, 'A Search into the Nature of Society,' in *The Fable of the Bees or Private Vices, Public Benefits*, ed. Douglas Garman (London: Wishart and Co., 1934), p. 196.
27 Ibid., pp. 195–6.
28 Ibid., pp. 200, 230.
29 Ibid., p. 248.
30 Ibid., p. 244.
31 Ibid., p. 172.
32 Bernard Mandeville, *Arete-logia or, an Enquiry into the Original of Moral Virtue* (London: Cleur and Campbell, 1728), p. 101.
33 Ibid., p. 14.
34 Ibid., p. 15.
35 John Gay, *The Fundamental Principle of Virtue or Morality*, in J.B. Schneewind, ed., *Moral Philosophy from Montaigne to Kant* (Cambridge: Cambridge University Press, 1990), vol. 2, p. 410.
36 Ibid.
37 Ibid., p. 79.

38 Bernard Mandeville, *Free Thoughts on Religion, the Church and National Happiness* (London: J. Brotherton, 1723), p. 215.
39 John Locke, *The Works* (London: Thomas Tegg, 1823), vol. 6, pp. 62–3.
40 Mandeville, *Fable of the Bees*, p. 95.
41 Mandeville, *Free Thoughts*, pp. 251, 361.
42 Ibid., pp. 118–19.
43 For thoughtful accounts of Mandeville's legacy in the eighteenth century, see Donna T. Andrew, *Philanthropy and Police: London Charity in the Eighteenth Century* (Princeton: Princeton University Press, 1989), and E.J. Hundert, *The Enlightenment's Fable: Bernard Mandeville and the Discovery of Society* (Cambridge: Cambridge University Press, 1994).
44 Mandeville, *Free Thoughts*, p. 244.
45 Ibid., pp. 282, 285, 291.
46 Ibid., p. 241.
47 Ibid., chaps. 11–12.
48 Ibid., p. 361.
49 George Berkeley, Bishop of Cloyne, *The Works*, ed. T.E. Jessop (London: Thomas Nelson, 1948–57), vol. 3, p. 107.
50 Ibid., p. 52.
51 Ibid., p. 120.
52 Ibid., p. 133; cf, William Law, *Remarks upon a Late Book entitled The Fable of the Bees, or Private Vices, Public Benefits* (London: William & John Innys, 1725), p. 56.
53 Berkeley, *Works*, vol. 3, pp. 114–15.
54 Ibid., p. 115.
55 Ibid., vol. 6, p. 69.
56 Ibid., p. 23.
57 Ibid., vol. 7, p. 130.
58 Ibid., vol. 6, pp. 17–46.
59 William Law, *A Serious Call to a Devout and Holy Life* (1728) (London: J.M. Dent and Sons, 1955), p. 142.
60 Berkeley, *Works*, vol. 6, pp. 106–8, 112–14.
61 See Terence Penelhum, *Butler* (London: Routledge and Kegan Paul, 1985); Christopher Cunliffe, ed., *Joseph Butler's Moral and Religious Thought* (Oxford: Clarendon Press, 1992); Stephen Darwall, *The British Moralists and the Internal 'Ought': 1640–1740* (Cambridge: Cambridge University Press, 1995).
62 Joseph Butler, *Fifteen Sermons Preached at Rolls Chapel*, Sermon I, in *The Whole Works* (London: Thomas Tegg, 1839), p. 4.
63 Ibid., Sermon II, in *Works*, p. 19.

64 Ibid., Sermon III, p. 29.
65 David McNaughton, 'British Moralists of the Eighteenth Century: Shaftesbury, Butler and Price,' in Stuart Brown, ed., *British Philosophy and the Age of Enlightenment* (London: Routledge, 1996), p. 212.
66 Butler, *Fifteen Sermons*, preface, in *Works*, viii.
67 Butler, *Works*, p. 95.
68 Ibid.
69 Ibid., p. 251.
70 Ibid., pp. 192–3.
71 Ibid., pp. 268–70.
72 Penelhum, *Butler*, p.71.
73 Brian Hebblethwaite, 'Butler on Conscience and Virtue,' in Cunliffe, ed., *Joseph Butler's Moral and Religious Thought*, p.197.
74 Butler, *Fifteen Sermons*, III, in *Works*, p. 25.
75 Laurence Sterne, *The Abuses of Conscience* (York: Caesar Ward, 1750), pp. 25–6.
76 Stephen Darwall, 'Conscience as Self-Authorizing in Butler's Ethics,' in Canliffe, ed., *Joseph Butler's Moral and Religious Thought*, p. 209.
77 Butler, *Analogy*, in *Works*, p. 155.
78 Penelhum, *Butler*, p. 36.
79 Butler, *Sermons Preached Upon Public Occasions*, in *Works*, p. 221.
80 Ibid., pp. 253–4.
81 Alexander Pope, *Essay on Man* (Edinburgh: William Blackwell, 1901), pp. 59–60.
82 Butler, *Fifteen Sermons*, XIII, in *Works*, p. 138.
83 Daniel Defoe, *Moll Flanders* (New York: New American Library, 1981), p. 205.
84 Claude Adrien Helvétius, *A Treatise on Man; His Intellectual Faculties and His Education*, trans. W. Hooper (New York: Burt Franklin, 1969), vol. 1, p. 127.
85 Laurence Sterne, *The Sermons of Mr. Yorick* (London: J. Dodsley, 1777), pp. 111–12.

7: Professors and Nonprofessors of Presbyterian Conscience

1 David Hume, *The History of England* (London: William Pickering, 1826), vol. 6, p. 292.
2 James Moore, 'The Two Systems of Francis Hutcheson,' in M.A. Stewart, ed., *Studies in the Philosophy of the Scottish Enlightenment* (Oxford: Clarendon, 1990), p. 44.

Notes to pages 114–18   213

3 Roger L. Emerson, 'Science and Moral Philosophy,' in M.A. Stewart, ed., *Studies in the Philosophy of the Scottish Enlightenment*, p. 19.
4 V.P. Hope, *Virtue by Consensus: The Moral Philosophy of Hutcheson, Hume and Adam Smith* (Oxford: Clarendon, 1989), p. 23.
5 Francis Hutcheson, *Thoughts on Laughter and Observations on 'The Fable of the Bees' in Six Letters* (1724–25) (Bristol: Thoemmes Antiquarian Books, 1989), p. 4.
6 Francis Hutcheson, *An Inquiry into the Original of our Ideas of Beauty and Virtue: in Two Treatises* (London: J. Darby et al., 1726), pp. 82, 135, 87, 134.
7 Ibid., p. 256.
8 Donald Winch, 'Adam Smith: Scottish Moral Philosopher as Political Economist,' in Hiroshi Mizuta and Chuhei Sugiyama, eds., *Adam Smith: International Perspectives* (New York: St. Martin's Press, 1993), p. 94.
9 Archibald Campbell, *An Enquiry into the Original of Moral Virtue* (Edinburgh: Gavin Hamilton, 1733), p. 313.
10 Adam Ferguson, *Principles of Moral and Political Science* (Edinburgh: W. Creech, 1792), p. 174.
11 Francis Hutcheson, *On Human Nature: Reflections on Our Common Systems of Morality*, ed. Thomas Mautner (Cambridge: Cambridge University Press, 1993), p. 136.
12 Francis Hutcheson, *An Essay on the Nature and Conduct of the Passions and Affections with Illustrations on the Moral Sense, 1728* (Menston: Scolar Press, 1972), p. 128.
13 Ibid., pp. 283–4.
14 Ibid., p. 138.
15 Hutcheson, *Inquiry into Original*, p. 113.
16 Ibid., pp. 221–3.
17 Hutcheson, *Human Nature*, p. 142.
18 Voltaire, *Oeuvres Complètes* (Paris: Garnier, 1879), tome 20, p. 518.
19 Voltaire, *La Voix du sage et du peuple* (Amsterdam, 1750), p. 8.
20 Denis Diderot, *Oeuvres Complètes* (Paris: Société encyclopédique français et le Club français du livre, 1973), tome 11, p. 210.
21 Anthony Strugnell, *Diderot's Politics: A Study of Diderot's Political Thought after the Revolution* (The Hague: Martinus Nijhoff, 1973), pp. 224–5.
22 Charles Griswold, Jr, *Adam Smith and the Virtues of Enlightenment* (Cambridge: Cambridge University Press, 1999), pp. 266–7. To be sure, Griswold primarily has Smith in mind when asserting that Enlightenment thinkers supported a separation of church and state. Smith balanced his support for establishment religion [*Wealth of Nations* V.i.9] with support for a plurality of sects, each moderating the claims of others. But Griswold

includes Hobbes, Hume, and Voltaire with Bayle, Smith, and Kant as Enlightenment figures supporting separation of church and state, and thus he is at least half wrong with the Enlightenment in general as he is with Smith in particular.

23 Hume, *History of England*, vol. 4, pp. 26–7; Duncan Forbes, *Hume's Philosophical Politics* (Cambridge: Cambridge University Press, 1975), p. 214; David Miller, *Philosophy and Ideology in Hume's Political Thought* (Oxford: Clarendon, 1981), pp. 117–18, 157; George Davie, *The Scottish Enlightenment and Other Essays* (Edinburgh: Polygon, 1991), p. 17.
24 Hume, *History of England*, vol. 4, p. 361.
25 Ibid., vol. 7, pp. 36, 239.
26 Ibid., vol. 6, pp. 140, 273–4, 290–6, 496, 508; vol. 7, p. 29.
27 Ibid., vol. 4, p. 27.
28 John B. Stewart, *Opinion and Reform in Hume's Political Philosophy* (Princeton: Princeton University Press, 1992), p. 279.
29 Hume, *History of England*, vol. 7, p. 306. I do not wish to comment on this shameful judgment, other than to indicate that where Hobbes provided a philosophic justification of trial by jury, Hume used rhetoric to signal his agreement with Hobbes. Juries, Hume wrote, are institutions 'the best calculated for the preservation of liberty and the administration of justice, that was ever devised by the wit of man' (*History of England*, vol. 1, pp. 83–4.)
30 Ibid., pp. 73–4.
31 David Hume, *The Philosophical Works*, ed. T.H. Green and T.H. Grose (London: Longmans, Green and Co., 1875), vol. 2, pp. 462–3.
32 David Hume, *An Enquiry concerning the Principles of Morals: A Critical Edition*, ed. Tom L. Beauchamp (Oxford: Clarendon, 1998), p. 82.
33 Ibid., p. 103.
34 Hume, *Philosophical Works*, vol. 2, p. 253.
35 Ibid., pp. 85–6.
36 Robert Clayton, *Some Thoughts on Self-Love* (1753), cited in Tom L. Beauchamp's introduction to Hume, *Enquiry concerning the Principles of Morals*, lxxi.
37 Kames, *Essays* (1758), cited in Beauchamp's introduction to Hume's *Enquiry*, lxxiv.
38 Hume, *Enquiry concerning the Principles of Morals*, p. 91.
39 Ibid., p. 77.
40 Ibid.
41 Hume, *The Philosophic Works*, vol. 4, p. 15.
42 Ibid., p. 153.

43 Ibid., p. 15.
44 Harvey Chisick, 'David Hume and the Common People,' in Peter Jones, ed., *The 'Science of Man' in the Scottish Enlightenment: Hume, Reid and Their Contemporaries* (Edinburgh: Edinburgh University Press, 1989), p. 21.
45 R.A. Houston, *Social Change in the Age of Enlightenment: Edinburgh, 1660–1760* (Oxford: Clarendon, 1994), p. 289.
46 Hume, *Philosophical Works*, vol. 3, pp. 308–9.
47 Gilles Deleuze, *Empiricism and Subjectivity: An Essay on Hume's Theory of Human Nature*, trans. Constantin V. Boundas (New York: Columbia University Press, 1991), x.
48 J.G.A. Pocock, 'Post-Puritan England and the Problem of the Enlightenment,' in Perez Zagorin, ed., *Culture and Politics From Puritanism to the Enlightenment* (Berkeley: University of California Press, 1980), p. 92.
49 Knud Haakonssen, 'Enlightened Dissent: an Introduction,' in K. Haakonssen, ed., *Enlightenment and Religion: Rational Dissent in Eighteenth-Century Britain* (Cambridge: Cambridge University Press, 1996), pp. 2–3.
50 Cited in Donald Winch, 'Adam Smith: Scottish Moral Philosopher as Political Economist,' in Knud Haakonssen, ed., *Adam Smith* (Aldershot: Dartmouth, 1998), p. 507.
51 Ibid., p. 518.
52 Peter Minowitz, *Profits, Priests and Princes: Adam Smith's Emancipation of Economics from Politics and Religion* (Stanford: Stanford University Press, 1993), pp. 139, 188. Minowitz elaborates the Adam Smith problem in religious terms and, not surprisingly for a Straussian, resolves it by asserting that Smith was consistently atheist in both his major works. Minowitz's conclusion certainly overrides numerous statements to the contrary, but my basic difference with Minowitz is that I do not wish to put Smith's texts to an inquisition to determine the real intention underlying the statements. Rather, I judge Smith by what he wrote, and find *The Theory of Moral Sentiments* to combine Protestant conscience with enlightened scepticism about conscience.
53 Vivienne Brown, *Adam Smith's Discourse: Canonicity, Commerce and Conscience* (London: Routledge, 1994), chap. 2.
54 V.P. Hope, *Virtue by Consensus: The Moral Philosophy of Hutcheson, Hume, and Adam Smith* (Oxford: Clarendon, 1989), p. 9.
55 Knud Haakonssen, *The Science of a Legislator: The Natural Jurisprudence of David Hume and Adam Smith* (Cambridge: Cambridge University Press, 1981), p. 46.

56 D.D. Raphael, 'Adam Smith,' in David Daiches, Peter Jones, and Jean Jones, eds., *The Scottish Enlightenment, 1730–1790: A Hotbed of Genius* (Edinburgh: The Saltire Society, 1996), p. 88.
57 Adam Smith, *The Theory of Moral Sentiments*, 10th edition (London: T. Cadell, 1804), vol. 1, p. 264.
58 Mark Hulliung, *The Autocritique of Enlightenment: Rousseau and the Philosophes* (Cambridge: Harvard University Press, 1994), p. 75.
59 Smith, *Moral Sentiments*, vol. 1, p. 266.
60 Ibid., pp. 239–40.
61 Ibid., p. 263.
62 Ibid., p. 264.
63 Griswold, *Adam Smith and the Virtues of Enlightenment*, pp. 107, 131.
64 Smith, *Moral Sentiments*, vol. 1, p. 227.
65 Ibid., III.iv.4, p. 324.
66 Samuel Fleischacker, 'Philosophy in Moral Practice: Kant and Adam Smith,' in Haakonssen, ed., *Adam Smith*, p. 12.
67 Smith, *Moral Sentiments*, vol. 1, p. 259.
68 Ibid., pp. 253–4.
69 Ibid., pp. 255–6.
70 Ibid., p. 240.
71 Ibid., p. 233.
72 Ibid., vol. 2, pp. 262–4.
73 Ibid., VI.iii.31, vol. 2, p. 140.
74 Hume, *Enquiry concerning Principles of Morals*, lxxix.
75 T.D. Campbell and Ian Ross, 'The Theory and Practice of the Wise and Virtuous Man: Reflections on Adam Smith's Response to Hume's Deathbed Wish,' in Knud Haakonssen, ed., *Adam Smith*, p. 132.
76 Minowitz, *Profits, Priests and Princes*, p. 48.
77 Andrew Stewart Skinner, *A System of Social Science: Papers Relating to Adam Smith* (Oxford: Clarendon, 1996), p. 112.
78 Ibid., vol. 1, pp. 405–6.
79 Ibid., pp. 243–4.
80 Ibid., pp. 277–8. One might compare this with *The Wealth of Nations*, in which self-love, not benevolence or humanity, provides the most efficient allocation of goods and services (when money replaces the social currency of esteem, which holds sway in *The Theory of Moral Sentiments*).
81 Smith, *Moral Sentiments*, vol. 1, pp. 344–5; Fleischacker, 'Philosophy in Moral Practice,' in Haakonssen, ed., *Adam Smith*, p. 17.
82 Smith, *Moral Sentiments*, vol. 1, p. 292.

83 Minowitz, *Profits, Priests and Princes*, p. 218; Adam Smith, *The Theory of Moral Sentiments*, 4th edition (London: W. Strahan, 1774), III.ii, vol. 1, p. 208.
84 Smith, *Moral Sentiments*, 10th edition, vol. 1, p. 313.
85 Ibid, p. 297.
86 Ibid., vol. 2, pp. 79–80.
87 Haakonssen, *Science of a Legislator*, p. 62.
88 Smith, *Moral Sentiments*, vol. 2, p. 120.
89 Ibid., vol. 1, pp. 289–90.
90 Ibid., p. 282.
91 Outside the English world, Rousseau set forth the demands of conscience as 'the sublime science of simple souls' but had an ambiguous relationship to enlightened views on progress, and its vehicles – commerce and the arts and sciences. Kant may be the apex of the marriage of Protestantism and the Enlightenment, but his views on the sensual component of experience both in epistemology and morality do not accord with the sensualism, empiricism, and utilitarianism of the French, Scots, and American Enlightenment. Smith, Rousseau, and Kant combined the conflicting claims of Protestant conscience and enlightened reason in different ways. Hobbes before, and Hegel after, gave philosophic political expression to the dialectic of conscience and reason, but of eighteenth-century thinkers, Smith is the individual who stood most firmly in the Enlightenment and who provided an illuminating account of the meaning of conscience.
92 T.D. Campbell and I.S. Ross, 'The Utilitarianism of Adam Smith's Policy Advice,' in Haakonssen, ed., *Adam Smith*, p. 128.
93 Winch, 'Scottish Moral Philosopher,' in Haakonssen, ed., *Adam Smith*, p. 508.

8: Conscience as Tiger and Lamb

1 Mary Wollstonecraft, *A Vindication of the Rights of Woman*, in Janet Todd, ed., *Political Writings* (Toronto: University of Toronto Press, 1993), p. 169.
2 Norman Hampson, *The Enlightenment* (Harmondsworth: Penguin, 1968), p. 9, writes: 'It may be argued with equal plausibility that Rousseau was either one of the greatest writers of the Enlightenment or its most eloquent and effective opponent.' Mark Hulliung in his excellent study of Rousseau, *The Autocritique of Enlightenment: Rousseau and the Philosophes* (Cambridge: Harvard University Press, 1994), elaborates Rousseau's ambivalent relationship to Enlightenment thought.

218 Notes to pages 132–4

3 Thomas Paine, *Agrarian Justice* (Paris: W. Adlard, 1797), pp. 10–11.
4 Jean-Jacques Rousseau, *Oeuvres Complètes*, ed. Bernard Gagnebin et Marcel Raymond (Paris: Gallimard-Pléiade, 1959), t. 3, p. 30; *The First and Second Discourses*, trans. R.D. Masters and J. Masters (New York: St. Martin's Press, 1964), p. 64.
5 William Blake, *The Poems*, ed. W.H. Stevenson and David V. Erdman (London: Longman, 1971), p. 481; cf., pp. 733–5.
6 William Blake, *Complete Writings*, ed. Geoffrey Keynes (London: Oxford University Press, 1972), p. 385.
7 Ibid., p. 396.
8 Richard Watson, Bishop of Llandaff's sermon *The Wisdom and Goodness of God in Having made both Rich and Poor* can be found in Marilyn Butler, *Burke, Paine, Godwin, and the Revolution Controversy* (Cambridge: Cambridge University Press, 1984), pp. 145–8. William Wordsworth's response to Bishop Watson is also in Butler, pp. 224–6. Paine's *Agrarian Justice* was published in response to Watson's sermon. Blake saw in Watson's sermon everything he despised in the laws of Urizen, or Enlightenment reason.
9 Ibid., p. 386.
10 Christopher Hill, *The World Turned Upside Down* (Harmondsworth: Penguin, 1984), p. 372.
11 Paine, *Agrarian Justice*, vi.
12 Rousseau, *Oeuvres Complètes*, t. 4, pp. 702–3; *Emile or On Education*, ed. Allan Bloom (New York: Basic Books, 1979), p. 365.
13 Wollstonecraft, *Vindication of the Rights of Men*, in *Political Writings*, p. 9; Virginia Sapiro, *A Vindication of Political Virtue* (Chicago: University of Chicago Press, 1992), p. 53.
14 Rousseau, *Oeuvres Complètes*, t. 4, p. 523; *Emile*, p. 235.
15 Blake, *Complete Writings*, p. 42.
16 Rousseau, *Oeuvres Complètes*, t. 4, pp. 1108–12; cf., *Emile*, in t. 4, pp. 600–1.
17 Peter F. Fisher, in *The Valley of Vision: Blake as Prophet and Revolutionary*, ed. Northrop Frye (Toronto: University of Toronto Press, 1961), p. 153, asserts that conscience and reason become Los and Urizen in Blake's prophetic works. While most scholars agree that Urizen is reason, Los is usually identified with imagination, not conscience. I would think that a case might be made that Enitharmon, the female emanation of Urthona as Los is the male, is conscience. Enitharmon is the daughter of Urthona (the underground source of the smithy's forge) and Enion, the female emanation of compassionate, emotive Tharmas. See *Milton*, plates 6, 7.
18 See David V. Erdman, *Blake: Prophet against Empire* (Princeton: Princeton University Press, 1969), p. 179.

19 E.P. Thompson, *Witness against the Beast: William Blake and the Moral Law* (Cambridge: Cambridge University Press, 1993), p. 20.
20 Blake, *Poems*, p. 108.
21 Wollstonecraft, *Political Writings*, p. 193.
22 Blake, *Poems*, p. 108.
23 Georg Wilhelm Friedrich Hegel, *The Philosophy of History*, trans. J. Sibree (New York: Dover, 1956), p. 447.
24 William Wordsworth, *The Poetical Works*, ed. E. de Selincourt and H. Darbishire (Oxford: Clarendon, 1940–9), vol. 3, p. 391.
25 Jack Fruchtman, Jr, in *Thomas Paine and the Religion of Nature* (Baltimore: The Johns Hopkins University Press, 1993) and *Thomas Paine: Apostle of Freedom* (New York: Four Walls Eight Windows, 1994), stresses that Paine was a deeply religious thinker; while John Keane, in *Tom Paine: A Political Life* (London: Bloomsbury, 1995), asserts that Paine's politics were purely secular, independent of Quaker beliefs.
26 Edward H. Davidson and William J. Scheik, *Paine, Scripture and Authority: The Age of Reason as Religious and Political Idea* (London: Associated University Presses, 1994), p. 28.
27 Thomas Jefferson, *The Complete Jefferson*, ed. Saul K. Padover (New York: Duell, Sloan and Pearce, 1943), p. 1032.
28 Benjamin Franklin, *The Writings*, ed. Albert H. Smyth (New York: Macmillan, 1907), vol. 9, p. 262.
29 Voltaire, *Philosophical Dictionary*, cited in Peter Gay, *The Enlightenment: An Interpretation* (New York: Alfred Knopf, 1976), vol. 2, p. 527.
30 Franklin, *Writings*, vol. 9, pp. 520–2.
31 Thomas Paine, *Common Sense* (Edinburgh: Charles Elliot, 1776), p. 21.
32 Ibid., p. 54.
33 Thomas Paine, *Rights of Man, Common Sense and Other Political Writings* (Oxford: Oxford University Press, 1995), p. 137.
34 Paine, *Common Sense*, pp. 6, 8.
35 Jefferson, *Complete Jefferson*, p. 1057.
36 Paine, *Common Sense*, p. 83.
37 Keane, *Tom Paine*, p. 129; Arthur J. Mekeel, *The Quakers and the American Revolution* (York: Sessions Book Trust, 1996), pp. 15–16.
38 Paine, *Common Sense*, pp. 94, 98–9; Keane, *Tom Paine*, p. 130.
39 Paine, *Common Sense*, p. 56. Paine of course did not refer to the American attempts to obtain support of Native and Black Americans, and the limited success of these attempts.
40 William C. Kashatus III, *Conflict of Conviction: A Reappraisal of Quaker Involvement in the American Revolution* (Lanham: University Press of America, 1990), p. 26.

41 Mekeel, *Quakers*, pp. 230–3, 368–9.
42 Keane, in *Tom Paine*, p. 269, asserts that the status of 'my boy Joe' is uncertain. It would thus be inappropriate to refer to Samuel Johnson's dictum that the loudest yelpers for liberty are the drivers of black slaves.
43 Edmund Burke, *Reflections on the Revolution in France*, ed J.G.A. Pocock (Indianapolis: Hackett, 1987), p. 52.
44 Ibid.
45 Jeremy Bentham, *Anarchist Fallacies*, in Jeremy Waldron, ed., *Nonsense upon Stilts: Bentham, Burke and Marx on the Rights of Man* (London: Methuen, 1987), pp. 52–3.
46 Ibid., p. 74.
47 Paine, *Rights of Man*, p. 120.
48 Keane, *Tom Paine*, p. 307.
49 Thomas Paine, *The Complete Writings*, ed. Philip S. Foner (New York: Citadel Press, 1945), vol. 2, p. 737.
50 Keane, *Tom Paine*, p. 391.
51 Thomas Paine, *The Age of Reason*, in *Life and Writings of Thomas Paine* (New York: Vincent Parke, 1908), vol. 6, p. 2.
52 Ibid., pp. 4, 287, 318.
53 Blake, *Complete Writings*, pp. 383–96; Northrop Frye, *Fearful Symmetry: A Study of William Blake* (Princeton: Princeton University Press, 1947), p. 66; Erdman, *Blake: Prophet against Empire*, p. 301.
54 Blake, *Complete Writings*, p. 389.
55 Paine, *Agrarian Justice*, p. 29.
56 William Godwin, *Enquiry concerning Political Justice and Its Influence on Morals and Happiness*, ed. F.E.L. Priestley (Toronto: University of Toronto Press, 1946), vol. 2, pp. 429–30, 469.
57 Mark Philp, *Godwin's Political Justice* (London: Duckworth, 1986), p. 161.
58 Don Locke, *A Fantasy of Reason: The Life and Thought of William Godwin* (London: Routledge and Kegan Paul, 1980), pp. 340–1.
59 Godwin, *Political Justice*, vol. 3, p. 68.
60 Philp, *Godwin's Political Justice*, pp. 10, 19–22.
61 Godwin, *Political Justice*, vol. 1, pp. 181–2.
62 Ibid., vol. 2, p. 2.
63 Ibid., pp. 496–7.
64 Ibid., vol. 1, p. 212.
65 Ibid., vol. 2, p. 333.
66 Ibid., vol. 1, p. 175.
67 Ibid., vol. 2, p. 331.
68 Ibid., vol. 1, p. 176.

69 Ibid., p. 181.
70 Auden cited in Peter Ackroyd, *Blake* (London: Sinclair-Stevenson, 1995), p. 142.
71 Godwin, *Political Justice*, vol. 1, pp. 145, 151; vol. 2, p. 2.
72 Compare Godwin, *Political Justice*, vol. 1, p. 157, with Richard Price, *A Review of the Principle Questions in Morals* (3rd ed., 1787), ed. D.D. Raphael (Oxford: Clarendon, 1948), p. 180.
73 John P. Clark, *The Philosophic Anarchism of William Godwin* (Princeton: Princeton University Press, 1977), pp. 140–4.
74 Godwin, *Political Justice*, vol. 1, pp. 164–5.
75 Ibid., pp. 27–8, 42–3.
76 Ibid., p. 38.
77 A.J. Ayer, *Thomas Paine* (London: Faber & Faber, 1989), p. 111.
78 John Locke, *An Essay concerning Human Understanding*, ed. Peter N. Nidditch (Oxford: Clarendon, 1975), p. 10.
79 Ibid., II.viii.9.
80 John Locke, *Two Treatises of Government*, ed. Peter Laslett (Cambridge: Cambridge University Press, 1988), II, chap. 5.
81 Frye, *Fearful Symmetry*, p. 105.
82 Blake, *Poems*, p. 116.
83 David Hume, *The History of England* (London: William Pickering, 1826), vol. 8, p. 293.
84 David Hume, *The Philosophical Works*, ed. T.H. Green and T.H. Grose (London: Longmans, Green and Co., 1875), vol. 4, p. 5.
85 Ibid., p. 135.
86 Cited in Stewart Crehan, *Blake in Context* (Dublin: Gill and Macmillan, 1984), p. 290.
87 John Stuart Mill, *Collected Works*, ed. John Robson (Toronto: University of Toronto Press, 1988), vol. 27, p. 652.
88 Ibid., p. 647.
89 Blake, *Poems*, p. 832.
90 Lord Byron, *The Complete Poetical Works*, ed. J.J. McGann (Oxford: Clarendon, 1993), vol. 7, p. 30.
91 Frye, *Fearful Symmetry*, p. 217; Fischer, *Valley of Vision*, p. 138: Crehan, *Blake in Context*, p. 293; Thompson, *Witness against the Beast*, p. 229.
92 Blake, *Poems*, p. 861; Ackroyd, *Blake*, p. 348.
93 Brenda S. Webster, *Blake's Prophetic Psychology* (London: Macmillan, 1983); Frye, *Fearful Symmetry*, p. 301. Frye, however, saw that Blake thought conscience to be on the side of freedom rather than repression: 'Cockney cheek and the Nonconformist conscience, two of the resolute and persis-

tent saboteurs of the dark satanic mills in English life, combine in Blake to establish an incorruptibly mental court without appeal to which all apologies for the traditional and conventional are referred' (p. 413).

94 Frye, *Fearful Symmetry*, p. 216.
95 Blake, *Poems*, p. 158.
96 Blake, *Complete Writings*, p. 410.
97 Blake, *Poems*, opp. 329.
98 Ibid., p. 111.
99 Frye, *Fearful Symmetry*, p. 53.
100 Blake, *Complete Writings*, p. 459.
101 Ibid., p. 42.
102 Blake, *Poems*, p. 32.
103 Ibid., p. 460.
104 Ibid., p. 767.
105 Ackroyd, *Blake*, p. 252.
106 Blake, *Poems*, p. 430.
107 Ibid., p. 141.
108 Ibid., p. 733.
109 Ibid., p. 734.
110 Ibid., p. 524.
111 Ibid., p. 432.
112 Ibid., p. 792.
113 Thompson, *Witness against the Beast*, p. 221.
114 Ibid., pp. 5, 109.
115 Don Locke, in *A Fantasy of Reason*, p. 139, cited Godwin on women's equality: 'Till the softer sex has produced a Bacon, a Newton, a Hume or a Shakespeare, I will never believe it.' William Godwin, in *Memoirs of Wollstonecraft* (Oxford: Woodstock Books, 1993), indicated that when he and Wollstonecraft first met, she kept interrupting conversation he wished to have with Tom Paine, and asserted that her *Vindication of the Rights of Woman* was not 'to be placed in the first class of human productions' (p. 83).
116 William Blake, *The Writings*, ed. Geoffrey Keynes (London: Nonesuch Press, 1925), vol. 3, pp. 387–8.
117 Blake, *Poems*, p. 850.
118 Ibid., p. 680.

9: Individualist Conscience and Nationalist Prejudice

1 William Wordsworth, *The Poetical Works*, ed. E. de Selincourt and H. Darbishire (Oxford: Clarendon, 1940–9), vol. 3, p. 117.

2 John Stuart Mill, *Collected Works*, ed. John M. Robson (Toronto: University of Toronto Press, 1969–90), vol. 28, p. 98.
3 Ibid., vol. 21, pp. 115, 253.
4 Ibid., vol. 1, p. 161.
5 John Henry Newman, *A Letter to his Grace The Duke of Norfolk on the Occasion of Mr. Gladstone's Recent Expostulation* (London: Pickering, 1875), p. 4.
6 John Henry Cardinal Newman, *An Essay in Aid of A Grammar of Assent* (Notre Dame: University of Notre Dame Press, 1979), p. 110.
7 Newman, *Letter to Duke of Norfolk*, p. 53.
8 Ibid., p. 66.
9 *The Correspondence of John Stuart Mill and Auguste Comte*, trans. and ed. Oscar A. Haac (New Brunswick: Transaction Publishers, 1995), p. 351.
10 *Auguste Comte and Positivism*, in John Stuart Mill, *Collected Works*, vol. 10, pp. 301–2, 310–14, 321–2, 338, 357–8; vol. 1, pp. 219–21.
11 Newman, *Grammar of Assent*, p. 304.
12 Mill, *Collected Works*, vol 10, p. 74.
13 Ibid., vol. 21, p. 251.
14 Ibid., vol. 1, p. 613.
15 Ibid., pp. 188–9.
16 Mill, *Collected Works*, vol. 12, p. 128; also vol. 1, pp. 34–5. Mill asserted (vol. 6, p. 228): 'It is the grossest abuse of the powers of an instructor, to employ them in *principling* a pupil ... a process which tends to nothing but enslaving and (by necessary consequence) paralyzing the human mind.'
17 Ibid., vol. 1, p. 45.
18 Ibid., p. 51.
19 Ibid., vol. 10, pp. 95–6; cf., pp. 13–15.
20 Ibid., p. 107.
21 Ibid., p. 144.
22 D.G. Brown, 'Mill on Liberty and Morality,' *Philosophical Review* 81 (1972), 133–58; D.P. Dryer, 'Justice, Liberty, and the Principle of Utility in Mill,' and David Copp, 'The Iterated-Utilitarianism of J.S. Mill,' in Wesley Cooper, Kai Nielsen, and Steven Patten, eds., *New Essays in John Stuart Mill and Utilitarianism* (Guelph: Canadian Association for Publishing in Philosophy, 1979), 63–73, 75–98; David Lyons, *Rights, Welfare, and Mill's Moral Theory* (New York: Oxford University Press, 1994), pp. 50–6, 129–30.
23 Lyons, *Rights, Welfare, and Mill's Moral Theory*, p. 129.
24 *Coleridge's Writings*, vol. 2, *On Humanity*, ed. Anya Taylor (London: Macmillan, 1994), p. 228.

25 Coleridge, *Notebook*, 26, folio 41, cited in Mary Anne Perkins, *Coleridge's Philosophy: The Logos as Unifying Principle* (Oxford: Clarendon, 1994), pp. 74–5.
26 Samuel Taylor Coleridge, *The Collected Works*, ed. Lewis Patton and Peter Mann (Princeton: Princeton University Press, 1971), vol. 4, p. 523.
27 Matthew Arnold, *Culture and Anarchy*, ed. Samuel Lipman (New Haven: Yale University Press, 1994), p. 88.
28 *Coleridge's Writings*, vol. 1, *On Politics and Society*, ed. John Morrow (London: Macmillan, 1990), p. 92.
29 *Coleridge's Writings*, vol. 2, p. 155.
30 Ibid.
31 Richard Holmes, *Coleridge: Darker Reflections* (London: HarperCollins, 1998), p. 461.
32 *Coleridge's Writings*, vol. 2, p. 181; cited in Mill, *Collected Works*, vol. 10, pp. 148–9.
33 *Coleridge's Writings*, vol. 2, p. 218.
34 Ibid., p. 211.
35 Ibid., p. 172.
36 Ibid., p. 178.
37 Ibid., p. 173.
38 Mill, *Collected Works*, vol. 10, p. 143.
39 Ibid., pp. 147–50.
40 Christopher Turk, *Coleridge and Mill: A Study of Influence* (Aldershot: Avebury, 1988), p. 184.
41 James Mill, *Analysis of the Phenomena of the Human Mind* (New York: Augustus Kelley, 1967), p. 300.
42 Ibid.
43 Mill, *Collected Works*, vol. 1, p. 612.
44 Ibid.
45 Josephine Kamm, *John Stuart Mill in Love* (London: Gordon & Cremonesi, 1977), p. 15; Peter Glassman, *J.S. Mill: The Evolution of a Genius* (Gainesville: University Presses of Florida, 1985), p. 17; Michael St. John Packe, *The Life of John Stuart Mill* (London: Secker and Warburg, 1954), pp. 32–3.
46 Mill, *Collected Works*, vol. 1, p. 51.
47 Ibid., p. 36.
48 Ibid., vol. 10, p. 246.
49 Ibid., p. 231.
50 Ibid., vol. 9, p. 455.

Notes to pages 161–8   225

51 Ibid., vol. 15, p. 649.
52 Ralph Waldo Emerson, *The Complete Works* (London: A.P. Watt and Son, 1903), vol. 9, p. 84; Sören Kierkegaard, *Either/Or*, trans. Walter Lowrie (London: Oxford University Press, 1944), vol. 2, pp. 138, 141, 150, 188, 210, 214–7; Sören Kierkegaard, *The Journals*, trans. Alexander Dru (London: Oxford University Press, 1938), p. 151; Pierre-Joseph Proudhon, *De la Justice dans la Révolution et dans l'Église* (Paris: Fayard, 1990), p. 2353.
53 Mill, *Collected Works*, vol. 15, p. 649.
54 Stefan Collini, introduction to Mill, *Collected Works*, vol. 21, xvi.
55 Ibid., vol. 18, p. 156.
56 Ibid., pp. 84, 107, 111.
57 Ibid., p. 132.
58 Ibid., pp. 178–9.
59 Ibid., p. 198.
60 Ibid., vol. 10, pp. 408–9.
61 Ibid., p. 410.
62 Ibid.
63 Ibid., p. 160.
64 *The Correspondence of John Stuart Mill and Auguste Comte*, pp. 42, 317.
65 Mill, *Collected Works*, vol. 18, pp. 225–6.
66 Jeremy Bentham, *Fragment on Government*, ed. J.H. Burns and H.L.A. Hart (Cambridge: Cambridge University Press, 1988), p. 10.
67 Ibid., p. 276.
68 Ibid., p. 222.
69 Ibid., vol. 6, pp. 85–6.
70 Ibid., vol. 10, p. 142.
71 Alan Ryan, 'Sense and Sensibility in Mill's Political Thought,' in Michael Laine, ed., *A Cultivated Mind: Essays on J.S. Mill Presented to John M. Robson* (Toronto: University of Toronto Press, 1991), p. 127.
72 Mill, *Collected Works*, vol. 1, p. 89.
73 Ibid., vol. 18, pp. 244, 246.
74 Ibid., p. 248.
75 Ibid., vol. 15, p. 759.
76 Ibid., vol. 1, p. 249.
77 Ibid., p. 221; vol. 10, pp. 313–4.
78 Ibid., vol. 10, p. 301.
79 Ibid., p. 313.
80 Ibid., p. 321.
81 Ibid., pp. 321–2.

82 Ibid., p. 338.
83 Mill thought Greek civilization was based on the unfreedom of citizens, as well as slaves and women, and thought contemporary civilizations were progressing as collectivities while reducing individuality to a homogeneous grey uniformity (*Collected Works*, vol 18, pp. 226, 272–5). If Mill were taken to assert that religious tolerance and individual freedom are conditions of cultural flourishing, the literature of Tsarist (and Soviet) Russia would be a counter-example to his thesis, as would Saint John of the Cross and Saint Teresa of Avila, two products of forced conversion by the Spanish Inquisition. In his *Inaugural Address Delivered to the University of St. Andrews*, Mill stated that 'the freest thinkers have often been trained in the most slavish seminaries of learning' – for example, the Reformers in Catholic universities and enlightened sceptics in Jesuit institutions (*Collected Works*, vol. 21, p. 250).
84 Ibid., vol. 18, p. 262.
85 Ibid.
86 Ibid., p. 263.
87 Ibid., vol. 10, pp. 417, 487.
88 Ibid., p. 487.
89 A.O.J. Cockshutt, *The Unbelievers: English Agnostic Thought, 1840–1890* (London: Collins, 1964), p. 28.
90 Copp, 'The Iterated-Utilitarianism of J.S. Mill,' 88.
91 See Wendy Donner, *The Liberal Self* (Ithaca: Cornell University Press, 1991), and John Skorupski, 'Utilitarianism,' in Skorupski, ed., *The Cambridge Companion to Mill* (Cambridge: Cambridge University Press, 1998), pp. 276–7; John Skorupski, *John Stuart Mill* (London: Routledge, 1989), pp. 43, 250, 303–08, 330–2, 342.
92 Mill, *Collected Works*, vol. 10, pp. 95–8.
93 Bernard Semmel, *John Stuart Mill and the Pursuit of Virtue* (New Haven: Yale University Press, 1984), p. 198.
94 Mill, *Collected Works*, vol. 1, p. 145.
95 Ibid., pp. 109, 111.
96 Ibid., p. 233.
97 Alan Ryan, introduction to Mill, *Collected Works*, vol. 9, xiii.
98 Mill, *Collected Works*, vol. 10, p. 73.
99 Ibid., vol. 8, p. 952.
100 Ibid., pp. 49–51.
101 Ibid., vol. 10, p. 212; vol. 18, p. 224.
102 Skorupski, *John Stuart Mill*, p. 5.
103 Mill, *Collected Works*, vol. 9, pp. 492–3.

104 Alan Ryan, *The Philosophy of John Stuart Mill* (London: Macmillan, 1998), p. 120.
105 Mill, *Collected Works*, vol. 9, pp. 446–7.
106 Ibid., p. 456.
107 Ryan, *Philosophy of John Stuart Mill*, pp. 120–30.
108 Mill, *Collected Works*, vol. 9, p. 466.
109 Ibid., vol. 10, pp. 375, 393.
110 Skorupski, *John Stuart Mill*, p. 10.
111 Mill, *Collected Works*, vol. 9, p. 449.
112 Ibid., p. 194.
113 Ibid., pp. 196, 208.
114 Jonathan Loesburg, *Fictions of Consciousness: Mill, Newman, and the Reading of Victorian Prose* (New Brunswick: Rutgers University Press, 1986), p. 42.
115 Ryan, *Philosophy of John Stuart Mill*, p. 130.
116 Kierkegaard, *Either/Or*, vol. 2, p. 210.
117 Ibid., p. 138.
118 Ibid., p. 150.
119 Mill, *Collected Works*, vol. 27, p. 657.
120 Ibid., vol. 1, p. 355.
121 Ibid., p. 349.
122 Ibid., vol. 21, p. 252.
123 Ibid., p. 350.
124 *The Correspondence of John Stuart Mill and Auguste Comte*, pp. 351, 361, 365.
125 Mill, *Collected Works*, vol. 21, p. 113.
126 Thomas Babington, Lord Macaulay, *The Complete Works* (London: Longmans Green, 1897), vol. 9, p. 157.
127 Stefan Collini, 'From Sectarian Radical to National Possession: John Stuart Mill in English Culture, 1873–1945,' in Laine, ed., *A Cultivated Mind*, pp. 242–72.

Conclusion

1 Richard Rorty, *Contingency, Irony, and Solidarity* (Cambridge: Cambridge University Press, 1989), p. 63; Richard Rorty, 'Postmodern Bourgeois Liberalism' and 'The Priority of Democracy to Philosophy,' in *Philosophic Papers*, vol. 1 (Cambridge: Cambridge University Press, 1991).
2 Cited in John W. Graham, *Conscription and Conscience: A History 1916–1919* (London: Allen and Unwin, 1922), p. 196.

3 Michael Ignatieff, *The Warrior's Honor: Ethnic War and the Modern Conscience* (Toronto: Viking, 1998), p. 12.
4 Charles Griswold, Jr, *Adam Smith and the Virtues of Enlightenment* (Cambridge: Cambridge University Press, 1999), p. 19.
5 J.B. Schneewind, *The Invention of Autonomy: A History of Modern Moral Philosophy* (Cambridge: Cambridge University Press, 1998), pp. 8, 9.
6 Niklas Luhmann, 'The Individuality of the Individual,' in Thomas C. Heller, Morton Sosna, and David E. Wellbery, eds., *Reconstructing Individualism: Autonomy, Individuality and the Self in Western Thought* (Stanford: Stanford University Press, 1986), p. 316.
7 John Rawls, *A Theory of Justice* (Cambridge: Belknap Press, 1971), p. 380.
8 Ibid., pp. 365, 377.
9 Michael Walzer, *Spheres of Justice: A Defence of Pluralism and Equality* (Oxford: Martin Robertson, 1983), p. 278.
10 Michael Walzer, *Thick and Thin: Moral Argument at Home and Abroad* (Notre Dame: University of Notre Dame Press, 1994), p. 97.
11 Ibid., p. 98.
12 George Kateb, 'Socratic Integrity,' in Ian Shapiro and Robert Adams, eds., *Integrity and Conscience*, Nomos Series, XL (New York: New York University Press, 1998), p. 99.
13 Rorty, *Philosophic Papers* vol. 1, pp. 188–90.
14 Edward Andrew, *Shylock's Rights: A Grammar of Lockian Claims* (Toronto: University of Toronto Press, 1988), pp. 67–75.
15 Paul Ricoeur, *The Just*, trans. David Pellauer (Chicago: University of Chicago Press, 2000), p. 155.

Bibliography

Ackroyd, Peter. *Blake*. London: Sinclair-Stevenson, 1995.
Allen, J.W. *English Political Thought 1603–1644*. London: Methuen, 1938.
Ames, William. *Conscience with the Power and Cases Thereof*. N.p., 1639.
Andrew, Donna Trembowelski. *Philanthropy and Police: London Charity in the Eighteenth Century*. Princeton: Princeton University Press, 1989.
Andrew, Edward. *The Genealogy of Values: The Aesthetic Economy of Nietzsche and Proust*. Lantham, Md.: Rowman and Littlefield, 1995.
– *Shylock's Rights: A Grammar of Lockian Claims*. Toronto: University of Toronto Press, 1988.
Aquinas, St Thomas. *The Summa Theologica*, trans. Fathers of the English Dominican Province. New York: Benzinger Bros., 1938.
Arnold, Matthew. *Culture and Anarchy*, ed. Samuel Lipman. New Haven: Yale University Press, 1994.
Arsleff, Hans. 'Locke's Influence,' in Vere Chappell, ed., *The Cambridge Companion to Locke*. Cambridge: Cambridge University Press, 1994.
Ashcraft, Richard. *Revolutionary Politics and Locke's 'Two Treatises of Government.'* Princeton: Princeton University Press, 1986.
Ayer, A.J. *Thomas Paine*. London: Faber & Faber, 1989.
Bacon, Francis. *Essays*, ed. J.M. Mitchell. London: Macmillan, 1959.
Baldwin, William. *A Treatise of Morall Philosophie* (1547), enlarged by Thomas Palfreyman 1640. Gainesville, Fl.: Scholars' Facsimiles & Reprints, 1967.
Bayle, Pierre. *The Dictionary Historical and Critical of Mr. Peter Bayle*, 2nd edition, trans. Pierre des Maizeaux. London: Bettenham, 1734.
– *A General Dictionary*. London: James Bettenham, 1734–41.
– *A Philosophic Commentary on These Words of the Gospel, Luke XIV, 23, Compel them to come in, that my House may be full* (1686), trans. John Fox. London: J. Darby, 1708.

Baylor, Michael G. *Action and Person: Conscience in Late Scholasticism and the Young Luther.* Leiden: E.J. Brill, 1977.

Beattie, John M. 'London Juries in the 1690s,' in J.S. Cockburn and T.A. Green, eds., *Twelve Good Men and True: The Criminal Trial Jury in England, 1200–1800.* Princeton: Princeton University Press, 1988.

Belsey, Catherine. 'The Case of Hamlet's Conscience.' *Studies in Philology* 76 (1979).

Bentham, Jeremy. *Anarchist Fallacies*, in Jeremy Waldron, ed., *Nonsense upon Stilts: Bentham, Burke and Marx on the Rights of Man.* London: Methuen, 1987.

– *A Fragment on Government*, ed. J.H. Burns and H.L.A. Hart. Cambridge: Cambridge University Press, 1988.

Berkeley, George, Bishop of Cloyne. *The Works*, ed. T.E. Jessop. London: Thomas Nelson, 1948–57.

Berman, Harold J. *Law and Revolution: The Formation of the Western Legal Tradition.* Cambridge: Harvard University Press, 1983.

Bien, David P. *The Calas Affair: Persecution, Toleration, and Heresy in Eighteenth Century Toulouse.* Princeton: Princeton University Press, 1960.

Blake, William. *Complete Writings*, ed. Geoffrey Keynes. London: Oxford University Press, 1972.

– *The Poems*, ed. W.H. Stevenson and David V. Erdman. London: Longman, 1971.

Bodin, Jean. *The Six Bookes of a Commonweale*, facsimile reprint of 1606, trans. Richard Knolles, ed. Kenneth D. McCrae. Cambridge: Harvard University Press, 1962.

Boutcher, Warren. 'Florio's Montaigne: Translation and Pragmatic Humanism in the Sixteenth Century.' PhD thesis, University of Cambridge, 1991.

Bradley, Andrew. *Shakespearean Tragedy.* London: Macmillan, 1904.

Brown, D.G. 'Mill on Liberty and Morality.' *Philosophical Review* 81 (1972).

Brown, Stuart. *British Philosophy and the Age of Enlightenment.* London: Routledge, 1996.

Brown, Vivienne. *Adam Smith's Discourse: Canonicity, Commerce and Conscience.* London: Routledge, 1994.

Burke, Edmund. *Reflections on the Revolution in France*, ed. J.G.A. Pocock. Indianapolis: Hackett, 1987.

Burke, Peter. *Montaigne.* Oxford: Oxford University Press, 1981.

Butler, Joseph. *The Whole Works.* London: Thomas Tegg, 1839.

Butler, Marilyn. *Burke, Paine, Godwin, and the Revolution Controversy.* Cambridge: Cambridge University Press, 1984.

Butler, Samuel. *Hudibras.* London: J. Walker, 1817.

Byron, George Gordon, Lord. *The Complete Poetical Works*, ed. J.J. McGann. Oxford: Clarendon, 1993.
Calvin, John. *Institutes of the Christian Religion*, trans. John Allen. London: James Clark and Co., 1937.
Campbell, Archibald. *An Enquiry into the Original of Moral Virtue*. Edinburgh: Gavin Hamilton, 1733.
Campbell, T.D., and Ian Ross. 'The Theory and Practice of the Wise and Virtuous Man: Reflections on Adam Smith's Response to Hume's Deathbed Wish,' in Knud Haakonssen, ed., *Adam Smith*. Dartmouth: Aldershot, 1998.
– 'The Utilitarianism of Adam Smith's Policy Advice,' in Knud Haakonssen, ed., *Adam Smith*. Dartmouth: Aldershot, 1998.
Carey, Mary. *New Jerusalem's Glory*. London: n.p., 1651.
– *A Word in Season to the Kingdom of England*. London: Giles Calvert, 1647.
Chisick, Harvey. 'David Hume and the Common People,' in Peter Jones, ed., *The 'Science of Man' in the Scottish Enlightenment: Hume, Reid and Their Contemporaries*. Edinburgh: Edinburgh University Press, 1989.
Christopher, Georgia B. *Milton and the Science of the Saints*. Princeton: Princeton University Press, 1982.
Clark, John P. *The Philosophic Anarchism of William Godwin*. Princeton: Princeton University Press, 1977.
Clarkson, Laurence. *A Single Eye*. London: n.p., 1650.
Cockburn, James C. *A History of English Assizes, 1558–1714*. Cambridge: University Press, 1972.
Cockshutt, A.O.J. *The Unbelievers: English Agnostic Thought, 1840–1890*. London: Collins, 1964.
Coleridge, Samuel Taylor. *Coleridge's Writings*, vol. 1, *On Politics and Society*, ed. John Morrow. London, Macmillan, 1990.
– *Coleridge's Writings*, vol. 2, *On Humanity*, ed. Anya Taylor. London: Macmillan, 1994.
– *The Collected Works*, ed. Lewis Patton and Peter Mann. Princeton: Princeton University Press, 1971.
Collini, Stefan. 'From Sectarian Radical to National Possession: John Stuart Mill in English Culture, 1873–1945,' in Michael Laine, ed., *A Cultivated Mind: Essays on J.S. Mill Presented to John M. Robson*. Toronto: University of Toronto Press, 1991.
– Introduction to vol. 21 of J.S. Mill, *Collected Works*, ed. John Robson. Toronto: University of Toronto Press, 1969–90.
Copp, David. 'The Iterated-Utilitarianism of J.S. Mill,' in Wesley Cooper, Kai Nielsen, and Steven Patten, eds., *New Essays in John Stuart Mill and Utilitarianism*. Guelph: Canadian Association for Publishing in Philosophy, 1979.

Crehan, Stewart. *Blake in Context*. Dublin: Gill and Macmillan, 1984.
Cropsey, Joseph. Introduction to Thomas Hobbes, *A Dialogue between a Philosopher and a Student of the Common Laws of England*. Chicago: University of Chicago Press, 1971.
Cudworth, Ralph. *The True Intellectual System of the Universe*. London: Richard Royston, 1678.
Cunliffe, Christopher. *Joseph Butler's Moral and Religious Thought*. Oxford: Clarendon Press, 1992.
Darwall, Stephen. *The British Moralists and the Internal 'Ought': 1640–1740*. Cambridge: Cambridge University Press, 1995.
– 'Conscience as Self-Authorizing in Butler's Ethics,' in Christopher Cunliffe, ed., *Joseph Butler's Moral and Religious Thought*. Oxford: Clarendon Press, 1992.
Davidson, Edward H., and William J. Scheik. *Paine, Scripture and Authority: The Age of Reason as Religious and Political Idea*. London: Associated University Presses, 1994.
Davie, George. *The Scottish Enlightenment and Other Essays*. Edinburgh: Polygon, 1991.
Davies, Catherine Glyn. *Conscience as Consciousness: The Idea of Self-Awareness in French Philosophic Writing from Descartes to Diderot*. Oxford: The Voltaire Society, 1990.
Defoe, Daniel. *A Letter to a Dissenter from his Friend at the Hague, concerning the Penal Laws and the Test; shewing that the Popular Plea for Liberty of Conscience is not concerned in that Question*. London: R. Baldwin, 1688.
– *A New Test of the Church of England's Loyalty: Or, Whiggish Loyalty and Church Liberty Compared*. London: n.p. 1702.
– *Moll Flanders*. New York: New American Library, 1981.
– *Persecution Anatomized*. London: n.p. 1705.
Dekker, Thomas. *The Dramatic Works*, ed. Fredson Bowers. Cambridge: Cambridge University Press, 1958.
Deleuze, Gilles. *Empiricism and Subjectivity: An Essay on Hume's Theory of Human Nature*, trans. Constantin V. Boundas. New York: Columbia University Press, 1991.
Diderot, Denis. *Le fils naturel*, in *Oeuvres Complètes*. Paris: Société encyclopédique français et le Club français du livre, 1969–73.
– *Political Writings*, trans. John Hope Mason and Robert Wokler. Cambridge: Cambridge University Press, 1992.
Diderot, Denis, et Jean D'Alembert. *L'Encyclopédie ou Dictionaire raisonné des sciences, des arts et des métiers* (1751). New York: Readex Microprint Corporation, 1969.

Disalvo, Jackie. *War of Titans: Blake's Critique of Milton and the Politics of Religion*. Pittsburgh: University of Pittsburgh Press, 1983.

Dodge, Guy Howard. *The Political Thought of the Huguenots of the Dispersion: With Special Reference to the Thought and Influence of Pierre Jurieu*. New York: Columbia University Press, 1947.

Donnelly, Jack, and Rhoda E. Howard, eds. *International Handbook of Human Rights*. Westport, Conn.: Greenwood, 1987.

Donner, Wendy. *The Liberal Self*. Ithaca: Cornell University Press, 1991.

Dryden, John. *The Poems*, ed. John Sargeaunt. London: Oxford University Press, 1910.

Dryer, D.P. 'Justice, Liberty, and the Principle of Utility in Mill,' in Wesley Cooper, Kai Nielsen, and Steven Patten, eds., *New Essays in John Stuart Mill and Utilitarianism*. Guelph: Canadian Association for Publishing in Philosophy, 1979.

Dunn, John. 'The Claim to Freedom of Conscience: Freedom of Speech, Freedom of Thought, Freedom of Worship?' in O.P. Grell, J.I. Israel, and N. Tyacke, eds., *From Persecution to Toleration: The Glorious Revolution and Reason in England*. Oxford: Clarendon Press, 1991.

– *The Political Thought of John Locke*. Cambridge: Cambridge University Press, 1969.

Dunn, Mary Maples. *William Penn: Politics and Conscience*. Princeton: Princeton University Press, 1967.

Dunn, Richard. 'William Penn's Odyssey: From Child of Light to Absentee Landlord,' in J. Morrell, P. Slack, and D. Woolf, eds., *Public Duty and Private Conscience in Seventeenth-Century England*. Oxford: Clarendon, 1993.

Eagleton, Terry. *William Shakespeare*. Oxford: Basil Blackwell, 1986.

Emerson, Ralph Waldo. *The Complete Works*. London: A.P. Watt and Son, 1903.

Emerson, Roger L. 'Science and Moral Philosophy,' in M.A. Stewart, ed., *Studies in the Philosophy of the Scottish Enlightenment*. Oxford: Clarendon Press, 1990.

Erdman, David V. *Blake: Prophet against Empire*. Princeton: Princeton University Press, 1969.

Erikson, Erik. *Young Man Luther*. London: Faber and Faber, 1958.

Ernst, James E. *The Political Thought of Roger Williams*. Seattle: University of Washington Press, 1979.

Ewin, R.E. *Virtues and Rights: The Moral Philosophy of Thomas Hobbes*. Boulder: Westview, 1991.

Ferguson, Adam. *Principles of Moral and Political Science*. Edinburgh: W. Creech, 1792.

Fisher, Peter F. *The Valley of Vision: Blake as Prophet and Revolutionary*, ed. Northrop Frye. Toronto: University of Toronto Press, 1961.

Fleischacker, Samuel. 'Philosophy in Moral Practice: Kant and Adam Smith,' in Knud Haakonssen, ed., *Adam Smith*. Dartmouth: Aldershot, 1998.

Fleissner, Robert F. *The Prince and the Professor: The Wittenberg Connection in Marlowe, Shakespeare, Goethe, and Frost*. Heidelberg: Carl Winter, 1986.

Forbes, Duncan. *Hume's Philosophical Politics*. Cambridge: Cambridge University Press, 1975.

Fox, John. *The Book of the Martyrs*. London: The Book Society, 1931.

Foxgrover, David Lee. 'John Calvin's Understanding of Conscience.' PhD dissertation, Claremont Graduate School, 1978.

Franklin, Benjamin. *The Writings*, ed. Albert Henry Smyth. New York: Macmillan, 1907.

Freud, Sigmund. *The Interpretation of Dreams*. London: George Allen and Unwin, 1982.

- *New Introductory Lectures on Psychoanalysis and Other Works*, trans. James Strachey. London: Hogarth Press, 1964.

- *The Origins of Psycho-Analysis: Letters to Wilhelm Fleiss, Drafts and Notes: 1887–1902*, ed. Marie Bonaparte, Anna Freud, and Ernst Kris, trans. Eric Mosbacher and James Strachey. London: Imago, 1954.

Fruchtman, Jack Jr. *Thomas Paine and the Religion of Nature*. Baltimore: The Johns Hopkins University Press, 1993.

- *Thomas Paine: Apostle of Freedom*. New York: Four Walls Eight Windows, 1994.

Frye, Northrop. *Fearful Symmetry: A Study of William Blake*. Princeton: Princeton University Press, 1947.

- *Five Essays on Milton's Epic*. London: Routledge and Kegan Paul, 1966.

Frye, Roland Mushat. *The Renaissance Hamlet: Issues and Response in 1600*. Princeton: Princeton University Press, 1984.

- *Shakespeare and Christian Doctrine*. Princeton: Princeton University Press, 1963.

Furness, Horace Howard. *The Varorium Shakespeare*. Philadelphia: J.B. Lippincott, 1908.

Gay, John. *The Fundamental Principle of Virtue or Morality*, in J.B. Schneewind, ed., *Moral Philosophy from Montaigne to Kant*. Cambridge: Cambridge University Press, 1990.

Gay, Peter. *The Enlightenment: An Interpretation*. New York: Alfred Knopf, 1976.

- ed. *John Locke on Education*. New York: Columbia University Press, 1964.

Geisst, Charles R. *The Political Thought of Milton*. London: Macmillan, 1984.

Glassman, Peter. *J.S. Mill: The Evolution of a Genius*. Gainesville: University Presses of Florida, 1985.

Glausser, Wayne. 'Three Approaches to Locke and the Slave Trade.' *Journal of the History of Ideas* 21 (1990).

Godwin, William. *Enquiry concerning Political Justice and Its Influence on Morals and Happiness*, ed. F.E.L. Priestley. Toronto: University of Toronto Press, 1946.

– *History of the Commonwealth of England from Its Commencement, to the Restoration of Charles the Second*. London: Henry Colburn, 1824.

– *Memoirs of Mary Wollstonecraft*. Oxford: Woodstock Books, 1993.

Goethe, Johann Wolfgang von. *Maxims and Reflections*, trans. Thomas Bailey Saunders. London: Macmillan, 1908.

Goldie, Mark. 'John Locke's Circle and James II.' *The Historical Journal* 35 (1992).

Gollanz, Israel. *The Sources of Hamlet*. London: Oxford University Press, 1926.

Gottried, Rudolf B. *A Conscience Undeflowered: A Lecture on Thomas More*. Lunenburg, Vt.: Stinehour Press, 1957.

Graham, John W. *Conscription and Conscience: A History of 1916–1919*. London: Allen & Unwin, 1998.

Grant, Ruth. *John Locke's Liberalism*. Chicago: University of Chicago Press, 1987.

Green, Thomas A. 'The English Criminal Trial Jury and the Law-Finding Traditions,' in J.S. Cockburn and T.A. Green, eds., *Twelve Good Men and True: The Criminal Trial Jury in England, 1200–1800*. Princeton: Princeton University Press, 1988.

– *Verdict According to Conscience*. Chicago: University of Chicago Press, 1985.

Greenblatt, Stephen. *Renaissance Self-Fashioning: From More to Shakespeare*. Chicago: University of Chicago Press, 1980.

– *Shakespearean Negotiations: The Circulation of Social Energy in Renaissance England*. Berkeley: University of California Press, 1988.

Griswold, Charles, Jr, *Adam Smith and the Virtues of Enlightenment*. Cambridge: Cambridge University Press, 1999.

Gunn, J.A.W. *Politics and the Public Interest in the Seventeenth Century*. Toronto: University of Toronto Press, 1969.

Haakonssen, Knud. 'Enlightened Dissent,' in K. Haakonssen, ed., *Enlightenment and Religion: Rational Dissent in Eighteenth-Century Britain*. Cambridge: Cambridge University Press, 1996.

– *The Science of a Legislator: The Natural Jurisprudence of David Hume and Adam Smith*. Cambridge: Cambridge University Press, 1981.

Hampson, Norman. *The Enlightenment*. Harmondsworth: Penguin, 1968.

Haydn, Hiram. *The Counter-Renaissance*. New York: Charles Scribner's Sons, 1950.
Hebblethwaite, Brian. 'Butler on Conscience and Virtue,' in Christopher Cunliffe, ed., *Joseph Butler's Moral and Religious Thought*. Oxford: Clarendon, 1992.
Hegel, Georg Wilhelm Friedrich. *The Philosophy of History*, trans. J. Sibree. New York: Dover, 1956.
Heidegger, Martin. *Being and Time*, trans. J. Macquarrie and E. Robinson. New York: Harper and Row, 1962.
Helvétius, Claude Adrien. *De l'esprit*. New York: Burt Franklin, 1810, reprinted 1970.
– *A Treatise on Man; His Intellectual Faculties and His Education*, trans. W. Hooper. New York: Burt Franklin, 1969.
Hill, Christopher, *The English Bible and the Seventeenth-Century Revolution*. London: Allen Lane, 1993.
– *Liberty against the Law: Some Seventeenth-Century Controversies*. London: Allen Lane, 1996.
– *Milton and the English Revolution*. London: Faber & Faber, 1979.
– *The World Turned Upside Down*. Harmondsworth: Penguin, 1984.
Hill, Thomas E., Jr. *Autonomy and Self-Respect*. Cambridge: Cambridge University Press, 1991.
– 'Four Conceptions of Conscience,' in Ian Shapiro and Robert Adams, eds., *Integrity and Conscience*. Nomos Series, XL. New York: New York University Press, 1998.
Hobbes, Thomas. *The English Works*, ed. W. Molesworth. London: J. Bohn, 1840.
– *Leviathan*, ed. M. Oakeshott. New York: Collier, 1968.
Holbach, Paul Henri Thiry, baron d'. 'Common Sense, or Natural Ideas Opposed to Supernatural,' in Isaac Kramnick, ed., *The Portable Enlightenment Reader*. Harmondsworth: Penguin, 1995.
Holmes, Richard. *Coleridge: Darker Reflections*. London: HarperCollins, 1998.
Holmes, Stephen. 'Political Psychology in Hobbes's *Behemoth*,' in M.G. Dietz, ed., *Thomas Hobbes and Political Theory*. Lawrence: University of Kansas, 1990.
Hope, V.P. *Virtue by Consensus: The Moral Philosophy of Hutcheson, Hume, and Adam Smith*. Oxford: Clarendon, 1989.
Houston, R.A. *Social Change in the Age of Enlightenment: Edinburgh, 1660–1760*. Oxford: Clarendon, 1994.
Howells, R.J. *Pierre Jurieu: Antinomian Radical*. Durham: University of Durham, 1983.

Hubberthorn, Richard, Samuel Fisher, and Francis Howgill. *Persecution Inconsistent with Christianity, Humane Society, and the Honour of Princes.* London: n.p., 1670.

Hughes, Martin. 'Locke on Taxation and Suffrage.' *History of Political Thought* 11 (1990).

Hulliung, Mark. *The Autocritique of Enlightenment: Rousseau and the Philosophes.* Cambridge: Harvard University Press, 1994.

Hume, David. *An Enquiry concerning the Principles of Morals*, ed. Tom L. Beauchamp. Oxford: Clarendon, 1998.

– *The History of England.* London: William Pickering, 1826.

– *The Philosophical Works*, ed. T.H. Green and T.H. Grose. London: Longmans, Green and Co., 1875.

Hundert, E.J. *The Enlightenment's Fable: Bernard Mandeville and the Discovery of Society.* Cambridge: Cambridge University Press, 1994.

Hutcheson, Francis. *An Essay on the Nature and Conduct of the Passions and Affections with Illustrations on the Moral Sense, 1728.* Menston: Scolar Press, 1972.

– *An Inquiry into the Original of our Ideas of Beauty and Virtue: in Two Treatises.* London: J. Darby et al., 1726.

– *On Human Nature: Reflections on Our Common Systems of Morality*, ed. Thomas Mautner. Cambridge: Cambridge University Press, 1993.

– *Thoughts on Laughter and Observations on 'The Fable of the Bees' in Six Letters* (1724–25). Bristol: Thoemmes Antiquarian Books, 1989.

Ignatieff, Michael. *The Warrior's Honor: Ethnic War and the Modern Conscience.* Toronto: Viking, 1998.

Izubuchi, Hiroshi. 'A Hamlet of Our Own: Some Japanese Adaptations,' in Yoshiko Uéno, ed., *Hamlet in Japan.* New York: AMS Press, 1995.

James I. *The Political Works of James I*, reprinted from 1616 edition, ed. Charles H. McIlwain. Cambridge: Harvard University Press, 1918.

Jefferson, Thomas. *The Complete Jefferson*, ed. Saul K. Padover. New York: Duell, Sloan and Pearce, 1943.

Jones, J.R. 'The Revolution in Context,' in J.R. Jones, ed., *Liberty Secured? Britain before and after 1688.* Stanford: Stanford University Press, 1992.

Jonsen, Albert R., and Stephen Toulmin. *The Abuse of Casuistry: A History of Moral Reasoning.* Berkeley: University of California Press, 1988.

Jordan, W.K. *Development of Religious Toleration.* Gloucester, Mass.: Peter Smith, 1965.

Jourdan, Serena. *The Sparrow and the Flea: The Sense of Providence in Shakespeare and Montaigne.* Salzburg: Institut für Anglistik und Amerikanistik, 1983.

Kamm, Josephine. *John Stuart Mill in Love.* London: Gordon & Cremonesi, 1977.

Kant, Immanuel. *Foundation of the Metaphysics of Morals and What Is Enlightenment?* trans. Lewis White Beck. Chicago: University of Chicago Press, 1950.
Kashatus, William C. III. *Conflict of Conviction: A Reappraisal of Quaker Involvement in the American Revolution*. Lanham: University Press of America, 1990.
Kateb, George. 'Socratic Integrity,' in Ian Shapiro and Robert Adams, eds., *Integrity and Conscience*. Nomos Series, XL. New York: New York University Press, 1998.
Keane, John. *Tom Paine: A Political Life*. London: Bloomsbury, 1995.
Kierkegaard, Sören, *Either/Or*, trans. Walter Lowrie. London: Oxford University Press, 1944.
– *The Journals*, trans. Alexander Dru. London: Oxford University Press, 1938.
Knox, John. *The First Blast of the Trumpet against the Monstrous Regiment of Women*. Geneva: J. Crespin, 1558.
Kramnick, Isaac. *The Portable Enlightenment Reader*. Harmondsworth: Penguin, 1995.
Lake, Peter. *Anglicans and Puritans? Presbyterianism and English Conformist Thought from Whitgift to Hooker*. London: Unwin Hyman, 1988.
Langbein, John. *Torture and the Law of Proof: Europe and England in the Ancien Régime*. Chicago: University of Chicago Press, 1977.
Law, William, *Remarks upon a Late Book entitled The Fable of the Bees, or Private Vices, Public Benefits*. London: William & John Innys, 1725.
– *A Serious Call to a Devout and Holy Life* (1728). London: J.M. Dent and Sons, 1955.
LeComte, Edward. *Milton and Sex*. London: Macmillan, 1978.
Leites, Edmund. 'Casuistry and Character,' in E. Leites, ed., *Conscience and Casuistry in Early Modern Europe*. Cambridge: Cambridge University Press, 1988.
A Letter to a Member of Parliament for Liberty of Conscience, By a Person of Honour. London: Richard Baldwin, 1689.
Lewis, C.S. *Studies in Words*. Cambridge, Cambridge University Press, 1991.
Locke, Don. *A Fantasy of Reason: The Life and Thought of William Godwin*. London: Routledge and Kegan Paul, 1980.
Locke, John. *The Educational Writings*, ed. J.L. Axtell. Cambridge: Cambridge University Press, 1968.
– *An Essay concerning Human Understanding*. London: Thomas Bassett, 1690.
– *An Essay concerning Human Understanding*, ed. Peter N. Nidditch. Oxford: Clarendon, 1975.
– *A Letter concerning Toleration*, in *The Works*. London: Thomas Tegg, 1823.

- *A New Method of making Common-Place-Books*. London: J. Greenwood, 1706.
- *The Reasonableness of Christianity*. London: George Vertue, 1836.
- *Two Treatises of Government*, ed. Peter Laslett. Cambridge: Cambridge University Press, 1988.
- *The Works*. London: Thomas Tegg, 1823.

Loesburg, Jonathan. *Fictions of Consciousness: Mill, Newman and the Reading of Victorian Prose*. New Brunswick, N.J.: Rutgers University Press, 1986.

Luhmann, Niklas. 'The Individuality of the Individual,' in Thomas C. Heller, Morton Sosna, and David E. Wellbery, eds., *Reconstructing Individualism: Autonomy, Individuality and the Self in Western Thought*. Stanford: Stanford University Press, 1986.

Lupton, Julia Reinhard, and Kenneth Reinhard. *After Oedipus: Shakespeare in Psychoanalysis*. Ithaca: Cornell University Press, 1993.

Luther, Martin. *Lectures on Romans*, trans. and ed. Wilhelm Pauck. London: SCM Press, 1961.

- *Works*, ed. Jaroslav Pelikan. St. Louis: Concordia Publishing House, 1958.

Lyon, David. *Rights, Welfare, and Mill's Moral Theory*. New York: Oxford University Press, 1994.

Macaulay, Thomas Babington, Lord. *The Complete Works*. London: Longmans Green, 1897.

Macpherson, C.B. *The Political Theory of Possessive Individualism*. Oxford: Oxford University Press, 1962.

Mandeville, Bernard. *Arete-logia or, an Enquiry into the Original of Moral Virtue*. London: Cleur and Campbell, 1728.

- *Free Thoughts on Religion, the Church and National Happiness*. London: J. Brotherton, 1723.
- 'A Search into the Nature of Society,' in Douglas Garman, ed., *The Fable of the Bees or Private Vices, Public Benefits*. London: Wishart and Co., 1934.

Marshall, John, *John Locke: Resistance, Religion and Responsibility*. Cambridge: Cambridge University Press, 1994.

Marx, Karl, and Friedrich Engels. *Manifesto of the Communist Party*, in *Selected Works*. Moscow: Progesss Publishers, 1968.

Matheson, Mark. 'Hamlet and "A Matter Tender and Dangerous,"' *Shakespeare Quarterly* 46 (1995).

McNaughton, David, 'British Moralists of the Eighteenth Century: Shaftesbury, Butler and Price,' in Stuart Brown, ed., *British Philosophy and the Age of Enlightenment*. London: Routledge, 1996.

Mekeel, Arthur J. *The Quakers and the American Revolution*. York: Sessions Book Trust, 1996.

Mercer, Peter. *Hamlet and the Acting of Revenge*. London: Macmillan, 1967.
Mill, James. *Analysis of the Phenomena of the Human Mind*. New York: Augustus Kelley, 1967.
Mill, John Stuart. *Collected Works*, ed. John M. Robson. Toronto: University of Toronto Press, 1969–90.
– *The Correspondence of John Stuart Mill and Auguste Comte*, trans. and ed. Oscar A. Haac. New Brunswick, N.J.: Transaction Publishers, 1995.
Miller, David. *Philosophy and Ideology in Hume's Political Thought*. Oxford: Clarendon, 1981.
Milton, John. *Areopagitica* in *The Prose of John Milton*, ed. J. Max Patrick. New York: New York University Press, 1968.
– *Complete Prose Works*. New Haven: Yale University Press, 1953–82.
– *The Poems*, ed. H. Darbishire. Oxford: Oxford University Press, 1961.
Minkowicz, Peter. *Profits, Priests and Princes: Adam Smith's Emancipation of Economics from Politics and Religion*. Stanford: Stanford University Press, 1993.
Montaigne, Michel de Montaigne. *The Essays*, trans. and ed. Jacob Zeitlin. New York: Alfred Knopf, 1934.
Moore, James, 'The Two Systems of Francis Hutcheson,' in M.A. Stewart, ed., *Studies in the Philosophy of the Scottish Enlightenment*. Oxford: Clarendon, 1990.
More, St Thomas, *The Complete Works*, ed. John Headley, trans. Sister Scholastica Mandeville. New Haven: Yale University Press, 1969.
Morris, Christopher. *Political Thought in England: Tyndale to Hooker*. London: Oxford University Press, 1965.
Newman, John Henry, Cardinal. *An Essay in Aid of A Grammar of Assent*. Notre Dame: University of Notre Dame Press, 1979.
– *A Letter to his Grace the Duke of Norfolk on the Occasion of Mr. Gladstone's Recent Expostulation*. London, Pickering, 1875.
Nietzsche, Friedrich. *The Will to Power*, trans. Walter Kaufmann. New York: Viking, 1968.
Nojima, Hidekatsu, 'The Mirror of Hamlet,' in Yoshiko Uèno, ed., *Hamlet in Japan*. New York: AMS Press, 1995.
Oesterberg, V. *Prince Hamlet's Age*. Koebenhavn: A.F. Fhoest, 1924.
Orr, Robert R., *Reason and Authority: The Thought of William Chillingworth* (Oxford: Clarendon, 1967).
Packe, Michael St John. *The Life of John Stuart Mill*. London: Secker and Warburg, 1954.
Paine, Thomas. *The Age of Reason*, in Daniel Edwin Wheller, ed., *Life and Writings of Thomas Paine*. New York: Vincent Parke, 1908.

- *Agrarian Justice*. Paris: W. Adlard, 1797.
- *Common Sense*. Edinburgh: Charles Elliot, 1776.
- *The Complete Writings*, ed. Philip S. Foner. New York: Citadel Press, 1945.
- *Rights of Man, Common Sense and Other Political Writings*, ed. Mark Philp. Oxford: Oxford University Press, 1995.

Pearson, Christian, SSF. 'Line upon Line: Here a Little, There a Little: Some Letters of Martin Luther,' in Peter Newman Brooks, ed., *Seven-Headed Luther: Essays in Commemoration of a Quincentenary 1483–1983*. Oxford: Clarendon, 1983.

Pelikan, Jaroslav. *Obedient Rebels: Catholic Substance and Protestant Principle in Luther's Reformation*. London: SCM Press, 1964.

- *Spirit versus Structure: Luther and the Institutions of the Church*. London: Collins, 1968.

Penelhum, Terence. *Butler*. London: Routledge and Kegan Paul, 1985.

Perkins, Mary Anne. *Coleridge's Philosophy: The Logos as Unifying Principle*. Oxford: Clarendon, 1994.

Perkins, William, *The Whole Treatise of the Cases of Conscience, Distinguished Into Three Books*. Cambridge: John Legat, 1606.

- *The Work of William Perkins*, ed. Ian Breward. Abington: Appleford, 1970.

Philp, Mark. *Godwin's Political Justice*. London: Duckworth, 1986.

Pieper, Josef. *The Four Cardinal Virtues*. Notre Dame: Notre Dame University Press, 1966.

Pierce, C.A. *Conscience in the New Testament*. London: SCM Press, 1955.

Pocock, J.G.A. 'Post-Puritan England and the Problem of the Enlightenment,' in Perez Zagorin, ed., *Culture and Politics from Puritanism to the Enlightenment*. Berkeley: University of California Press, 1980.

Pope, Alexander. *Essay on Man*. Edinburgh: William Blackwell, 1901.

Porter, Roy. 'The Enlightenment in England,' in R. Porter and M. Teich, eds., *The Enlightenment in National Context*. Cambridge: Cambridge University Press, 1981.

Potts, Timothy C. *Conscience in Medieval Philosophy*. Cambridge: Cambridge University Press, 1980.

Price, Richard. *A Review of the Principle Questions in Morals* (3rd ed., 1787), ed. D.D. Raphael. Oxford: Clarendon, 1948.

Prosser, Eleanor. *Hamlet and Revenge*. Stanford: University Press, 1971.

Proudhon, Pierre-Joseph. *De la Justice dans la Révolution et dans l'Église*. Paris: Fayard, 1990.

Rabieh, Michael S. 'The Reasonableness of Locke, or the Questionableness of Christianity.' *The Journal of Politics* 53 (1991).

Raphael, D.D. 'Adam Smith,' in David Daiches, Peter Jones, and Jean Jones, eds., *The Scottish Enlightenment, 1730–1790: A Hotbed of Genius*. Edinburgh: The Saltire Society, 1996.

Rauschning, Herman. *Hitler Speaks*. London: Thornton Butterworth, 1939.

Rawls, John. *A Theory of Justice*. Cambridge: Belknap Press, 1971.

Ricoeur, Paul. *The Just*, trans. David Pellauer. Chicago: University of Chicago Press, 2000.

Roper, Lynda. *Oedipus and the Devil: Witchcraft, Sexuality and Religion in Early Modern Europe*. London: Routledge, 1995.

Rorty, Richard. *Contingency, Irony, and Solidarity*. Cambridge: Cambridge University Press, 1989.

– *Philosophic Papers*, vol. 1. Cambridge: Cambridge University Press, 1991.

Rose, Elliot. *Cases of Conscience*. Cambridge: Cambridge University Press, 1975.

Rousseau, Jean-Jacques. *Emile or On Education*, ed. Allan Bloom. New York: Basic Books, 1979.

– *The First and Second Discourses*, trans. R.D. Masters and J. Masters. New York: St. Martin's Press, 1964.

– *Julie or the New Heloise*, trans. Philip Stewart and Jean Vaché, vol. 6 of Roger Masters and Christopher Kelly, eds., *The Collective Writings of Rousseau*. Hanover, N.H.: University Press of New England, 1997.

– *Oeuvres Complètes*, ed. Bernard Gagnebin and Marcel Raymond. Paris: Gallimard-Pléiade, 1959.

Rowse, A.L., *Milton the Puritan*. London: Macmillan, 1977.

Rupp, Gordon. 'Luther against "The Turk, The Pope And The Devil,"' in Peter Newman Brooks, ed., *Seven-Headed Luther: Essays in Commemoration of a Quincentenary 1483–1983*. Oxford: Clarendon, 1983.

Rutherford, Samuel. *A Free Disputation against pretended Liberty of Conscience*. London: Andrew Crook, 1649.

Ryan, Alan. Introduction to vol. 9 of J.S. Mill, *The Collected Works*, ed. John Robson. Toronto: University of Toronto Press, 1969–90.

– *The Philosophy of John Stuart Mill*. London: Macmillan, 1998.

– 'Sense and Sensibility in Mill's Political Thought,' in Michael Laine, ed., *A Cultivated Mind: Essays on J.S. Mill Presented to John M. Robson*. Toronto: University of Toronto Press, 1991.

Ryle, Gilbert. *Collected Papers*. Bristol: Thoemmes, 1990.

Sabean, David Warren. *Power in the Blood: Popular Culture and Village Discourse in Early Modern Germany*. Cambridge: Cambridge University Press, 1984.

Samson, Margaret. '"Will You Hear What a Casuist He Is?": Thomas Hobbes as Director of Conscience.' *History of Political Thought* 11 (1990).
Sanderson, Robert. *The Works in Six Volumes*, ed. W. Jacobson. Oxford: Oxford University Press, 1854.
– *Bishop Sanderson's Lectures on Conscience and Human Law* (1647), ed. and trans. C. Wordsworth. Lincoln: James Williamson, 1877.
Sapiro, Virginia. *A Vindication of Political Virtue*. Chicago: University of Chicago Press, 1992.
Schneewind, J.B. *The Invention of Autonomy: A History of Modern Moral Philosophy*. Cambridge: Cambridge University Press, 1998.
– *Moral Philosophy from Montaigne to Kant*. Cambridge: Cambridge University Press, 1990.
Schochet, Gordon J. 'John Locke and Religious Toleration,' in Lois G. Schwoerer, ed., *The Revolution of 1688–1689: Changing Perspectives*. Cambridge: Cambridge University, 1992.
– 'Why Should History Matter? Political Theory and the History of Discourse,' in J.G.A. Pocock, G.J. Schochet, and L.G. Schwoerer, eds., *The Varieties of British Political Thought, 1500–1800*. Cambridge: Cambridge University Press, 1993.
Semmel, Bernard. *John Stuart Mill and the Pursuit of Virtue*. New Haven: Yale University Press, 1984.
Shaftesbury, Anthony Ashley Cooper, 3rd Earl of. *Characteristics of Men, Manners, Opinions, Times, etc.* London: Grant Richards, 1900.
– *Complete Works*, ed. G. Hemmerlich and W. Benda. Stuttgart: Frommann-Holzboog, 1981.
Simmons, A. John. *On the Edge of Anarchy: Locke, Consent and the Limits of Society*. Princeton: Princeton University Press, 1993.
Skinner, Andrew Stewart. *A System of Social Science: Papers Relating to Adam Smith*. Oxford: Clarendon, 1996.
Skorupski, John. *John Stuart Mill*. London: Routledge, 1989.
– 'Utilitarianism,' in John Skorupski, ed., *The Cambridge Companion to Mill*. Cambridge: Cambridge University Press, 1998.
Smith, Adam. *Lectures on Justice, Police, Revenue and Arms* (1763), ed. E. Cannan. New York: Augustus Kelley, 1964.
– *The Theory of Moral Sentiments*, 10th ed. London: T. Cadell, 1804.
Spinoza, Benedict de. *Tractatus Theologico-Politicus*, chap. 14, in A.G. Wernham, trans. and ed., *The Political Works*. Oxford: Clarendon, 1958.
Sterne, Laurence. *The Abuses of Conscience*. York: Caesar Ward, 1750.
– *The Sermons of Mr. Yorick*. London: J. Dodsley, 1777.

Stewart, John B. *Opinion and Reform in Hume's Political Philosophy*. Princeton: Princeton University Press, 1992.

Stoner, James R., Jr. *Common Law and Liberal Theory: Coke, Hobbes and the Origins of American Constitutionalism*. Lawrence: University of Kansas Press, 1992.

Strauss, Gerald. '"Barrabas": Luther as Barrabas,' in Peter Newman Brooks, ed., *Seven-Headed Luther: Essays in Commemoration of a Quincentenary 1483–1983*. Oxford: Clarendon, 1983.

Strugnell, Anthony. *Diderot's Politics: A Study of Diderot's Political Thought after the Revolution*. The Hague: Martinus Nijhoff, 1973.

Swift, Jonathan. *The Prose Works*, ed. H. Davis. Oxford: Blackwell, 1948.

Takahashi, Yasumari. 'Hamlet and the Anxiety of Modern Japan.' *Shakespeare Survey* 48 (1995).

Tarkov, Nathan. *Locke's Education for Liberty*. Chicago: University of Chicago Press, 1984.

Taylor, Jeremy. *Ductor Dubitantium, or The Rule of Conscience in all her General Measures: Serving as a great Instrument for the determination of Cases of Conscience*. London: Norton, 1676.

Thompson, E.P. *Witness against the Beast: William Blake and the Moral Law*. Cambridge: Cambridge University Press, 1993.

Tuck, Richard. *Hobbes*. Oxford: Oxford University Press, 1989.

Tully, James. *An Approach to Political Philosophy: Locke in Contexts*. Cambridge: Cambridge University Press, 1993.

– ed. *John Locke, A Letter concerning Toleration*. Indianapolis: Hackett, 1983.

Turk, Christopher. *Coleridge and Mill: A Study of Influence*. Aldershot: Avebury, 1988.

Tyndale, William. *The Obedience of a Christian Man*. Menston: Scolar Press, 1970.

– *The Works*, ed. Stanley Lawrence Greenslade. Glasgow: Blackie, 1983.

Valdesso, John. *Divine Considerations*. Cambridge: Roger Daniel, 1646.

Virt, Guenter. 'Conscience in Conflict?' in Gerhard Zecha and Paul Weingartner, eds., *Conscience: An Interdisciplinary View*. Dordrecht: D. Reidel, 1987.

Voltaire, *Lettres philosophiques*, ed. Gustave Lanson. Paris: Edouard Cornély, 1909.

– *Oeuvres Complètes*. Paris: Garnier, 1879.

– *La Voix du sage et du peuple*. Amsterdam: n.p., 1750.

Waldron, Jeremy. *Liberal Rights: Collected Papers 1981–1991*. Cambridge: Cambridge University Press, 1993.

Walwin, William. *Juries Justified: or A WORD OF CORRECTION to Mr. Henry Robinson; for His seven Objections against Trial of Causes, by Juries of twelve men*. London: Robert Wood, 1651.
Walzer, Michael. *The Revolution of the Saints: A Study in the Origins of Radical Politics*. London: Weidenfeld and Nicolson, 1966.
– *Spheres of Justice: A Defence of Pluralism and Equality*. Oxford: Martin Robertson, 1983.
– *Thick and Thin: Moral Argument at Home and Abroad*. Notre Dame: University of Notre Dame Press, 1994.
Webster, Brenda S. *Blake's Prophetic Psychology*. London: Macmillan, 1983.
Werblowsky, R.J. Zwi. 'The Concept of Conscience in Jewish Perspective,' trans. Richard Francis Carrington Hull, in Curatorium of the C.G. Jung Institute, *Conscience*. Evanston: Northwestern University Press, 1970.
Whitaker, Mark. 'Hobbes View of the Reformation.' *History of Political Thought* 9 (1988).
Wilson, J. Dover. *What Happens in Hamlet*. Cambridge: University Press, 1951.
Winch, Donald. 'Adam Smith: Scottish Moral Philosopher as Political Economist,' in Hiroshi Mizuta and Chuhei Sugiyama, eds., *Adam Smith: International Perspectives*. New York: St. Martin's Press, 1993.
– 'Adam Smith: Scottish Moral Philosopher as Political Economist,' in Knud Haakonssen, ed., *Adam Smith*. Dartmouth: Aldershot, 1998.
Wollstonecraft, Mary. *A Vindication of the Rights of Woman*, in Janet Todd, ed., *The Political Writings of Mary Wollstonecraft*. Toronto: University of Toronto Press, 1993.
Wood, Neal. *The Politics of Locke's Philosophy: A Social Study of 'An Essay concerning Human Understanding.'* Berkeley: University of California Press, 1983.
Wootton, David, ed. *John Locke: Political Writings*. London: Penguin, 1993.
Wordsworth, William. *The Poetical Works*, ed. E. de Selincourt and H. Darbishire. Oxford: Clarendon, 1940–49.
Yolton, John W. *A Locke Dictionary*. Oxford: Blackwell, 1993.
Zagorin, Perez. *A History of Political Thought in The English Revolution*. London: Routledge and Kegan Paul, 1954.
– *Milton: Aristocrat and Rebel; The Poet and His Politics*. Woodbridge, Suffolk: D.S. Brewer, 1992.

Index

Abdiel, 51–2, 56
abortion, 181, 183
Act of Supremacy, 27
Act of Uniformity, 27, 30
afterlife. *See* destiny of soul and; immortality
Agrarian Justice, 131, 133, 140
American Revolution, 131, 135, 137–8
Ames, William, 28–30
Anabaptists, 20
anti-Catholicism, 56, 60–1, 63, 86–92, 94, 105, 111, 154
Aquinas, Saint Thomas, 17–19, 23, 41
Aristotle, 15, 18, 70
Arnold, Matthew, 157
Ashcraft, Richard, 95
atheism/atheists, 32, 80, 88–9, 102, 105–6, 108, 123, 129, 132, 135, 140–1, 148, 154, 167, 215 n. 52
Aubrey, John, 181
Auden, W.H., 142
Augustine, Saint, 21
autonomy, moral, 8, 35, 191 n.5
Ayer, A.J., 143

Bacon, Francis, 44–5, 65, 146–9, 156; *The Advancement of Learning*, 144

Baldwin, William, 27; *A Treatise of Morall Philosophie*, 27
Bayle, Pierre, 30, 32, 35, 90–1, 177, 179; *Commentaire Philosophique*, 91; on the Conscienciaries, 32; on Melanchthon, Philip, 35; on rights of conscience, 30, 90–1
Beethoven, Ludwig van, 135, 175
Bentham, Jeremy, 3–4, 6, 9, 55, 139, 149, 151, 154–6, 161, 165, 169, 170–1, 188; on natural rights, 3, 139, 151
Berkeley, Bishop George, 5, 99, 105–7, 111; *Alciphron*, 105–6; on conscience as innate and unchangeable, 106; *An Essay toward Preventing the Ruin of Great Britain*, 106; on Locke, 106; on obedience to government, 106; opposition to Shaftesbury and Mandeville, 5, 99, 105; opposition to view of morality as manners or taste, 105–6; on religion as necessary for morality, 105–6
Berman, Harold, 19
Bible, 16–17, 25–8, 56–7, 60, 64, 66–7, 69, 88, 140–1, 148, 151, 167–8. *See*

also New Testament; Old Testament
Bilson, Thomas, 28; *The True Difference between Christian Subjection and Unchristian Rebellion*, 28
Black Americans, 137, 138, 219 n.39
Blake, William, 5–8, 10, 131–5, 140–1, 143–52, 156–7, 168–9, 179–80, 187, 218n.8, 218n.17, 221n.93; on British hostility to speculative philosophy, 145; and Byron, 147; on church establishment, 132, 152; on class tensions, 144–5; on commercial civilization, 144; conscience: — and desire, 7, 134; — infallibility of, 132–3; — primacy of, 132–3, 187; on deism, 132, 148–50; egalitarianism of, 132–3; on Enlightenment, 144–6, 148–52, 156, 218n.8; — on constraints of Enlightenment reason, 146, 148; on French Revolution, 147, 149; *The French Revolution*, 149; and Frye, Northrop, 53, 144, 147, 221n.93; *The Ghost of Abel*, 147; and 'god of this world,' 147–8; *Jerusalem*, 146, 150; *King Edward the Third*, 148; *The Laocoon*, 148; and Locke, 133, 144–5, 147–9, 156; *London*, 144; *Newton*, 144; and Paine, 132, 140–1, 152; and Rousseau, 131–4, 149–50; *Vala, or the Four Zoas*, 149–50; and Wordsworth, 147
Bodin, Jean, 63–4
Bradley, A.C., 38, 44
Burke, Edmund, 3–4, 138–40, 149, 151; on natural rights 3, 139, 151; on right of private judgment, 138–9; *Reflections on the Revolution in France*, 139

Butler, Bishop Joseph, 5, 8, 13, 99, 107–12, 116–17, 119; *The Analogy of Religion*, 108; and Anscombe, G.E.M., 109; on church establishment, 111; on conscience as supreme authority, 108–9, 111; *Fifteen Sermons*, 108; *Of Personal Identity*, 108; on reason versus revelation, 110; on relation between conscience, prudence, and benevolence, 13, 107–8; on sociability of humans, 107
Butler, Samuel, 50–1
Byron, Lord, 134, 146–7; *Cain, a Mystery*, 147; *The Island*, 146

Calvin, Jean, 12–13, 23–5, 150, 178; ambivalence about conscience, 24; on civil disobedience, 24–5; on conscience versus law, 24–5; on equity, 25
Campbell, T.D., 126, 129
Carey, Mary, 31, 57
Carlstadt, Andrew, 16–19
Carlyle, Thomas, 155, 174
Carmichael, Gershom, 114
casuistry, 31
Catholic Church, 24, 60–1, 64, 158, 167–8, 179
Catholicism, 6, 20, 28, 38, 41, 56, 60–1, 63, 87–92, 94–5, 97, 105, 109, 111, 150, 153–4, 157, 166–8, 175–6. See *also* anti-Catholicism
Charles I, 56, 61, 66
Chillingworth, William, 28, 30
Chisick, Harvey, 121
Christ. *See* Jesus
Christianity, 14–15, 24
Church of England, 27, 30, 65, 105, 112, 158

Clarkson, Laurence, 31
Coke, Sir Edward, 67, 73–4
Colasterion, 58
Coleridge, Samuel Taylor, 5, 128, 134, 156–9, 162, 164, 170, 172, 179; on Catholicism, 157–8; on church establishment, 157–8; on conscience: priority over consciousness, 5, 156–7, 172, 187; *On the Constitution of the Church and State*, 157; on Enlightenment, 156–7; on love of one's own, 157; *Osario*, 157; on Protestantism, 157
Collini, Stefan, 162, 176
Comte, Auguste, 6, 154, 156, 167–8, 175
Condorcet, Marquis de, 126
conscience: as accessible to simple souls, 132; as anarchic, 178; and antinomianism, 5, 16, 19–20, 28, 32–3, 53–8, 60–2, 77, 86, 134; and benevolence or good-heartedness, 12, 13; and choice, 3, 6, 15, 60, 84, 168–9, 174–5, 187–9 (*see also* conscience, freedom of); Christian conscience supplanting classical reason, 15; and civil disobedience, 6, 13, 21, 24, 182 (*see also* conscience, and conscientious objection); objection; compared to natural law, 14, 19, 23; compared to theoretical understanding, 29; and conscientious objection, 6, 25, 136–7, 165, 182; and consciousness, 7, 35, 38, 48, 172–4, 187; as divine guide, divine judgement, divine law, divine light, or divine voice, 4, 14, 17–18, 29, 31, 51, 56, 109, 132, 152, 154; egalitarian views of, 9, 14–15, 28, 122, 132, 178–9, 187; etymology, 7, 12, 14, 18, 36–8, 83–4, 184, 206n.19; fallibility of, 15–16, 18, 29–30, 57, 66, 69, 77, 142; forensic metaphors (witness, jury, prosecutor, judge), 4, 23–5, 29–30, 108 (*see also* conscience, as legislator); freedom of, 3, 6, 9–10, 20–33, 53–65, 69–70, 86–92, 105, 111, 117–18, 132, 136, 141–2, 154, 156–7, 163–70, 174, 179, 186, 204n.65; and freedom of action, 165; in *Hamlet*, 4, 34–49; heresy and, 54, 60, 65; as heroic or bold, 4, 56, 62; as homeless, 5, 65, 181; and honour, 5, 39–40, 99–100; and humility, 50–1, 62, 140; and immortality, 14–15; as impartial spectator, 5, 49, 123, 125, 127–9; as individual judgment, 8–9, 29, 54, 69, 77, 187; as inner guide, light, or voice, 4, 51, 56–7, 77, 132–3, 137; institutionalization of, 5, 68–9, 74, 76–8, 96, 98, 178; intellectual vs moral-religious, 35; and Kateb's prescriptions, 184–6; and legal authority, 5–6, 8, 10, 13, 19–33, 53–62, 66, 69, 77, 92–6, 106. 165, 181–2 (*see also* conscience, and civil disobedience; conscience, and conscientious objection; conscience, forensic metaphors); as legislator, 4, 23, 30–1, 78, 86, 106, 109; pangs/pains of, 17, 28–9, 101, 105, 127, 161–2; pluralized, 184–6; and prudence, 5, 8, 13, 17–19, 30, 37, 40–1, 44–7, 77–8, 85, 107–8, 110, 112, 135; and reason, 3–4, 5–11, 12, 15, 18, 23, 28, 66, 76–7, 82–6, 94, 106–7, 109–10, 131, 133–4, 139, 145–6, 148, 151, 154, 167, 179, 182, 185, 187–9, 218 n. 17; and religious

ritual observance, 10, 13, 20, 24, 28, 111; retrospective vs. prospective, 4, 6, 29–30; revolution and (see conscience, legal authority and); as rhetoric, 178; and romanticism, 132, 134; and Walzer's prescriptions, 184–6; without religion, 32, 101, 105–6, 184; and Word of God, 16, 20

Conscienciaries, 32

Cudworth, Ralph, 7, 36, 83, 206n.19; *The True Intellectual System of the Universe*, 7, 83

D'Alembert, Jean, 83, 126; *Encyclopédie*, 83

Declaration of Indulgence, 90, 95

Defence of the Realm Act, 177

Defoe, Daniel, 90, 112; *Moll Flanders*, 112; *Robinson Crusoe*, 125

deism: deists, 9, 132, 135–6, 140–1, 144, 148–50, 152

Dekker, Thomas, 52; *If This Be Not a Good Play, the Devil Is in It*, 52

Deleuze, Gilles, 122

Descartes, René, 144

Diderot, Denis, 9, 10, 13, 55, 65, 83, 100, 105, 117–18, 122, 126, 128, 133, 152, 156, 161, 170, 179, 188; on church establishment, 65, 105, 117; on criticizing while obeying bad laws, 55; *Encyclopédie*, 83; on solitary individuals as vicious, 10

Diet of Worms, 15, 37

divorce, 26–7, 53, 58–9

Dryden, John, 26, 50–1, 62, 140, 152; *The Hind and the Panther*, 26

Dunn, John, 67, 89, 96

Eagleton, Terry, 36

Eck, Johann von, 15–16

Edict of Nantes, 91

Elizabeth I, 27, 43

Emerson, Ralph Waldo, 162

Engels, Friedrich, 55; *The Communist Manifesto*, 55

English Civil War, 10, 32, 53, 59, 65, 67

Enlightenment, 5–10, 13, 23, 36–7, 52, 64–5, 71, 81–2, 100, 104, 109, 112, 117–18, 121–2, 124, 128–9, 131–2, 143–52, 156–7, 164, 166–8, 170, 178–81, 186–9, 217n.91, 217n.2; American, 10, 217n.91; French, 152; religious scepticism or indifference, 9; Scottish, 5, 114–15, 152, 179

Erasmus, Desiderius, 20

Erikson, Erik, 22–3

Exclusion Crisis, 89, 97

Ewin, R.E., 65, 204n.65

Fawkes, Guy, 45

Ferguson, Adam, 115, 122

Fichte, Johann Gottlieb, 174, 177

final judgment. *See* immortality, destiny of soul and

Foucault, Michel, 177, 186

Fox, George, 31

Foxe, John, 27; *The Book of Martyrs*, 27

Franklin, Benjamin, 79, 136

French Revolution, 10, 131, 135, 138, 147, 149–50

Freud, Sigmund, 7, 22, 37, 42, 45, 147, 161, 168; on conscience as superego, 7, 161; on *Hamlet*, 7, 37; as thoughtless heir of Enlightenment, 37, 147

Frye, Northrop, 53–4, 144, 147, 221n.93

Frye, Roland, 38, 43

Furness, Horace Howard, 35; *Varorium Shakespeare*, 35

Gay, John, 104
George III, 149
Gibbon, Edward, 145, 150
Gladstone, William, 153, 156, 176; *The State in Its Relations with the Church*, 176
Glorious Revolution, 10, 75, 82, 89–91, 94–5, 97, 114, 137, 166
glory. *See* honour
Godwin, William, 5, 66, 121–2, 131, 133, 140–4, 151, 153, 164, 169, 178, 180, 222n.115; biblical support for distributive justice, 121–2, 140–1, 151; on conscience as socially constructed, 143; on conscience as synonymous with reason, 133, 151; on conscience versus law, 141–2; libertarianism of, 66, 141; and Mill, J. S., 142–3; *Political Justice*, 140, 142; on primacy of conscience, 141–2; religious beliefs of, 140–1; on women, 151, 222n.115
Goethe, Johann Wolfgang von, 35, 42
Green, Thomas, 74, 181, 204n.65
Greenblatt, Stephen, 26, 36
Griswold, Charles, Jr, 117, 125, 179–81; *Adam Smith and the Virtues of Enlightenment*, 179
Gunpowder Plot, 60, 72; Guy Fawkes and, 45

Haakonssen, Knud, 82, 122, 124, 128
Hamilton, Sir William, 161, 171–2
Hamlet. *See* Shakespeare
Hampson, Norman, 65
Hartley, David, 170

Hegel, G.W.F., 42, 48, 76, 135, 158, 174, 177, 217n.91; *Phenomenology of Spirit*, 48; *Philosophy of Right*, 158
Heidegger, Martin, 12, 132, 177; *Being and Time*, 132
hell. *See* immortality, destiny of soul and
Helvétius, Claude Adrien, 9, 102, 112, 122, 156, 161, 170
Henry VIII, 26–7, 43, 158
Hill, Christopher, 23, 26, 57, 60, 133
Hill, Thomas E., Jr, 191n.5; *Autonomy and Self-Respect*, 191n.5
Hitler, Adolf, 12
Hobbes, Thomas, 4, 5, 6, 9, 10, 26, 46, 52, 61, 63–78, 81, 92, 96, 98, 101, 105, 107, 111, 115, 118–19, 125, 142–3, 149, 152, 165, 174, 178–9, 181–3, 186, 188, 204n.65, 214n.29, 217n.91; ambivalence over Protestant conscience, 5, 66–7; anti-egalitarianism of, 67; *Behemoth*, 67; and Coke, Sir Edward, 67, 73–4; on conscience as opinion versus conscience as knowledge, 68–9; on conscription, 165, 182–3; *Dialogue of the Common Laws*, 72–3; and Dunn, John, 67; egalitarianism of, 5–6, 66, 74, 78, 84; as Enlightenment thinker, 64–5; and Ewin, R.E., 65, 204n.65; as foremost English political philosopher, 5, 63; on freedom from self-incrimination, 70; on freedom of inner conscience, 69–70, 129; and Hume, 118–19; and Hutcheson, Francis, 115; institutionalization of conscience, 5, 68–9, 74, 76–8, 96, 98, 178–9, 183–4; and Jordan, W.K., 68–9; on jurors/jury, 5, 65–8, 72–8, 96, 98, 178, 181–2,

188, 204n.65, 214n.29; — equitable discretion of jurors, 72–7; on law as public conscience, 69; *Leviathan*, 69, 71–2, 165; and Locke, 65, 81, 92, 96; rights of subjects, 5, 67–78; scepticism of, 9–10, 64–5; tolerance of, 9; on torture, 70

Holbach, Paul-Henri Thiry, Baron d', 9, 102, 122, 133, 156, 161, 170

Holmes, Richard, 157

honour, 5, 37, 39–40, 47, 49, 99, 103–4, 106, 112, 116, 118, 185

Hooker, Richard, 28–9

Huguenots, 63

Hulliung, Mark, 124

Hume, David, 5, 9, 10, 13, 65, 105, 111, 114, 117–22, 124–9, 133, 143, 145, 150, 152, 156, 159, 161, 166, 170, 179, 188, 214n.29; on Church establishment, 10, 105, 117–18, 152, 159, 166; conservatism of, 121–2; *Dialogues concerning Natural Religion*, 119; and Diderot, 117, 122; *An Enquiry concerning the Principles of Morals*, 119; eschewed the word conscience, 117, 119; *History of England*, 117; and Hobbes, 118–19, 214 n. 29; his love of fame, 120; and Mandeville, 121; on Presbyterianism, 114, 118, 122; sceptical tolerance of, 9; scepticism of, 114, 118; and Smith, 121–2, 124–9; on social approbation, 119–21, 126; *Treatise of Human Nature*, 119; on uselessness of solitude, 10; and Voltaire, 117

Hundert, E. J., 211n.43

Hutcheson, Francis, 5, 13, 114–17, 119, 122, 125, 179; *An Inquiry into the Original of our Ideas of Beauty and Virtue*, 115; on moral sense, 115–17; opposition to Hobbes, Locke, Mandeville, and Pufendorf, 115; on sense of honour, 116; and Shaftesbury, 115; on social approbation, 115–16, 119; on social nature of humans, 115–16

Ignatieff, Michael, 178

immortality, destiny of soul and, 14–15, 17, 25, 28–9, 32, 35, 37–8, 44–5, 47, 85, 108, 180

incest, 43, 184

Isabella, Harriet, 160

Islam, 15, 167

James I of Great Britain (James VI of Scotland), 28, 43–5

James II, 75, 89–91, 95, 97

Jefferson, Thomas, 89, 135–6, 163, 179

Jesus, 14, 15, 20, 24, 56–8, 59, 63, 104, 144, 151–2, 169

Jews, 15

Johnson, Samuel, 53, 121, 220n.42

Jones, J.R., 90

Jordan, W.K., 63, 68–9

Joyce, James, 12; *Ulysses*, 12

Judaism, 15, 28

judgment, final. *See* afterlife

Jurieu, Pierre, 9, 63, 91

juries: jurors, 5, 65–8, 72–8, 96–8, 165, 178, 181–2, 184, 188, 204n.65, 214n.29

Kames, Lord Henry Home, 120

Kant, Immanuel, 6, 8, 23, 30, 55, 63, 76, 107, 110, 119, 128, 157, 171–2, 174, 177, 179, 181, 191n.5, 217n.91, as exemplar of Enlightenment, 8

Kateb, George, 184–6

Keane, John, 137, 140, 219n.25, 220n.42
Kierkegaard, Søren, 7, 110, 128, 162, 168, 174, 177, 186
Knox, John, 24, 27–8, 52, 128; *The First Blast of the Trumpet against the Monstrous Regiment of Women*, 27
Kramnick, Isaac, 64

Lacan, Jacques, 45
Lake, Peter, 28
last judgment. *See* immortality, destiny of soul and, 25
Laud, William, 61
law: divine, 4, 13–14, 17–19, 23, 25, 80, 92; natural, 19, 23, 25, 80, 92
Law, William, 105–7
Leibniz, Gottfried Wilhelm, 83, 144
Levellers, 5, 31, 61, 74
Lewis, C.S., 4, 30, 37, 59
liberalism, 90, 153, 177–9, 182–4, 186; and anti-Catholicism, 90; and choice, 183; deconstructs conscience while championing freedom of conscience, 177; freedom of conscience as fundamental to, 186; and Rorty, 177, 186
Lilburne, John, 31, 74
Locke, John, 5, 7, 8, 9, 10, 13, 52, 57, 58, 61, 63, 65, 76, 79–104, 106–8, 114–15, 118, 140, 143–9, 152–3, 156, 178–81, 206n.19; accused of Hobbism, 79–80; as American ideologist, 79; anti-Catholicism of, 61, 63, 86–92, 94; and Bayle, Pierre, 90–1; and Berkeley, 106–7; and Butler, 108; on 'celestially focussed self-interest,' 100–1; on consciousness, social construction of, 80–2, 84; and Coste, Pierre, 83; on divorce, 58; and Dunn, John, 89, 96; *Essay concerning Human Understanding*, 7, 79–80, 83–5, 114, 144; *An Essay concerning Toleration*, 86–8; excommunicated conscience, 181; on freedom of conscience, 61, 86–92; *The Fundamental Constitutions of Carolina*, 97; and Goldie, Mark, 90, 95; and Hobbes, 65, 81, 92, 96; on humanity, social construction of, 84; and Hutcheson, Francis, 115; inconsistency of thought, 5, 79, 93; inegalitarianism of, 57, 84, 86; on innate ideas, 80; intolerance of, 9, 61, 63, 86–92; and juries/jurors, 97–8; and Jurieu, Pierre, 91; and Laslett, Peter, 93, 96; and Le Clerc, Jean, 83; *Letters concerning Toleration*, 61, 76, 80, 84–5, 87–93, 104, 178; nominalism of, 84; on public opinion, 80–2, 88; — substitution of public opinion for conscience, 80–2; on reason versus conscience, 76, 82–6; on reason and revelation, 82–3; *The Reasonableness of Christianity*, 85; *Report to the Board of Trade*, 97; and revolution, 92–6, 98; on rights of conscience, 5, 65, 90, 93–4; and Shaftesbury, third Earl of, 79–80, 86, 99–100; and Simmons, A.J., 94; *Some Thoughts concerning Education*, 82; on substitution of public opinion for conscience, 80; on toleration, 85–91; translations of Locke's 'consciousness,' 83–4; and Tully, James, 83, 89–90, 95; *Two Tracts on Government*, 86, 93; *Two Treatises of Government*, 80, 84–5, 92–4, 96, 114,

178; and Waldron, Jeremy, 88–9; and Wolff, Christian, 83; and Wootton, David, 79, 89, 91; and Yolton, John, 93
Luhmann, Niklas, 180
Luther, Martin, 4, 15–24, 26, 32, 35–8, 52, 59, 116, 128, 150–1, 178; and antinomianism, 16, 19–20; and Aquinas, Saint Thomas, 4, 17–19, 23; *Concerning Worldly Government*, 20; on conscience and law, 20–3, 32; dependence of conscience on Scripture, 16; egalitarianism of, 22, 32; *The Freedom of a Christian*, 20; on legal authority, 19–23; and More, Saint Thomas, 16–17; on the peasant war, 20; on private revenge, 36, 38; and scriptural authority, 16–17, 20; and subjectivism, 16–17, 32
Lutherans, 38
Lyons, David, 155

Macaulay, Thomas Babington, 176
Mandeville, Bernard, 5, 52, 99, 103–5, 107, 111–12, 115–16, 121, 126, 152, 179; *Arete-logia or, an Enquiry into the Original of Moral Virtue*, 104; on the clergy, 104–5; *Fable of the Bees*, 99, 103; and Hutcheson, Francis, 115; on opposition between honour and religion and trade, 103–4; on public approval, 103–4, 112; and Shaftesbury, third Earl of, 99, 103–4; on toleration, 104–5
Marshall, John, 86, 89
Mary Stuart (Mary, Queen of Scots), 24, 27–8, 43, 52
Mary Tudor (Mary I; Bloody Mary), 27

Marx, Karl, 55; *The Communist Manifesto*, 55
Matheson, Mark, 38
McNaughton, David, 108
Melanchthon, Philip, 35
Mercer, Peter, 45
Mill, Harriet Burrow, 160
Mill, James, 5, 154–6, 159–64, 170–1; ambivalence of John Stuart Mill, 160, 170; *Analysis of the Phenomena of the Human Mind*, 159, 161; educational theories, 155, 159; on socialization by praise and blame, 155, 159–60
Mill, John Stuart, 5–8, 142–3, 145, 153–82, 184, 187–8, 191n.5, 226n.83; *Autobiography*, 155, 160, 170; and Bentham, 155, 160, 169; on Catholicism, 6, 153–4, 166–8, 175; on choice, 168–9, 174–5, 187; on church establishment, 158–9, 166, 179; and Coleridge, 157, 170; and Collini, Stefan, 162, 176; and Comte, 6, 154, 167–8, 175; on conscience: — as acquired, 154–6, 169, 175, 187–8; — ambivalence toward, 155, 169, 174; — freedom of, 155, 163–6, 174; — and social approbation, 6, 154–6, 160–2; on conscientious objection, 165; on consciousness, primacy of, 172–4; on conscription, 165; education of, 155, 160, 170; on the English, 153–4, 174–6; *Examination of Hamilton*, 171–2; and Freud, 161; and Hamilton, Sir William, 161, 171–2; and Hobbes, 165; irreligion of, 154, 164; and Jesus, 169; and Kierkegaard, 174; and Mansell, Henry, 171; and Marmontel, Jean

François, 170; and Mill, Harriet Burrow (mother), 160; and Mill, James (father), 154–6, 159–64, 170–1; naturalism of, 171–2, 187; *On Liberty*, 156, 164–8, 171, 174; as outsider, 162–3; on personal identity, 173–4, 187; on poetry, 145, 175; and Protestantism, 153–4, 167–8, 175–6; on public opinion/social approbation, 154–6, 160, 162–4, 172; and religion, 153–4, 162–4, 166–9; and Ryan, Alan, 166, 171–3; as secular Protestant, 153, 167–8; *System of Logic*, 171; and Taylor, Harriet, 170; tensions in his thought, 155–6, 161–3, 170–4; and Tocqueville, 163; on toleration, 157, 165–6, 226n.83; *Utilitarianism*, 155–6, 161, 163, 171–2; utilitarianism of, 171

Milton, John, 4, 9, 10, 13, 26, 48, 51–63, 65, 88, 96, 106, 110, 116, 128, 150, 153–4, 174, 178–9; Abdiel, 51–2, 56; anti-Catholicism of, 56, 60–1, 63; and antinomianism, 53–8, 60–2; *Areopagitica*, 55; and brother Christopher Milton, 53; *Colasterion*, 58; on conscience and revolution, 53, 56, 62; conscience as divine light/voice or inner light/voice, 51, 56–7; conscience as standing against the crowd, 52; on divorce, 58–9; *The Doctrine and Discipline of Divorce*, 53, 58; *Eikonoklastes*, 56; on freedom of Biblical interpretation, 54, 56–7; on freedom of conscience, 53–62; intolerance of, 9, 56–7, 60–1; and C.S. Lewis, 59; on liberty versus licence, 53–4; and Montaigne, 62; *Paradise Lost*, 51–3, 57, 59–60; and A.L. Rowse, 51–2, 59; and Samuel Rutherford, 55–7; self-confidence of Milton's conscience, 51–2; *The Tenure of Kings and Magistrates*, 61; *Tetrachordon*, 58; on women, 58–9

Minowitz, Peter, 123, 126, 129, 215n.52

Mohammed, 15

Monmouth Rebellion, 89

Montaigne, Michel de, 4, 7, 35, 40, 47, 49, 62, 64, 70, 83, 177, 197n.4; *Essays*, 35

moral sense, 100–2, 105, 115–17, 136, 155

More, Saint Thomas, 16–17, 26–7; on heresy, 26–7; on Lutheranism, 16–17, 26; on Tyndale, 26; *Utopia*, 27

Morgentaler case, 75

Moses, 15, 58

Mozart, Wolfgang Amadeus, 175

Muenzer, Thomas, 16–19

Muggleton, Lodowick, 31

nationalism, 25

Native Americans, 137–8, 219n.39

natural taste. *See* moral taste

Newman, John Henry, Cardinal, 107, 153–4, 156; on compatibility of Catholicism and English citizenship, 153–4; on conscience, 153–4; — primacy of conscience, 154

New Testament, 13, 14

Newton, Isaac, 79–80, 144–9, 156; *Opticks*, 144; *Principia*, 144

Nietzsche, Friedrich, 14, 177

Old Testament, 12, 24, 59

Orr, Robert, 28

Paine, Thomas, 5, 27, 121, 131–3, 135–41, 143–4, 149, 151–3, 169, 178–9, 218n.8, 219n.25, 219n.39, 222n.115; *The Age of Reason*, 140; *Agrarian Justice*, 131, 133, 140; on Bible, 140, 151; on Black Americans, 137, 219n.39; and Burke, 138–40; on capitalism, 121–2, 131–2, 143; on church establishment, 135, 152; *Common Sense*, 131, 135–7; on conscience as synonymous with reason, 133, 151; on conscientious objection, 136–7; on economic redistribution, 131–2, 140; on Native Americans, 137, 219n.39; and Quakers, 135, 137; religious beliefs, 135–6; *The Rights of Man*, 27, 131, 136, 139–40; and Smith, 131

Pascal, Blaise, 26, 129

Paul, Saint, 13, 14, 57, 178

Peace of Augsburg, 90

Pelikan, Jaroslav, 16

Penn, William, 90

Perkins, William, 28, 30, 37

Philip of Hesse, 22, 59

Pieper, Josef, 17–18, 41

Pierce, C.A., 14; *Conscience in the New Testament*, 14

Plato, 15, 143

Pocock, J.G.A., 82, 122

Pope, Alexander, 53, 111; *Essay on Man*, 53, 111

Popish Plot, 97

poverty, 130–1

Presbyterianism, 5, 28, 53, 114, 118, 122

Price, Richard, 152, 178

Priestley, F.E.L., 141, 178

Priestley, Joseph, 145

Proast, Jonas, 104

Protestantism, 6, 8, 10, 16, 25, 28, 32, 41, 54, 56, 64–5, 67, 76–7, 82, 84, 87–8, 91–2, 96, 113, 118, 122, 124, 128–9, 133, 136, 153–4, 157, 167–8, 174–6, 178–80, 185, 217n.91; and certainty, 9, 64; and deism, 136; and equality, 67, 84; and individualism, 10, 96, 124, 168–9; as inner-directed, 28, 130, 133; and liberalism, 167; and nationalism, 25; and scriptural authority, 16–17, 28, 54, 87–8; and tolerance, 154, 167

Protestants, 32, 38, 60, 87, 89–91, 105, 108, 110, 150, 169, 176

Proudhon, Pierre-Joseph, 162, 164

public approbation/approval/esteem. *See* public opinion

public opinion, 5–6, 8–9, 12, 23, 36, 52–3, 80–2, 88, 99, 101–4, 112, 115–16, 119–29, 132–4, 136, 146, 148, 154–6, 159–64, 169, 172, 174, 178–81, 187–9

Pufendorf, Samuel von, 115

punishment, 17, 25–9, 37, 44–5, 69–71, 97, 101, 105, 108, 112, 137, 172

Quakers, 61, 86, 90, 135, 137

Quebec Act, 137

Rainborough, Col. Thomas, 95

rationalism: Catholic, 23; classical, 23; Enlightenment, 23, 174; Socratic, 185. *See also* reason

Rawls, John, 128, 181–2

reason: Enlightenment, 5, 7, 9, 146, 148, 187; and inequality, 9, 187; as prudential calculation, 3, 8; as public opinion, 7–8, 187; relation

to conscience (*see* conscience, and reason); as universalistic, 8
Reeve, John, 31
Reformation, Protestant, 10, 22–3, 36, 66–7, 155, 168, 178
republicanism, 53, 56, 61–2, 182, 185
reputation. *See* public opinion
revelation. *See* scriptural authority
revenge, 36, 38–9, 42, 45–6
Richelieu, Cardinal Armand-Jean du Plessis, 63
Ricoeur, Paul, 189
rights, 3–4, 12, 14; human, 3, 11–12, 189; of individual/private judgment, 3–4, 138, 141; natural, 3, 138–43, 151, 165; property, 19, 29, 140–1, 158, 163, 178
Roman Catholic Church. *See* Catholic Church
Roman Catholics. *See* Catholics
Rorty, Richard, 177, 186
Ross, Ian, 126, 129
Rousseau, Jean-Jacques, 7, 8, 10, 13, 30, 76, 119, 122, 128, 131–4, 142–3, 149–51, 157, 177, 179–80, 187, 217n.91, 217n.2; *Confessions*, 150; conscience: — and desire, 134; — as divine voice, 132; — egalitarian view of, 122, 132; — as innate, 7; — as legislator, 30; — as nonconformist, 134; and Diderot, 10; *Discourse on the Arts and the Sciences*, 132; *Emile*, 134; on inequality, 131; *Julie or the New Heloise*, 13; on women, 133
Rowse, A.L. *See* Milton, John, A.L. Rowse on
Russell, Bertrand, 82, 177–8, 182
Rutherford, Samuel, 26, 55–7
Ryan, Alan, 166, 171–3

Rye House Plot, 89
Ryle, Gilbert, 8, 82

Salmasius, Claude, 61–2
Sanderson, Robert, 28–30
Sartre, Jean-Paul, 177
Satan, 53, 150
Saxo Grammaticus, 42, 46
Schneewind, J.B., 179–81, 191n.5; *The Invention of Autonomy: A History of Modern Philosophy*, 179, 191n.5
Schochet, Gordon, 63, 95
scriptural authority, 16–17, 54, 87–8, 116
Semple, Francis, 91–2; *A Discourse Between Law and Conscience When they were both Banished from Parliament*, 91
Shaftesbury, first Earl of, 96–7
Shaftesbury, third Earl of (Antony Ashley Cooper), 5, 7, 13, 79–80, 86, 99–109, 111–13, 115–16; and Hutcheson, Francis, 115; *An Inquiry concerning Virtue and Merit*, 100; on moral sense, 100–2, 115; on moral versus religious conscience, 100; on sociability of humans, 100–3, 108; on social approbation, 101–3; on taste (moral and aesthetic), 102–3
Shakespeare, William, 4, 34–8, 42, 44, 47, 50, 179; *Hamlet*, 4, 6–7, 27, 34–49, 51–2, 56, 65, 197n.4; — Claudius, 36–7, 39–47; — debate about Hamlet's age, 44, 199 n. 34; — debate about meaning of conscience, 36–9; — and Freud, 7, 37, 42; — Gertrude, 37, 42–4; — and Goethe, 35, 42; — Hamlet's conscience in relation to prudence

and honour, 4, 39–47; — and Hegel, 42, 48; — Laertes, 39–41, 46–7; — and C.S. Lewis, 37; — and Montaigne, 4, 35, 40, 49; — Ophelia, 41–2; — punishment for regicide, 37, 44–5; — reflective consciousness, 4, 35–6; — and religious beliefs, 37–9, 41, 43–5, 47–8; — and Voltaire, 36–7, 39, 41; *Richard III*, 34–5

Smith, Adam, 5, 13, 49, 98, 115, 119, 121–9, 131, 143–4, 159, 179, 181, 213n.22, 215n.52, 217n.91; the 'Adam Smith problem,' 122–3, 215n.52; on beggars, 129; conscience as 'impartial spectator,' 5, 49, 123, 125, 127–9; — difficulties in establishing standpoint of 'impartial spectator', 128–9; Griswold, Charles, Jr, 125; and Haakonssen, Knud, 124, 128; and Hume, 121–2, 124–9; and juries, 98; and Mandeville, 126; and Minowitz, Peter, 123, 126, 129, 215n.52; relation between praise and praiseworthiness, 124, 126; on self-conception as dependent on others, 125, 127; on social approbation, 119, 123–7, 129; *The Theory of Moral Sentiments*, 122–3, 126–7, 129, 159, 215n52, 216n.80; *The Wealth of Nations*, 115, 121–3, 126, 216n.80; and Winch, Donald, 123, 129–30

social approbation/approval/censure/esteem. *See* public opinion

Socrates, 40, 185

soul, immortality of. *See* immortality, destiny of soul and

Spinoza, Benedict de, 26, 52, 68, 104
state of nature, 65, 81, 94, 125
Sterne, Laurence, 109, 112–13
Steuart, Sir James, 122
Stewart, Dugald, 122
St John, Oliver, 65
Stoner, James R., Jr, 72, 204n.65
Strafford, 1st Earl of, 56, 61, 65, 66
subjectivism, 3–4, 14, 16–18, 23–4, 32, 35–6, 66, 76, 179, 187, 197n.4
subjectivity. *See* subjectivism
Swift, Jonathan, 99, 107

taste, moral, 102–3
taxation, moral choice and, 183
Taylor, Harriet, 170
Taylor, Jeremy, 28–30; *Ductor Dubitantium*, 29
Test Act, 90
Thompson, E.P., 134, 151
Tocqueville, Alexis de, 5, 159, 163–4
tolerance; toleration, 55, 61, 63–5, 68, 86–91, 104–5, 111, 117, 136, 157, 165–6, 179, 187, 204n.65, 226n.83; and scepticism, 9–10, 64–5, 105, 166, 174, 187
torture, 70–1
Tully, James, 83, 89, 95
Tyndale, William, 25–6; *The Obedience of a Christian Man*, 25

Universal Declaration of Human Rights, 3, 11–12, 189
Universities, 5, 1; Scottish, 5, 114; — University of Glasgow, 126

Valdes, Juan de, 39–40
Voltaire (François-Marie Arouet), 9, 10, 36–7, 39, 41, 64, 65, 71, 105, 117–18, 128, 132, 136, 149–50, 152,

156, 179; *La Voix du sage et du people*, 65

Walwyn, William, 31, 76; *Juries Justified*, 76
Walzer, Michael, 184–6
War of Independence. *See* American Revolution
Ward, William George, 161–3
Watson, Bishop Richard, 132–3, 140, 149, 152, 218n.8
Whichcote, Benjamin, 66
William of Orange, 91
Williams, Roger, 54–5, 57, 61, 88; *The Hireling Ministry*, 88
Wilson, Dover, 38, 43
Winch, Donald, 115, 123, 129–30

Wollstonecraft, Mary, 5, 8, 131, 133–4, 139–40, 143, 149, 151, 178, 222n.115; on conscience as sole authority, 133; on conscience as synonymous with reason, 133, 151; *A Vindication of the Rights of Men*, 139; *A Vindication of the Rights of Woman*, 131, 134, 222n.115; on women, 133, 151
women, 58–9, 84, 133–4, 151, 154, 160, 181, 222n.115
Wordsworth, William, 134, 135, 146–7, 153, 179, 218n.8; *The Excursion*, 146–7; *The Pilgrim Fathers*, 135; *The Prelude*, 135

Yeats, William Butler, 107

www.ingramcontent.com/pod-product-compliance
Lightning Source LLC
Chambersburg PA
CBHW020401080526
44584CB00014B/1127